# MOTORMOUTH IN MY MIND

**Calm Racing Thoughts, Tune Up The Overthinking Mind, And Maintain Your Mental Sanity.**

By Lynn R. Davis

Published By Lynn R. Davis

## Disclaimer

This book is a work of personal reflection and faith-based metaphor. The stories shared are drawn from the author's lived experiences. References to Ford vehicles are included as part of those experiences and are not intended to imply any affiliation with, or endorsement by, the Ford Motor Company or any dealership.

All trademarks and brand names remain the property of their respective owners.

Scripture quotations, where used, are taken from the Holy Bible. This book is not intended as professional mental health, medical, or legal advice. Readers seeking support in these areas should consult qualified professionals.

# Table of contents

# INTRODUCTION
# Buckle Up

**Introduction**

One of my earliest memories is standing in the driveway, holding out a screwdriver to my dad while he worked under the hood of one of our old Fords. The sun was hot, the smell of motor oil hung in the air, and my job was simple: hand him the right tool when he called for it. Flathead, Phillips — I learned the difference not from a classroom, but from the sound of his voice and the look of his hand reaching out for what he needed.

I didn't know it then, but God was teaching me something bigger in those moments. I thought I was just helping Dad fix a car, but really, I was learning about listening, about guidance, and about how the right tool in the right hand can change everything. Who knew those little driveway lessons would one day become the very metaphors I'd use to talk about the motormouth in my mind?

Because here's the truth: I don't talk much, but my mind talks a lot. In fact, it talks nonstop. So much that it's safe to say my mind is a motormouth.

The mind affects the entire body, just as the motor affects the entire usability of the car. When the motor is off, nothing works the way it should. And when my mind is off, it feels the same way.

Now let me pause and be real with you: I am not a mechanic, lol. I'm no expert on cars. But I've had plenty of impactful experiences with them — some fond, some hair-raising — and every single one has left me with lessons I'll never forget. So if I mislabel a tool or mix up a part, laugh with me. Charge it to my head, not my heart. Leave me a comment so we can laugh about it together.

Here's what I do know: my expectation is that you're a believer, and the Holy Spirit will relay the message that's most important for you to hear. I never in a million years thought I'd be sharing a message like this, but that's how I know it has a higher purpose — for me, and for you.

In this book, we're going to look under the hood of the motormouth in our minds. First, at the breakdowns — the moments we stall out, flood, grind, or overheat. And then, at the maintenance — the ways God rebuilds, refills, stabilizes, and renews us.

Think of this as your roadmap:

- **Breakdowns:** Revved Up and Going Nowhere, Flooded Engine, Grinding Gears, Check Engine Light, Throwing a Rod, Overheated Mind.
- **Maintenance:** The Rebuilt Life, The Oil of the Mind, Stabilized by the Mounts... and more.

**Buckle Up**

So buckle up. We've got some stories to share, lessons to learn, and repairs to make. And I promise — by the time we're through, you'll see your own mind a little differently. Not as a motormouth that wears you down, but as a finely tuned engine that, with God's help, can take you exactly where you're meant to go.

CHAPTER 1

# Revved Up and Going Nowhere

**Chapter One: Revved Up and Going Nowhere**

When I was a little girl growing up in the seventies, the driveway was one of my classrooms, and my dad was the teacher. No chalkboards, no textbooks—just a Ford with the hood popped open and a handful of tools scattered across an old rag.

The smell of motor oil hung in the air, the sun baked down on the metal, and I stood by like a pint-sized assistant. My job wasn't complicated, but it felt important. Dad would call out for a flathead screwdriver, and I would quickly scan the tools until I picked the right one. Then he'd ask for a Phillips, and I'd learn the difference: one with a single straight groove, the other with a cross. I was proud every time I got it right—proud that I could help in a world that felt far bigger than me.

I didn't understand the mechanics. I couldn't tell you what a carburetor did, but I did know it was possible to flood one. Nor did I understand why something called a timing belt caused so much stress when it broke. But I could hand my dad the right tool, and in that simple act, I felt like I was part of the solution.

But here's the thing about cars—sometimes the repair is bigger than one man and his tool set. I remember those days when my dad would frown, wipe his hands on an old rag, and mutter, "This one's tricky." That's when he'd call in the big guns: my uncles.

My uncles were the legends of our family when it came to cars. Shade tree mechanics, people called them, because they could work wonders with an engine parked right under a tree in the backyard. To me, they were like magicians. They could take a car apart, piece by piece, down to the bare bones, and put it back together again better than it was before. When they showed up, there was no panic. No worry. They didn't throw their hands up in despair and say, "This car is finished." No, they got to work—sleeves rolled up, voices calm and confident. They had seen it all before: blown gaskets, stubborn bolts, engines that refused to turn over. And they knew exactly what to do.

All these years later, I realize that what I saw under the hood of those Fords was more than car repair. It was a picture of life, and more specifically, a picture of the mind.

## The Motormouth Mind

If I'm honest, my mind has often felt like one of those old cars that just won't cooperate. Some days it sputters and stalls, coughing out smoke and noise. Other days it revs too high, stuck in overdrive, my thoughts racing fast but getting me nowhere. It feels like life itself is pressing down hard on the gas pedal, flooding my brain with negative thoughts until everything chokes and stalls.

That's what I call the motormouth in my mind.

It talks too much, too fast, too loud. It interrupts my peace, questions my worth, criticizes my choices, and narrates my day with constant chatter that leaves me exhausted.

The motormouth in my mind cranks up with things like:

- *"You'll never get it right."*
- *"Everyone's judging you."*
- *"What if it all falls apart?"*
- *"You should have known better."*

It's like sitting in a parked car with the engine revving, the radio blasting static, and the windows rattling from the noise. You can't think straight with all that chaos. And worse—you're not moving anywhere. You want to shift gears and turn down the volume, but the dial is broken and the shifter cable has snapped. Basically, you're stuck.

Unless, of course, you get under the hood—or better yet, call on Someone who actually knows how to fix it.

**God, the Master Mechanic**

My dad could fix a lot. My uncles could fix almost anything. But God? God can fix everything.

He is the Master Mechanic of the mind. He doesn't just pop the hood, tap around, and hope for the best. He designed the engine in the first place. He knows how every gear, piston, and spark plug is supposed to function. He knows when things are misaligned, when the system is flooded, and when something deep inside needs a full rebuild.

*"Be transformed by the renewing of your mind"* (Romans 12:2). That's divine

maintenance. That's a tune-up straight from the Creator.

When my thoughts sputter with doubt, God replaces them with faith.

When my mind floods with fear, He drains the excess and restores calm.

When my gears grind with worry, He oils them with peace.

And when I stall out completely, He reminds me it's His power—not mine—that gets me moving again.

**Your Role: Handing Over What He Asks For**

Back in the driveway, I didn't fix the car. My dad did. My uncles did. My part was small but important: handing over the right tools when they asked.

That's our role with God, too. We don't have to fix the motormouth in our minds all by ourselves. But we can hand Him what He asks for:

- **Surrender.** Hand Him your fear.
- **Prayer.** Hand Him your worry.
- **Trust.** Hand Him your plans.

We don't need to know the full mechanics of how He'll repair us. We just need to trust Him enough to place the tools in His hands.

**Reflection**

If your mind were an engine right now, what sound would it be making?

- Sputtering with doubt?
- Revving with anxiety?
- Grinding with stress?
- Or stalling out from exhaustion?

Whatever it is, picture the Master Mechanic standing beside you. He's calm. He's capable. And all He's asking is that you hand Him the tool He needs—your surrender, your prayer, your trust.

**Prayer**

Father, You know the motormouth in my mind. You hear every clunky thought, every grinding fear, every stalled-out worry. I confess that I've tried to fix myself, and I've flooded my own engine more times than I can count. But today, I choose to hand You the tools.

Be my Master Mechanic. Tune my thoughts. Align my heart. Replace the lies with truth, the fear with peace, and the noise with stillness. Fill me with the premium fuel of Your Word so my mind runs steady, smooth, and strong.

I trust You with every rattle and every repair. In Jesus' name, Amen.

**Final Encouragement**

And don't worry if you're not quite sure—or if you feel anxious that you don't understand exactly what's being asked of you. Because He always knows just what's needed.

**Chapter One Takeaways**

- The motormouth in your mind is noisy, distracting, and exhausting — like an engine revving in park.
- Just because there's motion doesn't mean there's progress.
- Trust the Master Mechanic — God knows exactly what's needed under the hood of your life.
- You don't have to fix everything yourself.

CHAPTER 2

# Flooded Engine, Flooded Mind

**Chapter Two: Flooded Engine, Flooded Mind**

The first car I remember is a bright red 1970

Ford Thunderbird. It felt massive to me as a child — all steel and chrome, with a hood that seemed to stretch a mile long. That car carried our family through everyday life, but it also taught me some of my earliest lessons about patience, pressure, and trust.

I remember one particular afternoon when my dad was working under the hood. He needed me to help start the car. From where he stood, head bent over the engine, he called out, “When I tell you to turn it, turn the key like this.” He pantomimed the motion with his hand, twisting an invisible ignition.

I climbed into the driver’s seat, legs too short to touch the pedals, and wrapped my small hand around the key. I felt the weight of responsibility settle over me. This wasn’t just playtime — this was real help. I listened carefully, waiting for his signal.

“Now!” he yelled. I turned the key, and the engine cranked. Once, twice — but instead of coming to life, it coughed and choked. “Stop, stop!” Dad called. I froze, heart pounding.

“I think I might have flooded it,” he said, wiping his forehead as he poked his head up from under the hood. "If you pump it too much, that's what can happen."

I felt bad for him. Whatever flooding meant, it was clear it wasn't a good thing.

That was the day I learned what it meant to flood an engine — too much fuel, too fast, and the whole system stalls out.

And years later, I realized: the same thing happens in the mind.

**Flooded Engine, Flooded Mind**

That lesson with the red Ford Thunderbird stuck with me: an engine can have everything it needs — fuel, spark, power — and still fail to start if it's flooded. Too much at once overwhelms the system, and instead of roaring to life, it coughs, sputters, and stalls. The same thing happens in the mind.

When I flood my thoughts with "what ifs" and "should haves," my brain chokes on the overload. Instead of moving forward, I stall. When I pump fear and self-criticism into every situation, I'm just like that flooded engine: overfueled but under-functioning.

Flooding the mind looks like:

- Replaying the same mistake on loop until you're stuck in guilt.
- Imagining ten different worst-case scenarios before you've even taken one step.
- Running through endless to-do lists but never making progress.
- Asking "what if" until your spirit is paralyzed.

Just like my dad told me, the solution isn't to keep pressing harder.

Back then, I didn't understand what he meant about stopping, letting it breathe, waiting, resetting, and only then trying again. But I see it now. It wasn't just car talk — it was a life lesson.

I'm no mechanic, and I still don't fully understand the science of flooding an engine. But I can see the truth in the experience: when you flood something, whether it's an engine or your own thoughts, pressing harder only makes it worse. The reset, the pause, the waiting — that's what brings it back to life.

**God's Breath in a Flooded Mind**

What my dad told me about that Ford Thunderbird makes even more sense to me now as an adult. A flooded engine doesn't need *more gas*. It needs to pause, breathe, and reset. The system has to clear out the excess before it can run again.

The same is true for the mind.

When my thoughts are flooded with fear, self-doubt, or endless "what-ifs," the answer isn't to push harder. It isn't to pump more mental fuel into an already overwhelmed brain. The answer is to stop. To be still. To let God breathe fresh air into the chaos.

*"Be still, and know that I am God"* (Psalm 46:10). That's more than a comforting verse — it's a divine reset. Stillness makes room for God's Spirit to do what overthinking never can. His breath clears out the clutter. His Word is the fresh air that ventilates the soul.

Flooding happens when we try to power everything ourselves. Peace comes when we let the Master Mechanic lift the hood, wave us back from the driver's seat, and take over.

**Steps to Un-Flood the Mind**

Just like a car engine, a flooded mind doesn't need more fuel. It needs a reset. Here are four simple steps you can practice when the motormouth in your mind cranks too loud and your thoughts feel flooded:

**1. Stop pressing the issue.**

In the car, pressing the gas only makes the flooding worse. In your mind, pressing harder into the "what ifs" and negative loops does the same thing. Pause. Don't add more pressure. Don't keep replaying the scenario. The first step is to take your foot off the mental gas pedal.

**2. Let it breathe.**

An engine needs air to clear the extra fuel. Your mind needs space to clear the noise. This might look like stepping away, taking a deep breath, opening your Bible, or simply sitting in silence for a moment. God's Spirit is the breath that clears out the overload.

**3. Reset.**

Once the excess has had time to clear, you can try again — but slowly. For the mind, this means anchoring yourself with one small truth. One scripture. One prayer. Not fifty. Just one. A single verse, whispered aloud, can reset your perspective in ways that frantic thinking never will.

**4. Trust the Mechanic.**

At the end of the day, you aren't the one who repairs the engine — God is. Your role is to pause, breathe, and hand Him the tools. He knows exactly what's wrong and how to fix it. Don't worry if you don't fully understand what's happening inside your own mind — He does. And He always knows just what's needed.

**Reflection**

Think about a recent time when your mind felt flooded.

- What did it sound like — racing thoughts, constant what-ifs, replaying the same scenario?
- How did your body react — tight chest, shallow breathing, restless energy?
- What would it look like for you to "stop pressing the issue" and instead let God's Spirit breathe fresh air into your thoughts?

Write down one area of your life right now where you need to step back, let it breathe, and trust the Master Mechanic.

**Prayer**

Father, You know how easily I flood my mind with too much at once. I press harder, I add more fuel, and I end up stalling instead of moving forward. Today, I choose to pause. I take my foot off the gas and make room for You to breathe fresh air into my thoughts. Reset my spirit with Your peace. Anchor me with one truth, one scripture, one prayer that clears out the clutter and steadies my heart. Teach me to trust You as my Master Mechanic, knowing You understand exactly what's needed, even when I don't.

In Jesus' name, Amen.

**Chapter 2: Takeaways**

- Too much, too fast, too soon can flood both an engine and a mind.
- Sometimes the solution isn't pressing harder but stopping, breathing, and resetting.
- Trust God's timing instead of forcing your own.
- Even when you don't understand what's happening, the Master Mechanic does

CHAPTER 3

# The Grinding Gears of Worry

**Chapter Three: The Grinding Gears of Worry**

I remember one Sunday morning on the way to church when my mom was driving. We were turning into the parking lot, dressed up and ready for service, when suddenly—*bam*—another car bumped us from behind.

It wasn't hard. Just a fender bender. But I still remember the jolt, the way my mom's body stiffened, the sound of metal on metal. For a moment, it felt bigger than it was. My young mind went straight to panic: *What happened? Are we okay? Is the car ruined?*

I think we got rid of that car shortly after. Looking back, that little bump barely left a scratch. But it left an impression on me about how easily worry can take over. Sometimes life dings us, and it's not catastrophic—it's just a small bump. But our minds treat it like a collision. We replay it, brace for it, expect it to happen again. That's the way worry works. It magnifies every bump, every noise, every possibility, until the gears in your mind grind against each other.

**Worry Is Mental Grinding**

If you've ever heard the sound of grinding gears in a car, you know it's awful. Metal scraping metal, the transmission straining, the whole vehicle shuddering because something is out of sync. It doesn't move the car forward—it only makes noise and damage.

That's exactly what worry does in the mind.

- You're not moving forward, but your thoughts are straining.
- You're stuck between neutral and drive, grinding instead of flowing.
- You can't enjoy the ride because you're bracing for the next bump.

Worry isn't progress—it's friction. It eats up your peace the way grinding gears eat up a transmission.

**What Jesus Said About Worry**

Jesus knew the cost of worry when He said, *"Do not worry about tomorrow, for tomorrow will worry about itself. Each day has enough trouble of its own"* (Matthew 6:34).

Worry is like sitting in the car with the clutch halfway pressed, revving the engine but never shifting into gear. You use up energy but go nowhere. You wear yourself out waiting for the next "bump from behind" instead of trusting the One who sees the whole road ahead.

God didn't design your mind to grind. He designed it to shift smoothly with His Spirit—grace for today, strength for this moment, peace for right now.

**Shifting Out of Worry**

Worry always reminds me of my dad's reddish orange 1980s Ford truck. He only had it for a few years, but he loved that truck. Mama couldn't drive a stick shift, so it was his alone. Mama swore that was why he bought it.

I remember sitting on the front bench seat, watching him shift the gears. To me, it looked so smooth, almost like a dance—clutch, shift, release, and the truck would glide forward in rhythm with him. I never learned to drive a standard myself, but to this day I envy people who can. It just looks so cool.

But when those gears grind? Oh my goodness, the sound made me grimace every time. Metal scraping metal, the whole truck jerking with resistance. You couldn't ignore it.

I figured the grinding meant something wasn't connecting the way it should.

That's exactly what worry feels like in the mind. Smooth shifting is trust. Grinding is worry. One keeps you moving forward. The other just makes noise and wears you down.

Here are four ways to shift out of worry and into trust:

**1. Notice the grind.**

When my dad shifted smoothly, you hardly noticed. But when the gears ground, everyone in the truck winced. In the same way, worry is easy to spot if you pay attention. Notice when your mind is stuck replaying fears or "what ifs." Naming it is the first step to shifting out of it.

**2. Press the clutch and pause.**

You can't shift gears without pressing the clutch. Spiritually, pressing pause is your clutch moment. Breathe. Pray. Loosen your grip on control so you can change mental gears.

**3. Shift with truth.**

My dad knew exactly which gear to move into. For us, that gear is truth. Replace the grinding thought—*"What if everything falls apart?"*—with the steady truth—*"God holds all things together" (Colossians 1:17).* Shift intentionally into peace.

**4. Trust the Driver.**

At the end of the day, I wasn't the one driving the burnt orange-looking truck—my dad was. And in life, I'm not the ultimate Driver either—God is. Worry comes from thinking it's all on me. Trust comes when I remember who's really behind the wheel.

**Reflection**

What are the gears in your life that worry keeps grinding?

- Are you stuck between neutral and drive in your thoughts?

- Do you keep replaying a "fender bender" moment that wasn't as big as it felt?
- Where do you need to ease off, breathe, and let God handle the next shift?

Write down one worry you've been grinding on and what it would look like to trust the Driver instead.

**Prayer**

Father, You know how easily I get caught in the grinding gears of worry. I replay moments, brace for bumps, and strain against things I can't control. I confess that worry has worn me down, just like grinding wears down a car. Today, I choose to notice the grind, press pause, and shift with Your truth. Teach me to rest in the fact that You are the Driver, and You know the way. Smooth out the rough places in my mind, and guide me forward in Your peace.

In Jesus' name, Amen.

**Chapter 3: Takeaways**

- Worry wears you down like grinding gears wear down a transmission.
- Forcing things before they're ready creates more damage than progress.
- The motormouth tells you, *"You'll never get it right,"* but God says, *"Be still — I've got the clutch."*
- Smooth shifts happen when you let God set the rhythm.

# CHAPTER 4
# Check Engine Light of Anxiety

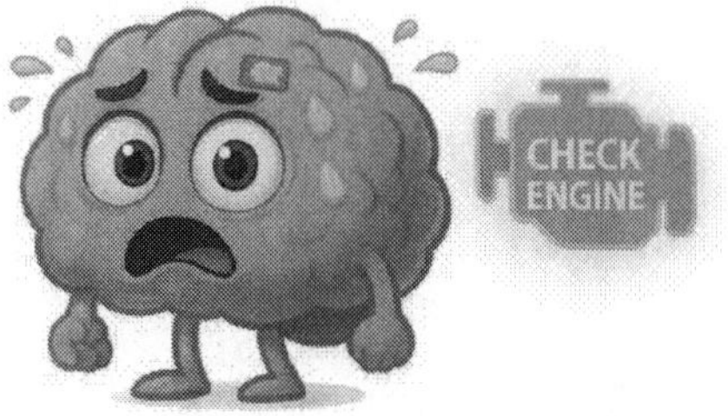


**Chapter Four: The Check Engine Light of Anxiety**

The first time I ever noticed a *check engine* light come on, it was in my mama's 1985 Ford Tempo. I still remember the way that car jerked, like it was gasping for breath, and suddenly that little light glowed red and steady on the dashboard. My heart jumped. Even as a kid, I knew that wasn't good.

My uncles were called in to take a look. They were the ones who always knew what to do when cars acted up. They poked and prodded, lifted the hood, and finally shook their heads. “The transmission’s a goner,” they said. That car had to be pulled home, tail tucked between its legs.

That one light—the size of a coin—changed the whole day. One minute we were driving, the next we were stranded. It felt like the car was announcing its doom with that glowing message: *something is seriously wrong.*

**When the Warning Light Flashes in Your Mind**

That little light reminds me of anxiety. Anxiety is like the check engine light of the mind. One moment you’re moving through life, and the next you feel a sudden jolt. Your chest tightens, your thoughts race, and a bright warning seems to flash across your soul: *something is seriously wrong.*

Just like that Ford Tempo, anxiety makes you feel like you're about to break down completely. It convinces you the transmission of your life is shot, the whole system is failing, and you'll never make it to where you're going. But here's the truth: the light isn't the problem itself. The light is just a signal.

**The Light Is Not the End**

The *check engine* light never fixed the Tempo. But it also didn't destroy it. All that light did was say, *Pay attention. Something under the hood needs care.*

That's how anxiety works. It's a signal that something inside—your body, your thoughts, your spirit—needs attention. The problem comes when we either ignore the light or panic at its presence.

Ignoring anxiety is like putting a piece of tape over the dashboard light. Pretending it's not there won't stop the problem underneath from growing worse.

Panicking over anxiety is like assuming the entire car is totaled the second the light flickers on. But sometimes the issue is small. Sometimes it's just a sensor. Sometimes it's nothing more than a momentary reset.

The light is not the end. It's an invitation.

**God and Your Warning Lights**

God doesn't shame us when the check engine light of anxiety flashes. He doesn't say, *How dare you feel this way?* He doesn't roll His eyes and mutter, *You again?*

Instead, He invites us to bring it to Him.

Philippians 4:6-7 says, *"Do not be anxious about anything, but in every situation, by prayer and petition, with thanksgiving, present your requests to God. And the peace of God, which transcends all understanding, will guard your hearts and your minds in Christ Jesus."*

Do you see it? God doesn't say, *Ignore the light.* He says, *Bring the light to Me.* Prayer is like pulling into His garage, lifting the hood, and letting Him diagnose what's really happening underneath.

Anxiety might make you feel stranded, but peace is always waiting when you hand the keys over to the Master Mechanic.

**Four Ways to Respond to Anxiety's Check Engine Light**

Just like you don't keep driving a car that's jerking with a warning light blazing, you don't have to keep running with unchecked anxiety. Here are four ways to respond:

**1. Don't ignore it.**

The worst thing you can do with a warning light is pretend it isn't there. The same goes for anxiety. Acknowledge it. Name it. Say, *Father, I feel anxious. My thoughts are racing. My heart feels heavy, but I know you have me in Your hands.* That simple act opens the door to healing.

**2. Don't panic.**

The light is a signal, not a sentence. When it flashes, don't assume you're ruined, broken, or hopeless. Anxiety doesn't mean your whole life is falling apart—it means something inside needs attention.

**3. Pull over and pause.**

In a car, you stop to prevent more damage. In life, you can stop, too. Step away. Take a breath. Pray. Journal. Let your mind catch its breath. This is where Psalm 46:10 becomes real: *"Be still, and know that I am God."*

**4. Take it to the Mechanic.**

The Master Mechanic knows what's under the hood. He sees every wire, every piston, every worn-out place in your heart. Invite Him in. Ask Him, *Father, what is this anxiety signaling? Show me, fix me, heal me.* He always knows what's needed—even when you don't.

### Reflection

Think about your own "check engine" light moments:

- What signals tell you that anxiety is flashing in your life?
- Do you tend to ignore the warning, or do you panic as if the car is totaled?
- What would it look like to pull over, pause, and invite the Master Mechanic to take a look?

Write down one specific way you'll respond differently the next time your "light" comes on.

**Prayer**

Father, You know the warning lights in my life. You know when my heart races, when my chest tightens, when anxiety jerks me off course. I confess that I've either ignored those signals or panicked at their presence. But today, I choose to see them for what they are—not the end, but an invitation.

Teach me not to fear the light, but to use it as a reminder to bring everything to You. Be my Mechanic, my Comforter, my Peace. Reset my mind with stillness, guard my heart with Your promises, and help me keep moving forward in trust.

In Jesus' name, Amen.

**Chapter 4: Takeaways**

- Anxiety is like a check engine light — it's a warning, not a death sentence.
- Ignoring small signs can lead to bigger breakdowns.
- The motormouth says panic, but God says, *"Bring it to Me — I'll carry you."*
- Don't fear the signal; let it remind you to lean on the Master Mechanic.

# Chapter 5
# Throwing a Rod

**Chapter Five: Throwing a Rod**

The phrase "throwing a rod" didn't mean much to me as a child. I only knew it was serious because of how the grown-ups around me reacted. The first time I heard it, we were driving home from a fishing trip in a late-seventies brown Pontiac.

It wasn't just our car on the road that night — it was a caravan of family vehicles. My grandfather, my mom's brothers, my uncles — we had all gone fishing together down in Corpus Christi. The salty air still clung to our clothes, and the trunk carried the day's catch packed into coolers. The trip had been good, but the ride home took a hard turn.

Somewhere in the middle of the night, on a dark stretch of highway, our Pontiac jerked, sputtered, and gave up. We coasted to the side of the road, stranded in the dark.

Flashlights clicked on, hoods went up, and my uncles peered inside. It didn't take long for the diagnosis. Shaking their heads, they said, "It threw a rod."

As a kid, the words sounded strange to me, almost comical — like the car had lost its temper and hurled something. But the serious tone in my uncles' voices told me the truth. This wasn't just a small repair. This was major. The Pontiac was finished for the night. But here's the part I'll never forget: we weren't left alone on that highway. Our family pulled together. One of the other cars in the caravan hooked a chain to ours, and they towed us all the way home.

I didn't understand what "throwing a rod" meant mechanically. But I understood what it meant emotionally: something broke, and we had to be carried.

**When Stress Breaks You Down**

Engines don't throw a rod without warning. There are always signs: strange noises, persistent knocking, oil leaks, or something rattling under the hood. The car is trying to tell you something isn't right. If you ignore it, push harder, and keep running it under strain, one day the stress becomes too much. Something inside breaks loose, and the engine tears itself apart.

That's what happened to the Pontiac. And that's what happens to us.

Stress builds. Worries stack. Life pushes harder and faster. And though the signs are there — constant fatigue, snapping at people you love, the dull ache of burnout, headaches that don't go away — we ignore them. We say, *Just one more week. Just one more project. Just one more responsibility.*

Until one day, something inside us snaps. We "throw a rod."

- Burnout drops us flat.
- Anxiety overwhelms like a tidal wave.
- Depression takes hold and won't let go.
- Anger erupts suddenly, shocking even us.

- Our body breaks down, reminding us we can't outrun stress forever.

Throwing a rod feels like collapse. It feels like being stranded on the side of the road in the middle of the night, powerless to keep moving.

**When Your Mind Throws a Rod**

Sometimes life brings us to the breaking point. Our minds throw the metaphorical rod, and we feel like we can't move forward anymore. The pressure becomes too much, and something deep inside us breaks loose.

It looks like the panic attack that comes out of nowhere.

It feels like the exhaustion that keeps you in bed all day.

It sounds like the whisper, *"You can't do this anymore."*

And maybe you've felt that. Maybe you've been there — sidelined, stranded, convinced your "engine" is finished.

But here's the good news: just like my family that night on the highway, God doesn't leave you there.

When our car threw a rod, the Pontiac couldn't move itself another inch. But my uncles didn't leave us behind. They hooked our car to theirs and pulled us all the way home.

That's what God does for us. When we break down, when we can't take another step, when our own strength fails — He carries us. Isaiah 46:4 says, *"I have made you and I will carry you; I will sustain you and I will rescue you."*

Your breakdown doesn't mean your journey is over. It means it's time to let the Master

Mechanic hook His strength to your weakness and tow you safely until you're restored.

**Preventing a Breakdown**

Of course, prevention matters too. Just like mechanics encourage regular maintenance to avoid catastrophic failures, God calls us to rhythms that protect our hearts and minds. Here are four ways to keep from "throwing a rod":

**1. Pay attention to the signs.**

Engines knock and rattle before they break. Our souls do the same. Fatigue, irritability, numbness — they're warning signs. Don't brush them off. They're your soul saying, *I need attention.*

**2. Slow down the speed.**

Engines blow faster when they're pushed hard. So do people. You can't live at full throttle every day. Even Jesus withdrew to quiet places to rest and pray. If the Son of God slowed down, so should you.

**3. Schedule maintenance.**

Engines need oil changes and tune-ups. We need spiritual maintenance, too. Prayer, worship, Sabbath rest, journaling, and community aren't luxuries — they're the practices that keep us from breaking under pressure.

**4. Let God rebuild.**

Sometimes breakdowns do happen. Maybe you've already thrown a rod. Maybe you feel beyond repair. But God is the Master Rebuilder. He doesn't scrap you for parts. He restores. He takes what stress destroyed and makes it new. Ezekiel 36:26 promises, *"I will give you a new heart and put a new spirit in you."*

**Reflection**

Think about your own life:

- Have you ever felt like you "threw a rod" — a breaking point where stress, worry, or exhaustion sidelined you?
- What warning signs did you notice but ignore?
- What would it look like to let God carry you — or even tow you — when you can't move on your own?

Write down one area where you feel at risk of breaking down, and how you can release that weight to God before it takes you out.

**Prayer**

Father, I confess I've carried more than I was built to bear. I've ignored the rattles, pushed through the warning signs, and demanded more of myself than You ever asked. And I feel the weight of it.

Sometimes the motormouth in my mind throws a rod. I've collapsed under stress and pressure, and I've felt stranded on the side of life's highway. But thank You that I'm never left behind. You carry me. You hook Your strength to my weakness and pull me when I can't go on.

Teach me to notice the signs. Teach me to slow down. Teach me to release my burdens into Your hands. And for every place inside me that already feels broken, be my Rebuilder. Restore me. Renew me. Repair what stress has torn apart.

In Jesus' name, Amen.

**Chapter 5: Takeaways**

- Sometimes life's stress feels like a total breakdown — like an engine throwing a rod.
- Even when you collapse, you are not abandoned.
- The motormouth says, *"You're finished."* God says, *"I'll hook you up and pull you home."*
- Community and faith can tow you through when you can't move on your own.

# Chapter 6
# The Overheated Mind

**Chapter Six: Overheated Mind**

I'll never forget the day my mom's Ford

Aerostar overheated. We were driving when suddenly steam began to pour out from under the hood. The van jerked and shuddered, and the temperature gauge shot up. We had no choice but to pull over.

When the hood came up, the problem was clear: the radiator hose had busted. The engine was too hot, and without coolant it couldn't regulate itself. To get home, we had to do the only thing we could — pour water into the radiator, drive a little ways, stop again, add more water, and repeat until we finally made it back.

As a kid, I didn't understand all the mechanics of overheating. But I knew this much: when a car gets too hot, you can't ignore it. If you keep pushing it, you'll blow the engine.

And now, all these years later, I realize: our minds can overheat too.

**The Overheated Mind**

Engines overheat when they're under too much strain without proper cooling. The same thing happens to our thoughts and emotions.

When the motormouth in my mind runs too hot, I feel it:

- My patience evaporates.
- My words get sharp.
- My energy dries up.
- My body sends signals — a racing heart, a pounding head, tense shoulders.

And just like the Aerostar that day, sometimes I try to keep driving anyway. But when you ignore the steam and the warning signs, the damage gets worse. Eventually, something seizes up inside.

**The Living Water That Cools Us**

That day with the Aerostar, we couldn't fix the radiator hose on the side of the road. All we could do was pour water in to keep the engine from burning up completely. It wasn't a permanent fix, but it was enough to get us home.

Spiritually, God does the same thing for us when we're overheated.

Jesus said in John 7:37, *"Let anyone who is thirsty come to me and drink."* He called Himself Living Water, the refreshment that never runs dry. When my mind runs too hot, His Spirit is what cools me down. His presence doesn't just patch the leak — it replenishes my soul.

Prayer is pouring water into the overheated places. Worship is pouring water into the cracks. Time in Scripture is water for a dry, boiling spirit. And Sabbath rest is the deep refill that keeps me from running too hot in the first place.

**Four Ways to Cool an Overheated Mind**

**1. Recognize the steam.**

Engines don't overheat quietly. Neither do we. The steam of an overheated mind looks like irritability, anger, exhaustion, or emotional outbursts. Notice it before it burns you out.

**2. Pull over before you blow.**

When you see the warning signs, stop. Take a pause. Step away. Sit down with God instead of pushing forward in your own strength.

**3. Pour in Living Water.**

Temporary water kept the Aerostar running until we got home. Spiritually, prayer, scripture, worship, and silence are ways God pours His Living Water into us. It cools us, refreshes us, and keeps us moving.

**4. Fix the hose.**

Adding water helped us make it home, but we couldn't ignore the busted radiator hose forever. Sometimes you need more than a quick refill. You need God to repair what's broken — whether that's your boundaries, your rest habits, or your willingness to trust Him with what's overheating your heart.

**Reflection**

Think about the last time your mind or emotions overheated.

- What did your "steam" look like — snapping at loved ones, tears, shutting down?
- Did you stop and refill, or did you try to push through?
- What would it look like to let God pour His Living Water into you before you burn out completely?

Write down one "hose" in your life that God might be pointing to — a place He wants to repair so you don't keep overheating.

**Prayer**

Father, sometimes the motormouth in my mind runs too hot. My patience boils over, my strength dries up, and I feel like steam is pouring out of me. I confess I've tried to keep going on my own, even when I knew I was overheated.

Teach me to stop before I break down. Pour Your Living Water into me when I'm thirsty and burned out. Cool my thoughts with Your peace. And Father, repair the broken places in me — the leaks, the busted hoses, the things I've ignored — so I can run steady and strong again.

In Jesus' name, Amen.

**Chapter 6: Takeaways**

- Just like a busted radiator overheats a car, overload overheats your mind.
- Pouring in "Living Water" restores and refreshes what heat has drained.
- The motormouth says, *"Push harder."* God says, *"Be still and drink deeply."*
- Cooling down in God's presence is not laziness — it's survival.

# CHAPTER 7
# The Rebuilt Life

**Chapter Seven: The Rebuilt Life**

Mama's Ford Tempo was the car in which I learned to drive. By the time I slid into that driver's seat, the car had already been through a lot. The transmission had given out once, and the motor had been rebuilt. Somehow, against the odds, it lasted a few more years after that repair.

When you rebuild an engine, you're not just patching a problem. You're giving the whole thing another chance at life. And that's what the Tempo got — a second chance.

But eventually, the transmission gave out again. And this time, it couldn't be saved. The car had run its course. It was time to let it go.

That old Ford Tempo taught me something I didn't understand at the time: rebuilding is possible, but even rebuilt engines don't last forever. At some point, you need something brand new.

And of course, the motormouth in my mind had plenty to say during seasons like that.

- *"You'll never recover from this."*
- *"That's too broken to ever be fixed."*
- *"Why even bother trying again?"*
- *"You're just going to fail like last time."*

That chatter is relentless. The motormouth convinces you that what's been damaged can't be restored, and what's been lost is gone forever.

But God's voice says something different: *"I will restore to you the years the locusts have eaten. I will rebuild. I will renew. I will give you a new heart and a new spirit."* (Joel 2:25, Ezekiel 36:26)

**When We Keep Trying to Rebuild**

That old car reminded me of how I sometimes treat my own life.

There are parts of me I've tried to keep patching together, hoping they'll carry me a little further. Habits I've tried to fix with willpower. Relationships I've tried to force back to life. Old ways of thinking I've tried to manage instead of releasing.

But here's the truth: sometimes there are parts of our lives we keep trying to rebuild, when God is asking us to release them.

We patch and repair, but He's saying, *"Stop nursing along what I want to replace."*

Because God doesn't just want us limping down the highway of life. He wants to bring us into something new.

Sometimes that new thing is a healthier relationship. Sometimes it's a new opportunity. Sometimes it's simply a renewed mind — a transformation in the way we think, feel, and live.

**The Flip Side: Restoration**

But there's a flip side, too. Sometimes the things we think are junk are really classics that just need the right expertise to restore them. And God specializes in restoring classics — the people others have given up on, the marriages the world says are over, the situations everyone else writes off as hopeless.

An old truck sitting in a junkyard might look finished to us. But with a new motor, and in the hands of the right mechanic, that same truck can be restored, polished, rebuilt, and celebrated as something rare and valuable.

God does the same with our lives. What we've written off as too broken, too wasted, or too far gone — He calls worthy of restoration.

Joel 2:25 says, *"I will restore to you the years that the swarming locust has eaten."* What you thought was wasted can be redeemed. What you thought was finished can be renewed.

And Psalm 23:3 reminds us: *"He restores my soul."* Restoration isn't just what God does; it's who He is.

**The Power of Renewal**

Romans 12:2 says, *"Do not conform to the pattern of this world, but be transformed by the renewing of your mind."*

Notice it doesn't say, *"be transformed by patching things up just enough to keep going."* It says *renew.* That's more than repair. Renewal is about God doing something fresh, something different, something only He can do.

In other words, we transform by renewing the motormouth in our minds — letting God silence the noisy chatter, repair what can be repaired, and replace what needs to go.

### Practical Ways God Rebuilds Us

Just like engines, sometimes God rebuilds us piece by piece, and sometimes He gives us a brand new start. Either way, here are some ways to lean into His renewing work:

**1. Release what's beyond repair.**
The Tempo couldn't last forever, no matter how many repairs were made. Likewise, there are seasons, habits, and even mindsets that God is asking you to let go. Don't cling to what He's asking you to release.

2. **Cooperate with the Mechanic.**
When an engine is being rebuilt, every piece is taken apart. It's a process. Spiritually, God sometimes dismantles things in us to put them back together right. Trust the process. Cooperate with what He's doing, even if it feels uncomfortable.

3. **Accept temporary fixes, but aim for lasting change.**
Just like water in an overheated engine can get you home but won't fix the busted hose, sometimes small practices (like taking a deep

breath or journaling) get us through a moment. But lasting renewal comes from deeper work — prayer, scripture, counseling, and allowing God to heal at the root.

4. **Embrace the new.**
Eventually, the Tempo had to go. Sometimes God closes the door on an old chapter to open the way for something brand new. Don't fear the replacement. A new season, a new calling, a renewed mind — they are gifts that keep you moving forward.

**Reflection**

- What parts of your life have you been patching, when God might be asking you to release them?
- Where has God already rebuilt or restored you — and how did that change your life?
- What "renewal" do you need in the motormouth of your mind today?

Take time to write down one area you're ready to stop patching and start surrendering to God for full renewal and restoration.

**Prayer**

Father, You know the motormouth in my mind and all the parts of my life I've tried to patch together. I confess that I've sometimes clung to things You were asking me to release. I've rebuilt the same broken pieces over and over, instead of trusting You for something new.

But thank You that You are also the God of restoration. What I've thought was wasted, You can redeem. What I thought was junk, You can polish into something timeless. You restore my soul, and You rebuild what feels beyond repair.

Today I choose to hand it all to You. Be my Rebuilder. Take apart what needs to go, renew what needs Your touch, and replace what is no longer serving my journey.

Transform me by renewing my mind. Silence the chatter. Steady my thoughts. Give me the courage to embrace the new seasons and opportunities You are bringing my way.

In Jesus' name, Amen.

**Chapter 7:Takeaways**

- God rebuilds what's broken — sometimes He restores, sometimes He replaces.
- What looks like junk to us may be a classic in the making to Him.
- The motormouth says, *"Too broken."* God says, *"Restored and renewed."*
- Trust the Master Mechanic's judgment on whether to rebuild or replace.

# Chapter 8
# The Oil of the Mind

**Chapter Eight: The Oil of the Mind**

One of the cars I owned had an oil leak that refused to be solved. The dealership mechanics told me they couldn't locate the exact leak without pulling the entire engine, which would cost what felt like a small fortune at the time.

So, I lived with it.

I kept a few bottles of 10w40 on hand in the trunk, just in case the oil got low. Every so often, I'd pop the hood, check the dipstick, and top it off. It worked — at least enough to keep the car running.

But here's the thing: ignoring the leak didn't make it go away. In fact, it left permanent stains on my driveway. Dark spots that never quite washed out. Even years later, the marks were there as evidence of the leak I chose to live with instead of fully repairing.

That old car taught me something: you can live with leaks for a while, but they always leave a mark.

**Oil Keeps Things Alive**

Oil is the lifeblood of an engine. Without it, metal grinds against metal, heat builds up, and eventually the motor seizes. Oil keeps everything running smooth, cool, and protected.

Spiritually, oil represents something even more important — the presence of God, the anointing of His Spirit, the refreshment of His Word.

- Psalm 23:5 says, *"You anoint my head with oil; my cup overflows."*
- In the parable of the ten virgins (Matthew 25), those without oil in their lamps were left unprepared when the bridegroom came.
- Throughout scripture, oil was used to consecrate, heal, and set apart for God's work.

In other words: just like an engine can't run without oil, your mind and spirit can't run without God's presence.

**The Motormouth and the Leaks**

When the motormouth in my mind runs unchecked, it leaks constantly.

- *"You're running out."*
- *"You don't have enough."*
- *"You can get by with just a little top-off — don't bother with the real fix."*

It convinces me that quick fixes will do, that topping off here and there is enough to keep going.

But the stains in my soul tell the truth. Leaks leave marks. Bitterness that spills out. Regret that stains relationships. Exhaustion that doesn't go away.

The motormouth says, *"Live with the leak."* But God says, *"Bring it to Me. I'll fix the source, not just the symptom."*

**Lessons from Oil Changes and Leaks**

The oil in my old car taught me lessons about the oil in my mind:

**1. Fresh oil keeps things smooth.**
Engines last longer when the oil is changed regularly. Our minds are steadier when we keep coming back to God for fresh encounters through prayer, worship, and His Word. Yesterday's oil can't keep you running forever.

**2. Ignoring leaks leaves stains.**
The stains on my driveway are a reminder:

what we tolerate spiritually leaves a mark. Unchecked sin, unspoken resentment, or neglected habits may not stop us immediately, but they leave scars on our hearts and relationships.

**3. Topping off is good, but not enough.**
I kept bottles of 10w40 on hand, and it worked for a while. But topping off isn't the same as a real fix. Spiritually, "topping off" looks like quick prayers only in emergencies, or opening the Bible only when we're desperate. It helps in the moment, but it won't replace a full renewal.

**4. The real fix costs something.**
Pulling the engine to find the leak felt too expensive, so I avoided it. Spiritually, surrender often feels costly too. Slowing down, confessing, seeking counsel, resting in God's presence — these require something of us. But the cost of neglect is always higher.

**God's Oil Never Runs Out**

The good news is this: God never lets us run dry when we stay connected to Him. His oil is abundant, overflowing, and always fresh.

Psalm 92:10 says, *"I have been anointed with fresh oil."*

God doesn't just want you topped off with yesterday's leftover. He wants to give you **fresh oil** for today's journey. He wants to anoint your mind, cool your anxieties, and keep your life running smooth under the hood.

### The Power of the Anointing

There's something else oil does in the spiritual sense: it breaks what binds. Isaiah 10:27 says, *"The yoke shall be destroyed because of the anointing."*

Think about that. The oil of God doesn't just keep things running smooth — it destroys the yokes of oppression, fear, anxiety, and bondage. The motormouth in your mind may chatter about what you'll never escape, but the anointing silences it.

The same way oil protects an engine from seizing, God's anointing protects your life from being locked up by the enemy's lies. Where the Spirit of the Lord is, the yoke is broken, and you are free.

**Reflection**

- Where in your life are you trying to "top off" instead of allowing God to do a full repair?
- What stains has ignoring the leaks left behind?
- What would it look like to invite God to give you **fresh oil** instead of running on fumes?

Write down one area where you've been patching or topping off, and pray about how God might be inviting you to a deeper renewal.

**Prayer**

Father, the motormouth in my mind runs dry without Your presence. I confess I've tried to patch the leaks, top off with quick fixes, and live with stains instead of letting You do the full repair.

Anoint me afresh with Your oil. Change what needs changing. Clean what's been stained. And keep me running smooth with Your Spirit every single day.

Thank You for fresh oil, Lord. Thank You for not just topping me off, but restoring me completely. Thank You that by Your anointing, every yoke is broken and I am free.

In Jesus' name, Amen.

**Chapter 8: Takeaways**

- Oil is to the engine what God's anointing is to your life — it keeps everything running smooth.
- Quick "top-offs" aren't enough; you need fresh oil daily.
- The motormouth says, *"Just live with the leak."* God says, *"My anointing breaks the yoke."*
- Don't ignore the stains — bring the leaks to God for a full repair.

Chapter 9

# Stabilized by the Mounts

**Chapter Nine: Stabilized by the Mounts**

My 20 year old Mazda 626 taught me a lesson I'll never forget about stability. One day, I noticed the car was shaking and vibrating badly. It wasn't just a little shimmy — the whole car trembled when it was running, and it felt like something under the hood was straining to hold together.

When I took it to the mechanic, the diagnosis came quick: *"It's your motor mounts."*

He explained that the mounts were worn out. I needed three in total, but there was one especially important one — the main mount in the front middle, near the radiator. That mount carried the most weight. Without it, the engine rocked back and forth like it was trying to shake itself loose.

The mechanic said something that stuck with me: *"When the mounts go bad, the whole engine rattles. And if you don't fix it, that vibration doesn't just stay in one place. It starts to affect other parts under the hood."*

That hit me.

Because isn't that what happens to us, too?

When we're not stabilized in life, when the foundations of our minds and spirits aren't secure, the rattling spreads. It shows up in our decisions, our relationships, our emotions, even our health. Instability doesn't stay in one place. It leaks out everywhere.

## The Trinity Holds Us Steady

Motor mounts do for engines what the Father, Son, and Holy Spirit do for us: they hold everything steady.

- The **Father** anchors us in His love.
- The **Son** secures us in His salvation.
- The **Spirit** steadies us in our daily walk.

Three mounts, one engine. Three Persons, one God.

And just like my Mazda needed all its mounts in place to stop shaking, we need the fullness of God — Father, Son, and Spirit — to keep us stable when life vibrates.

## When Life Shakes

Psalm 62:2 says, *“He alone is my rock and my salvation; He is my fortress, I will never be shaken.”*

But let’s be honest: we feel shaken all the time. Pressure rattles us. Disappointment shakes us. Anxiety vibrates through us like an engine straining under stress.

And the motormouth in my mind is quick to jump in with its commentary:

- *"You're about to fall apart."*
- *"You can't hold it together."*
- *"One wrong move and you'll shake yourself loose."*

But God whispers something different:

- *"Be still, and know that I am God."* (Psalm 46:10)
- *"You will not be shaken."* (Psalm 62:6)
- *"I am the One who holds all things together."* (Colossians 1:17)

**The Main Mount**

The mechanic told me one mount was especially important — the main one in the front, the one that carried the heaviest load.

Spiritually, Jesus is that main Mount. He's the One who bore the heaviest load at the cross. He carried the weight of our sin, shame, and brokenness. And because He carried it, we don't have to.

Hebrews 13:8 says, *"Jesus Christ is the same yesterday, today, and forever."* He doesn't wear out. He doesn't weaken. He doesn't crack under pressure. He is the Mount that holds steady when everything else is shaking.

**Practical Steps to Stay Stabilized**

**1. Know your foundation.**
The Father's love is unshakable. Nothing you do can make Him love you less. Rest in that anchor.

**2. Trust your Savior.**
Jesus has already secured your victory. You don't have to hold the weight of the world. He already carried it.

**3. Lean on the Spirit.**
The Holy Spirit steadies you daily, whispering truth when the motormouth gets loud. Listen for His guidance — He is your stabilizer in real time.

**4. Replace worn mounts.**
Just like my Mazda needed new mounts, sometimes we need to renew our trust in God. Where are you relying on your own strength instead of His? Let Him replace your shaky places with His strength.

### Reflection

- Where do you feel the "shaking" in your life right now?
- Which mount (Father's love, Son's salvation, Spirit's guidance) do you need to lean on most in this season?
- How have you seen God hold you steady in the past, even when everything else was rattling?

Write down one area of your life where you need God's stabilizing power, and pray over it this week.

### Prayer

Father, the motormouth in my mind tells me I'm falling apart, that I can't hold it together, and that one wrong move will shake me loose.

But I thank You that You are my Mounts — Father, Son, and Holy Spirit — the anchors that keep me steady.

Father, ground me in Your love. Jesus, secure me with Your salvation. Holy Spirit, steady me in my daily walk.

Replace my worn-out places with Your strength. Keep me from rattling loose under the pressures of life. And remind me that in You, I will not be shaken.

In Jesus' name, Amen.

**Chapter 9: Takeaways**

- Motor mounts keep the engine steady; the Father, Son, and Spirit keep your life steady.
- Instability spreads — if you're rattling inside, it will affect every other part of your life.
- The motormouth says, *"You're falling apart."* God says, *"You will not be shaken."*
- Stay anchored in the love of the Father, the salvation of the Son, and the guidance of the Spirit.

CHAPTER 10

# In God's Timing

**Chapter Ten: God's Timing Belt**

I remember hearing a loud squealing noise under the hood one day. At first, it was just annoying, but I knew something wasn't right. The sound got louder every time I started the car, and it made me wince.

When I finally took it in, the mechanic shook his head and said, *"That's your timing belt."*

I had no idea how important that belt was until he explained it to me. If the timing belt failed completely, the whole engine could be ruined. It had to be replaced before it snapped, or the damage would be far worse than the inconvenience of the noise.

### How the Timing Belt Works

I had to look this up to understand it better, but here's what I found about how the timing belt supports the motor's function: it keeps the engine's internal parts moving in perfect rhythm. This synchronized movement is crucial for allowing the engine to properly take in fuel and air and expel exhaust, leading to smooth and efficient engine operation.

Without the belt's steady rhythm, the engine falls out of sync, misfires, or even seizes completely.

And isn't that what happens when we try to run outside of God's timing? When we push ahead, lag behind, or refuse to listen to the Spirit's rhythm, our lives lose their smoothness. Things feel rough, exhausting, out of sync. But when we align with His timing, everything runs the way it was designed to.

### Timing Matters

The timing belt synchronizes everything under the hood. Spiritually, timing synchronizes everything in our lives with God's will.

When the belt slips, everything feels off. When we ignore God's timing, life feels the same way — misaligned, noisy, strained.

The squealing sound under my hood was a warning. And often, God gives us warnings too: restlessness, closed doors, delays. They're His way of telling us something is out of sync, urging us to trust His pace instead of forcing our own.

## The Motormouth and Timing

The motormouth in my mind is especially loud when it comes to timing.

- *"You're falling behind."*
- *"You should be further along by now."*
- *"Hurry up or you'll miss it."*

But God says something different:

- *"He has made everything beautiful in its time."* (Ecclesiastes 3:11)
- *"Those who wait on the Lord shall renew their strength."* (Isaiah 40:31)
- *"The vision awaits its appointed time... it will surely come; it will not delay."* (Habakkuk 2:3)

## The Belt of Truth

As I studied the timing belt, I couldn't help but think of another belt — the one Paul describes in Ephesians 6:14: *"Stand firm then, with the belt of truth buckled around your waist."*

The belt of truth holds the armor of God in place, just as the timing belt holds the engine's rhythm together. Without truth, everything else wobbles and falls apart.

So when the motormouth squeals about timing — telling you you're late, forgotten, or out of step — it's the belt of truth that steadies you. Truth says:

- God's timing is perfect.
- His plan will not fail.
- He is working all things together for your good.

**Encouragement for the Waiting**

Perhaps you are struggling with God's timing right now. Just know that His plans are perfect. Put on the whole armor of God, and pay particular attention to the **belt of truth** in this season of your life. When the motormouth tells you that you're behind, forgotten, or out of sync, the belt of truth holds everything together. Trust that God is synchronizing every detail for your good, and that in His time, it will all come together smoothly.

**Reflection**

- Where do you hear "squealing" in your life — signals that something is out of sync?
- How has the motormouth been lying to you about your timing?
- What scriptures (belt of truth) do you need to hold onto right now to stay steady?

**Prayer**

Father, the motormouth in my mind tells me I'm late, behind, or that I'll miss out. But I know Your timing is perfect.

Thank You for the timing belt reminders in my life — the squeals, the signals, the closed doors that keep me aligned with Your rhythm. Help me to trust Your timing, even when I don't understand it. Teach me to wear the belt of truth so I can stand firm against lies.

Synchronize my life with Your will, Lord. And remind me that in Your perfect time, everything will come together smoothly.

In Jesus' name, Amen.

**Chapter 10: Takeaways**

- The timing belt keeps the engine in sync; God's timing keeps your life in rhythm.
- Ignoring the "squeals" leads to breakdowns — pay attention to the warnings.
- The motormouth says, *"You're late, you'll miss it."* Truth says, *"God makes everything beautiful in its time."*
- Strap on the belt of truth to silence the lies about timing and trust God's perfect schedule.

# CHAPTER 11
# Tune Up the Motor

**Chapter Eleven: Tuning Up the Motor-mouth**

My dad didn't just teach me about tools

and repairs — he preached maintenance. He would say it often: *"Take care of the little things before they become big things."*

He taught me to keep the oil changed, because a motor can't survive running dry. He reminded me to take care of the brakes as soon as I heard that first squeal, because once they started grinding, it would mess up the rotors. He told me to replace wiper blades when they were worn, because you need a clear view to drive safely. He showed me the importance of putting the right gas in the car and inflating the tires to the proper pressure. And he always said to keep a spare in the trunk, just in case.

Back then, I thought he was just teaching me how to take care of a car. But years later, I realized — he was giving me wisdom for my soul.

**Spiritual Maintenance Lessons**

**1. Keep the oil changed.**
Oil = God's presence, His anointing. Stay filled with fresh encounters, not old leftovers. Without fresh oil, the motormouth in your mind will run hot and dry.

**2. Take care of the brakes when they squeal.**
Brakes = boundaries. When something feels off, don't ignore it. Stop before damage spreads. When you refuse to set boundaries, the motormouth cranks up with guilt and pressure. Boundaries silence that noise.

**3. Replace the wiper blades.**
Clear vision = discernment. Don't drive blind in the rain of life's chaos. Let God renew your perspective so you can see clearly. Otherwise, the motormouth convinces you you'll never find your way.

**4. Use the right fuel.**
Gas = what you feed your mind and spirit. Junk in, junk out. Fill yourself with God's Word, truth, and encouragement — not the toxic stuff that burns dirty. Feed on garbage, and the motormouth has plenty of fuel for its lies.

**5. Keep the tires properly inflated.**
Tires = balance. Too much or too little pressure leads to wear and blowouts. Spiritually, balance is key — between work and rest, giving and receiving, doing and being. If you don't maintain balance, the motormouth tells you you'll never keep up.

**6. Always have a spare.**
Life will throw curveballs. Faith is your spare — the backup hope and strength that keeps you moving when things go flat. The

motormouth says you're stranded for good. God says you've got what you need to keep rolling.

**Your Spiritual Tune-Up Checklist**

✓ **Spark Plugs → Rekindle Your Fire**
Ask God to reignite the spark of the Holy Spirit in you daily.

✓ **Air Filter → Breathe Clean**
Spend time in the Word to filter out lies, negativity, and worldly noise.

✓ **Fuel Filter → Guard Your Heart**
Watch what you allow into your spirit — keep your fuel pure with prayer and discernment.

✓ **Oil Change → Seek Fresh Anointing**
Don't run on yesterday's oil. Ask for fresh strength and presence for today's journey.

✓ **Belts & Hoses → Stay Connected**
Maintain strong connections with God and with the Body of Christ — relationships that keep you steady.

✓ **Battery → Stay Powered Through Prayer**
Keep your prayer life charged so you

always have power to start and keep moving.

✓ **Wheel Alignment → Check Your Path** Regularly align your life with God's Word so you stay on course.

**The Motormouth and Maintenance**

Here's the truth: the motormouth in my mind doesn't just go away forever. Like a car engine, it needs regular tune-ups. If I skip the oil changes, ignore the squealing brakes, or run on low fuel, the motormouth cranks right back up — louder than ever.

- When I skip prayer, the motormouth floods me with fear.
- When I ignore boundaries, the motormouth traps me in guilt and regret.
- When I let my vision blur, the motormouth convinces me I can't see my future clearly.
- When I fill myself with junk, the motormouth reminds me how empty I feel.

- When I lose balance, the motormouth whispers that I'll never get it right.

But when I stay tuned up — when I keep the oil fresh, listen to the squeals early, keep my vision clear, and fill my tank with God's Word — the motormouth loses its grip. It quiets down, and what was once noise becomes clarity.

That's the power of regular maintenance. It doesn't just keep the car running — it keeps the motormouth from running me.

**Don't Worry About the Price**

Here's the best part: Jesus already paid it all. The ultimate repair bill was covered at the cross. Every tune-up, every renewal, every act of restoration in your life is possible because the price has been paid in full.

So you don't have to fear breakdowns. You don't have to worry about whether you can afford the work it will take to get your mind back on track. All you have to do is bring it to the Master Mechanic.

### Scripture Anchors

- **Philippians 1:6** — *"He who began a good work in you will carry it on to completion until the day of Christ Jesus."*
- **Romans 8:32** — *"He who did not spare His own Son but gave Him up for us all—how will He not also, along with Him, graciously give us all things?"*
- **Colossians 3:10** — *"Put on the new self, which is being renewed in knowledge in the image of its Creator."*

### Reflection

- What spiritual maintenance steps are easiest for you — and which do you tend to put off?
- Where is God inviting you to schedule regular tune-ups instead of waiting for breakdowns?
- How does it change your perspective to know the cost of your renewal has already been paid?

**Prayer**

Father, thank You that You are the Master Mechanic of my mind and my life. Thank You that the cost has already been paid by Jesus, and I never have to fear the repair bill.

Help me to gather and use the tools You've given me. Remind me to schedule regular time with You. Teach me to care for this body, the temple of Your Spirit. Show me where the hoses and belts of my life need checking, and replace what's worn out with something new.

Tune me up, Lord. Adjust me, refine me, and keep me aligned with Your will. May my mind run smoothly, my heart stay steady, and my life bring glory to You.

In Jesus' name, Amen.

**Chapter 11: Takeaways**

- Regular maintenance prevents breakdowns — spiritually and mentally.
- The motormouth gets loud again if you neglect prayer, boundaries, balance, or truth.
- Dad's lessons on oil, brakes, wipers, fuel, tires, and spares apply directly to the care of your soul.
- The Master Mechanic handles the repairs, and the bill has already been paid by Jesus.
- Tune-ups keep your mind running smoothly and your life aligned with God's will.

# Epilogue: Dad's Last Ford

For those who've become a fan of Dad's Fords by now, you'll be glad to know he never stopped buying them. From the same dealership in town — Lief Johnson Ford. Dad stayed faithful to his favorite cars, just as he stayed faithful to everything he loved.

His last purchase was a Ford Explorer. He drove it faithfully until the day he retired from his forty-plus-year career as a custodian at the local elementary school. That Explorer now rests in the yard. Dad doesn't crank the motor anymore, and he'll never get rid of that Ford. I think it's growing flowers — like a living garden — as if even the car has joined him in retirement.

Just like all the Fords before it, that Explorer carries more than memories of miles. It carries the story of a man who worked hard, stayed loyal, and took care of what God entrusted to him.

And Dad's faithfulness wasn't only seen in the cars he drove. In 1998, when Mama went to be with the Lord, suddenly at the young age of forty-five, they had already been married for twenty-seven years. Dad had plenty of opportunities to let the motormouth grind away at his mind. But instead of giving in to despair, he put his trust in God. He stayed faithful to his faith, to us six children, and to the life they had built. That's the kind of strength you can't find under any hood. It only comes from the One who promises never to leave us nor forsake us.

And maybe that's the real lesson here. With commitment and dedication to renewing your mind, one day you will retire the stress, the worry, the anxiety, and the doubt. You can overcome any breakdown, because the

Master is your Mechanic, and He never leaves you nor forsakes you.

You'll take fishing trips. You'll go to church. You'll sit with your family and enjoy the simple moments. And you'll know what it feels like to live with the peace that passes all understanding — because the motormouth has finally quieted, the engine rests, and your mind runs smooth.

I guess you could say Dad's faith is Ford tough. And with God as your Master Mechanic, your faith will be strong too.

## Thank You for Reading

Thank you so much for taking this ride with me through *The Motormouth in My Mind*. I pray the stories, scriptures, and lessons spoke to your heart the same way they spoke to mine as I wrote them.

Books are meant to be shared. If this book encouraged you, strengthened you, or helped you quiet the motormouth in your mind, would you do me a favor?

Please take a few minutes to leave an honest review where you purchased this book. Your feedback not only helps me grow as an author, but it also helps other readers discover the message they might need at just the right time.

Your voice matters. Your story matters. And I am truly honored that you chose to spend time with mine.

With gratitude,
*Lynn R. Davis*

CHAPTER
Motormouth Metaphor Glossary

## Motormouth Metaphor Glossary

**Revving Engine** → Racing thoughts that spin fast but go nowhere. A mind stuck in overdrive.

**Flooded Engine** → Overloading your thoughts with too much, too fast, until everything stalls.

**Grinding Gears** → The strain of worry and stress wearing you down, like metal scraping metal.

**Check Engine Light** → Anxiety signaling that something deeper needs attention.

**Throwing a Rod** → Breaking down under pressure, feeling stranded and unable to move forward.

**Overheated Engine** → Stress or burnout from pushing too hard without rest or renewal.

**The Rebuilt Life** → God's restoration — taking what's broken and making it new again.

**Oil of the Mind** → The fresh anointing and presence of God that keeps your spirit running smoothly.

**Motor Mounts** → Stability found in the Father, Son, and Holy Spirit holding your life steady.

**Timing Belt** → God's timing bringing everything into alignment, synchronized for His purpose.

**Spiritual Tune-Up** → Ongoing maintenance of your mind and spirit — spark plugs of faith, air filter of God's Word, fuel filter of a guarded heart, and prayer as your power source.

Printed in Dunstable, United Kingdom

71675815R00067

# Contents

# Introduction

Buying a newly built, newly refurbished or newly converted property is a major decision. It is also a comparatively infrequent event, so most people have little practical experience of what is involved. Usually they have to rely on others.

The specific aim of this book is to help you check your newly built home more thoroughly than you might do otherwise. It will also help you to understand your rights and how the building "system" works. It gives you some general hints and tips about things to do and things to watch.

People mainly choose a newly built property because of its location, price and size. They usually assume that the building has been soundly constructed on good land. Sadly, there are many cases where this assumption has turned out to be seriously flawed. In the worst instances, quite appalling construction practices have led to people's lives being seriously disrupted or even devastated. No doubt they all thought they were buying their dream home not one that would become a nightmare. Some properties will, of course, be well built, others not. Usually there will be a lot of sales literature designed to stop you thinking you are being sold a bad house, one that has not been properly built or properly inspected.

So how are you going to know the difference? If you buy a property which has problems, what can you do?

**In practice the buyer of a newly built property has no right to a refund if it is faulty**. At best a claim can be made under a building warranty or guarantee scheme. If the land is contaminated, there is probably no warranty cover. Compare this with what happens when you buy even a humble pencil. If it is faulty, you take it back and have the right to a refund or a replacement as you wish.

The existence of a warranty, which is anyway limited in its scope (meaning that you are not covered for some things that might go wrong), is helpful but it is only as good as its provider and its limitations.

Many people think that when they buy a newly built property which has a 10-year construction warranty, this is a safe bet. They expect that the house has been properly built to comply with the law of the land, unless the vendor has disclosed otherwise. They expect that the builder will have checked the soundness of construction and the correct operation of the services. They expect that the Building Control Officer will have done a proper job inspecting the property before finally passing it. They also expect that any inspections by warranty providers are competent and that the underlying technical standards are properly devised. It is true that the UK has some of the most highly controlled building legislation in the world - but still avoidable problems do occur.

If there are faults for which you can make legitimate claims, the builder might try not to do the work, to delay it, hoping that you become fed up waiting, or do a bodged job. Even if the work is done satisfactorily, you will still need to allow the builder access to your home to do the remedial work. In the worst case, you and your furnishings will have to move out while major structural work is undertaken. There cannot be many people who would willingly pay the full price for a property with serious problems if they knew in advance.

## NHBC (National House-Building Council)

**NHBC (National House-Building Council)** has been in existence for nearly 70 years and it has set many high standards for building construction practice. This is welcome. That it has been needed for so many years is a reflection on the practices of sectors of the building industry. Be aware, though, that the NHBC does have its limitations. NHBC publicity implies that homeowners should not 'normally' need to have their own survey done. The NHBC wants you to rely on its inspectors, yet when you move in, you are given a brochure to help you check the property! Guidance given by the NHBC to solicitors, however, is more explicit, stating that its surveyors will visit sites every three to four weeks on average, concentrating on the parts that buyers cannot see and leaving owners to check the finishings for themselves!

Usually the property is mortgaged to a lender. The survey done for the lender (at the buyer's expense) is a valuation survey. Lenders are only concerned with security for the money advanced but obviously they do not want to have defective houses on their books.

It is also clear that if building control inspection is undertaken by NHBC Building Control Services Limited, probably the same person inspects for both Building Control compliance and for insurability. The wording used indicates that their inspectors cannot see everything and that a lot can happen in three or four weeks on a building site.

In its 10-year scheme the NHBC arranges that problems in the first two years are really down to the builder to solve but the NHBC will intervene if necessary.

The NHBC also says its scheme is fully transferable to second purchasers. However, on at least one occasion, claims to faults which the second purchaser found but which the first purchaser had failed to notice were disallowed. (Check the wording of your policy in case it has since changed.)

From the third to the tenth year, the owner's policy says that the NHBC will not allow any claims for structural timbers which are technically undersized if there is no apparent damage. What this seems to imply is that if the timbers are below their calculated and approved load-bearing capacity but the roof is not actually sagging, no remedial work will be authorised.

The small print regarding exclusions for this period also indicated to owners that NHBC would not meet a claim if the owner had other insurance for it!

NHBC is now facing competition from Zurich Municipal, and in the housing association market, Housing Association Property Mutual and more recently 'Shield'.

This whole market is undergoing a period of rapid transition – to the benefit of homeowners. Be clear what the terms of your home's policy are.

It is quite probable that there may be some unavoidable minor defects, such as natural shrinkage, which do not seriously inconvenience the buyer. What is unacceptable, for example, is a major UK building company selling a new house with a full construction warranty and Building Control certificates but with significant defects. This is not a hypothetical situation, but something which has happened on many occasions.

It is unfortunately no guarantee of quality that your house has been sold to you by a well-known builder. If your newly built house is illegally constructed, rectification orders will be served on you as the owner.

It is quite possible that having checked your house thoroughly, you may find that it is well built and inspected. There are, of course, builders and tradespeople who take a real pride in their work. The reputation of builders and inspectors who do a professional job should be recognised and if you are satisfied, you might like to write an appreciative letter to the people concerned. (Bear in mind, though, that if you were later to find a fault, the letter could be used as evidence against you.) Beware, too, of signing the builder's Satisfaction Form the instant you move in.

## How to Use This Book

The first part of this book is mainly about checking and surveying your new or potentially new home. It gives some suggestions about how to deal with faults and broadly outlines how the building "system" works. The second part covers lots of points individually in alphabetical order.

This sourcebook is designed to be used with other publications (a useful list appears on pages 164-8) some of which you should be able to find in your local public library. New house-building and refurbishment is conducted in the constantly moving sands of changing laws, changing regulations and changing technical standards. Homebuyers who encounter problems may end up doing the research themselves. Consulting a solicitor is an expensive option.

Those supplying construction insurance cover can also quickly change their inclusions and exclusions as part of their marketing strategy. The names and addresses of organisations can also change.

Please don't regard this source book as being definitive. The intention is to give pointers and suggestions. It concentrates on the potential problem areas and hopefully will enable you to take a systematic approach and to use any professional advisers more efficiently. Ultimately, it is entirely up to you what you do or do not do.

Good luck with your new home … you might just need it!

### The Housing Market

Currently there are around 200,000 new homes (including houses, flats and maisonettes) being built in the UK every year. Public housing accounts for about 25 per cent of the newly built market in value. About a quarter of properties are flats and three-quarters houses.

It is said that four-fifths of building firms employ less than 10 people and only about a third of building companies are registered with the NHBC.

Between 80 and 90 per cent of these properties are certified by NHBC against construction faults, with Zurich Municipal being a new insurer in this market; others are expected. Some are profit-making organisations. The NHBC is not.

According to the Department of the Environment, around 4.4 million new homes will be created between 1991 and 2016. The problem is where to put them. The government wants up to 60 per cent of these to be built on 'brown land' (land which has already been used for housing, industry or tipping refuse). There will also be pressure on the green belt for the remaining 40 per cent which will inevitably create considerable opposition by some environmentalists. This pressure will mean that properties will be squashed together – not good if you are next to difficult neighbours. Room sizes may be further reduced. Even today many people find their garages are too small for the average family saloon car.

The NHBC does, however, provide a newly built conversions insurance for buyers of refurbished flats and separately built homes newly converted from old structures. At present it dominates the building fault insurance market for privately-owned homes.

# Developers, Builders and Your Rights

The act of building a house is a complicated task, even for an experienced builder. Every house and the land on which it is built has its own character, its own problems.

Many people and organisations come together to build or convert properties and this is done within the context of local and national legal requirements, codes of practice and technical standards – which are constantly being updated. Much planning and coordination are involved and builders encounter many problems which we – as inhabitants – may never know. The builder may be let down by a supplier or have recruited someone whose work is just incompetent.

## The Laws

New houses are built within strict legislative frameworks. There are laws to be obeyed and penalties for breach. For example, the Building Act applies to the construction and structure of new buildings, extending to fire safety and energy-saving measures and access for the disabled. Similar Acts govern the installation and supply of services – mains electricity, gas, mains water, sewerage and telecommunications.

The laws that apply to a newly built property will probably be those in existence when the foundations were laid. If your property is a conversion or refurbishment, then it is likely that the regulations that apply will be those in existence when any plans were submitted for local authority approval or when services were installed. To be sure, make enquiries.

For example, older parts of a property, such as external walls, usually need not be rebuilt but the latest requirements for thermal insulation will have to be fulfilled. The people involved in the construction are supposed to know what regulations apply and take heed.

If a building is constructed without regulatory compliance, it may be illegal in that respect, and potentially dangerous. Any enforcement notice will be served on the owner or the occupier (you or the developer). There are penalties for breaching the law.

The builder, or developer, will have plans and a technical specification for the property. It is usually the builder or developer who initially owns the land and who funds the development. A commercial developer's aim is to make a profit through the sale of the property. Housing Associations can also be developers but usually not for a profit.

The developer has to apply for planning permission by lodging documents with the local authority – either a district council or metropolitan borough council. The planning application is open for public inspection and members of the public can raise objections within a specified time. The planning committee of the local authority will then make a decision. This may take into account development plans which the council itself has, as well as other factors. Politics may be involved.

You will be able to see the local council's planning file for your own property and can usually buy copies of the relevant pages, since copyright does not fully apply to plans which are put on the public record.

When a planning authority gives consent, a number of restrictions are usually applied. These restrictions are listed in the planning file; you can also

### Brochures – Selling a Dream

Major developers will provide you with glossy brochures, perhaps evoking the new lifestyle that will in theory be yours if you buy the property. The development has probably been given an evocative name without negative connotations. The sales literature is obviously designed to put the property in the best light, and psychological hooking methods may have been used to lure you into buying. To an extent, this is legitimate marketing.

Be aware that the glossy sales literature will probably state in very small print that the text is not actually a formal description of the property (and so is not governed by the Property Misdescriptions Act) nor is it part of any sales contract with you. The developer's legal adviser has insisted the wording is there.

The sales person giving you the brochure may not have emphasised that it is not entirely reliable. Nor, if the new plot happens to be on a landfill site, will that have always been mentioned. It is also unlikely that you will be told initially what the restrictive covenants are or whether the local authority has plans for some development that would adversely affect the value or enjoyment of the property.

check whether neighbouring properties comply. The planning authority may not permit the building of extensions if the land is suspected to be contaminated; it may require an open-plan site without fences. Often planning consent is given within a framework of governmental orders; there is usually a Local Development Plan, which you can ask to see in the local council offices.

The local authority is set up under statute and is empowered to take action to enforce any breach of planning consent. Violation of building regulations is a separate matter and is the province of the Building Control section of the local authority. Usually the Planning department and the Building Control department are separate divisions within the Environmental Services part of the local authority. Don't expect them to speak to each other!

Builders may start to build and then retrospectively apply for planning permission. If refused, the property may have to be demolished or be reinstated. The obtaining of planning permission is therefore important, particularly if what is involved is a change of use of the property or a site.

Having planning permission does not, however, mean that building control approval will be given to the specific structure intended or even that the site is economically viable or safe for building. Environmental and other factors may have to be taken into account. For example, the development may be in a Conservation Area or necessitate the removal of trees which are subject to Tree Preservation Orders. If a property is a Listed Building there are further restrictions on modifications.

Except for exempted building work (ask the council for details of exemptions if necessary), structural plans have to be deposited with a Building Control officer for examination for Building Act compliance. Usually an architect is involved here. The officer can approve, reject or propose amendments to the proposed plan.

### Who Does What?

Once building work begins, quantities of materials have to be estimated by a quantity surveyor and ordered on schedule by the clerk of works. A series of tradespeople have to be engaged to do their work, either as part of their employment with the developer or as subcontractors or employees of subcontracted firms.

Commonly, building firms will not employ people with all the necessary skills, so there is extensive use of subcontractors, e.g. groundworkers, bricklayers, joiners, plumbers, electricians, roofers, plasterers, and so on. There are standard contracts which many subcontractors use.

Various specialist designers can also be employed. A specialist may be called in to design the central heating and plumbing systems: some builders' merchants offer this as a service with a view to selling the parts. Kitchen, bathroom and bedroom planners may also be brought in to design the finishing elements.

### Who is Responsible?

Contractually the subcontractors are most probably legally responsible to the builder rather than to you. Faults in a new property should be reported in writing to the builder or developer who sold the home to you.

The builder will then be responsible for correcting faults in accordance with the contract with you or under law. This may end up with the builder invoking clauses in its contract with a subcontractor to have repairs made. It is very important to distinguish who has the legal responsibility and who might end up doing the work.

For example, under Building Regulations proper materials and workmanship must be used. Leaving aside any warranty claims, those builders or subcontractors using improper materials or workmanship can be prosecuted for breach of the appropriate Building Regulations. (These regulations differ in Scotland, Northern Ireland, and England and Wales.)

If construction warranty insurance exists, that may mean involving another set of people from a different organisation.

If you have construction fault insurance, some (but not all) unexpected faults can be remedied at no cost to you – but only if the fault actually occurs and it is then reported within the strict time limits, and if the warranty provider agrees and is still in business.

There are many injuries on building sites and the Health and Safety Executive will become involved if there is an accident. This can apply to accidents to workpeople who are effecting repairs in your home. To prevent accidents, the Construction (Design and Management) Regulations are now in force and require a Health and Safety file to be prepared for each significant site and for there to be a person responsible for health and safety matters on site. Hopefully, this will result in better practice and fewer injuries and deaths.

## Warranties

When you are being sold a new house, the marketing gloss may suggest that you can sleep soundly at night because you will have warranty cover. **Warranties are certainly useful but it is important to remember that they are always limited.** Further, warranties are usually time limited – you need to know the dates for when they start and finish. For electrical and gas appliances bought in a shop, the warranty usually starts from the date of purchase (and will be valid only if installed in accordance with the manufacturer's directions). However, in the case of house construction warranties, these may start not on the date of the purchase of the property, rather the date of completion of the building. This may be the date on which the property is signed off by the building inspector and on which the owner is first liable for council tax. This date may apply even if the property is not sold for years. Similarly, the end limit of construction warranty cover (probably ten years) may be ten years from the date of building completion rather than sale.

Unless the warranty terms say differently, a purchaser buying the vacant property after three years may have no initial two-year cover (provided for all faults by the NHBC scheme) but be left with only seven years of major fault guarantee insurance. (The purchaser may, of course, be under the impression that a 'ten year' cover was being given from the date of purchase.)

Clearly if you make a claim which is outside the time limits, even by one day, the warranty will not apply.

It will fall to you (or the property owner) to make a claim under the warranty. It is important that as owner, you record all claims in writing and state that they are warranty or guarantee claims. If you choose not to claim in writing, the developer or insurer may try to deny that they were told. It is their word against yours. If the developer does not agree with your claim, there could be the makings of a dispute. So consider asking for the fault to be inspected by the insurer (who will probably insist on a tidy deposit being paid, though this may be refundable.)

In any event you will have to wait until the developer is ready to do the work. Promises may be broken and it may take, as happened in one case, 18 months from the date of reporting the fault to the reluctant start of remedial work. Of course, the worst scenario is that the work is never done. **Remember, even the largest building company can go bankrupt or into liquidation, and thus be unable to do the work.**

You will also have to make your house available during this time, which could mean a certain amount of inconvenience. In the worse cases you might even be moved to a hotel or other new house temporarily – with all your furniture. The warranty scheme may pay for such accommodation; your policy document will tell you what is included and excluded.

Be wary of doing anything which may invalidate your warranty. If you wish to build an extension, your construction insurance may be invalidated because of work which is too near the foundations of the existing property. Any future problems will then have to be remedied at your own cost. A new extension is unlikely to be insured (though you could try to find a willing insurer).

## After-Sales Team

Most major developers have 'after-sales service' teams whose task it is to correct faulty and even uncompleted work. Some subcontracting companies even specialise in after-sales remedial work, so great are the problems. Don't, however, expect that a service team which has rectified faults in a neighbouring property will automatically visit you to see if your house has the same problems.

Remember, too, that a team is unlikely to inspect the property once it has been sold to you. The responsibility is entirely yours to inspect the property and to make any claims in a timely and written manner (in accordance with the claiming procedure) if anything appears to be wrong.

In other words, despite having paid a small fortune for the property and despite the sales hype about quality and your new lifestyle, you, the first occupant and owner, are expected to undertake the final quality control check. If you do not, you may never hear from the builder again. Major unreported faults may, however, be picked up by a prospective purchaser's surveyor when you try to sell the property. The result? The purchaser may withdraw the offer.

If you have bought a house from a builder without any construction insurance warranty, then you have contractual rights and can invoke any breaches of building law. You will however be left high and dry if the building company goes into liquidation.

A difficulty which we all have is that it is often not clear before purchase which properties are the good ones and which have problems. When you look round a new property for the first time you are taking in a general impression of the aesthetics, rather than looking for broken hinges. Once the property has been sold to you, the builder's main efforts are probably mostly directed to the next property under construction.

It has been said that a building developer, when pricing a new home, adds on a substantial percentage of money for after-sales service. But it is, of course, up to you to check your home and ask for the service.

If your new home is mortgaged, the lender may insist that you have insurance: it will help protect their investment. So it is also in their interest that your home is checked thoroughly. Consider employing your own surveyor (separate from the valuation surveyor the lender will employ). Remember, though, that independent inspection certificates do not actually certify that new houses comply with even the minimum relevant statutory requirements.

**The simple answer to the blunt question 'Does your certificate mean that my brand new home complies with all statutory requirements at the time it was sold to me?' will probably be a reluctant 'No'.**

Of course, it is supposed to do so according to the law, to the plans and to the builder's sales department, but there can be a great gap between what plans say and the grim reality of what sometimes happens on a working site, especially if the building developer is losing money or becoming greedy.

### SAFETY FIRST

No one has ever lived in your new home before you and so the utilities such as gas and electricity will all come under their first serious use with your occupancy. Although most, if not all, should work properly, you might encounter problems. Perhaps the drain hose from the washing machine might not be connected to the drain and a flood starts. It is worth remaining with each appliance when first used in case there is an immediate problem.

# The Land

If you are thinking of moving to a new locality, an Ordnance Survey map will give you a general idea of the geography and features such as rivers and roads. Large scale OS maps are available – ask at your local public library. The maps are never fully up to date and a new street may not appear for some years.

It is critical to have a plot of land which has access to the public highway. The access can either be direct, or over other land by written permission of the existing landowner and any subsequent owners.

Not to have access, even over a strip of land a metre wide between the plot and the highway, can mean that the owner cannot gain access to the plot without trespassing. The strip owner could even erect a wall. Sometimes these small strips of land are called "ransom strips", for obvious reasons. They tend to be discovered by accident, not being clearly shown on land maps.

The current and previous landowners of your plot may have applied restrictive covenants on future owners, limiting their freedom to act. Usually there is a chain of ownership and current owners can set conditions on subsequent owners. It can be quite complicated but the deeds will tell the story. Remember, such covenants must be observed, though they can be removed by a court.

It is a good idea to keep a working copy of the deeds in case you need to refer to them. You may also wish to find out who the owners of the adjacent land are and for what it is used. If the land is above mineworkings or an underground railway or tunnel, you can ask the relevant organisation for details.

You may also need to consider the stability of the land:

- ❒ Is it flat or sloping?
- ❒ Is it prone to flooding?
- ❒ Is it exposed?
- ❒ What is the soil type? This will determine the kinds of foundation used. Check local geological maps for information.
- ❒ Are there any problem trees or tree root systems?

A number of companies specialise in supplying land for building use and offer plot-finder services. If you are interested, look for the adverts in self-build magazines in major newsagents.

Any plot must have planning consent for both the building and its use. There are probably restrictions which you need to observe. It is unwise to buy a plot without it having planning consent, even consent in principle. However, the fact that a plot has planning consent does not mean that it is technically or economically feasible to build a house or that the structure will be approved for Building Act compliance.

Much land is registered by the Land Registry but some land is unregistered or indeed, is unregisterable since it is common land (see page 97).

It is wise to have a local authority search done before purchase as this should reveal any plans for new motorways, or bypasses in the vicinity. You should also be able to establish whether there is a nearby traffic route, railway, airport, sewerage works or a fish and chip shop!

## Contaminated Land

Contaminated land is used for building homes. The green belt cannot cope with the demand for housing, so many houses will be located on "brown" land. This is land which has been used before, other than for agriculture or parks. It may have been the site of previous houses or a long-gone industry or a landfill site. The sales brochures may not have been too forthcoming about that but remember the small print at the foot of the brochures disclaiming responsibility.

Some building companies specialise in building on "brown" land and many houses are safely erected to the enjoyment of the new owners. **"Brown" land does not mean bad land. Indeed, much of the land is perfectly serviceable.** However, there can be problem sites. Land may be contaminated with industrial waste – the topsoil may have high level of lead and other heavy metals, there may be waste solvents in the ground, or there may even be asbestos contamination. A problem with landfill sites is that the putrefying waste (such as domestic garbage) generates methane, an inflammable gas (see page 110).

This problem is now being taken very seriously. Special measures are taken to cover such tips with impermeable membranes and to pipe out the gas and perhaps even flare it off from a stack. Indeed, there are over 60 sites in the UK where waste methane is being used to generate electricity!

Not all new houses on such sites are affected but it is a potential problem which may very well have been glossed over by the sales people.

It is possible that greenfield sites could have been contaminated too; if so, the local authority may know about this.

Before industrial or commercial land changes hands these days, the purchaser conducts a survey and tries to identify any problems of contamination. Some companies are now providing a contaminated land database service which even if not completely definitive can be helpful. A proper survey can also be carried out, with soil sampling and analysis.

Although control over landfill sites is quite strict, old sites may be full of anything. Indeed it may not even be recorded where they all are. Historical records were often poorly kept or even non-existent.

The 1995 Environment Act placed a duty on certain local councils to inspect the land within their boundaries to identify contaminated land. The Act also requires the relevant authority to make the land "suitable for use". Before granting planning permission for a site, the authority will investigate and may then set conditions for any planning consent granted. These might include a ban on the building of any extensions in later years for fear of disturbing the underlying soil, or a requirement that contaminated soil be capped.

Inspection of the planning file should also give the background of the site and references to previous or associated files, which you can also research if necessary.

The developer is legally bound to comply with the planning consent but might not do so. If you want to know what the conditions are for your house, look at the district council's planning file which is open to public inspection. It is a serious matter if the planning consent has been breached. But even though the developer (if still in business) is culpable, you, as the property owner, could well be on the receiving end of any legal enforcement order.

Bear in mind that construction warranty schemes tend not to cover contaminated land. This is a major gap and the author hopes that insurance cover will be offered to newly built home owners in future.

A building surveyor who inspects your property may make no mention of contaminated land even if the surveyor knows that the land is in fact contaminated. This is because the subject may be outside the surveyor's professional indemnity insurance cover.

Affected soil can sometimes be treated *in situ.*. Sometimes soil solidification methods are used. These have been successfully used with soils which are contaminated with heavy metals. Additives such as cement are mixed with the soil until it becomes caked. This does, of course, mean that the land cannot be used for gardening.

Soil-capping methods may also be used. At its most basic, this can involve laying a heavy patio to cover the problem land. More sophisticated methods include the use of bacteria to "eat" the contaminants, but these are expensive. In some cases, the soil may be removed. This can, however, affect the groundwater level, which in turn will create problems with drinking water supplies or rivers.

Planning consents are usually given within the background of the development plan for the area prepared by the county council. This identifies zones for future development.

The Environment Agency has an important role to play in mitigating the effects of pollution and in stopping or minimising future pollution.

## Sloping Land

Severely sloping land may be at risk of slipping so the developer may have been required by the local planning authority to undertake civil engineering work to stabilise any embankments. Details will be found in the local council's planning file.

Land which is sloping needs to be properly drained too, otherwise there could be a mudslip. Keep a careful eye out for land which is bulging; there could be a serious problem in the making. Soil may bulge if there is a build-up of water behind it.

Foundations on sloping land may be of the stepped variety and the damp proof membrane will also then be stepped. See, for example, Chudley's *Building Construction Handbook*.

Basements of new homes which are on sloping sites are usually sealed against dampness. If any water gathers in the basement, this should be investigated.

Regular articles about contaminated land appear in trade journals, such as *Building Control* and *Building Homes*. Back numbers are available for reference in The British Library's Science Reference and Information Service's holdings in London.

# Construction Standards and Insurance

New houses are not built in a legislative vacuum. Rather there is a detailed legislative and regulatory framework. Your house should therefore have been built to minimum legal standards (at the least). So if you suspect there is a problem, refer to the relevant legislation.

If something is illegal, you as the owner of the property are responsible for rectification. In the worst cases, an enforcement notice could be served on you, as owner. For example, if a gas fire is illegally installed, a prohibition order may be served forbidding its use until repairs are effected and passed as complying with statutory requirements. Otherwise, using it may lead to an explosion, a fire or carbon monoxide poisoning.

The person and company who installed the fire in a dangerous way could be criminally indicted by the gas authority and will also be open to you for a civil claim for any damage.

If the property has construction insurance, provided by an organisation such as NHBC or Zurich Municipal, the technical standards set by the insurer are higher than those which must be met by the builder simply to comply with the law. If you have been provided with such insurance for the first 10 or 15 years of the property's life, it is the insurer's technical standards in force at the time your property was built which set the minimum standards.
Construction industry training courses endeavour to apply high standards. If construction standards fall, the builder may also be liable under Health and Safety legislation if there is an accident.

The builder may have provided carpets and curtains. These are unlikely to be covered in your construction insurance policy, but you may be allowed to claim for faulty materials by the terms of your purchase agreement.

If a washing machine and other manufactured electrical appliances have been installed but are faulty, you may not be able to reject these goods under the Sale of Goods Act; the goods have been supplied as fittings in the property rather than sold to you as a separately receipted transaction. You should, however, have common law rights, the manufacturer's guarantee and the builder's warranty.

## Construction Insurance

It is said that around 90 per cent of newly built homes are provided with a construction fault warranty. This is, however, a limited warranty, so if such a guarantee scheme applies to your home, you need to be very clear what the limitations are. Remember, too, that there is a time limit for reporting problems.

The NHBC has done a great deal to lift the standards of housebuilding and has a large number of inspectors throughout the UK who inspect houses as they are built and certify those which they judge fit for warranty cover. These certificates do not, however, mean that a property necessarily complies with all of the Technical Requirements set by them.

Insurers accept onto their register of housebuilders, developers and builders who appear to be competent technically and who agree to comply with the Membership Rules. One of the rules is that the housebuilder undertakes to build houses in compliance with the insurer's Technical

Requirements. The member has no choice other than absolute compliance. So if a registered property breaches Technical Requirements, the membership undertaking for registration is broken by the member. In case of a serious breach, the builder can be struck off the register.

Insurers publish their Technical Requirements in their Technical Manuals. Nowadays the NHBC Manual is printed in looseleaf form. A copy costs about £45 but individual sections can be purchased. Ask NHBC for a list of its publications. Zurich Municipal also has a manual. HAPM provides members with defect avoidance manuals and maintenance indicators.

As these manuals are somewhat technical, they are usually only seen by member companies rather than by homeowners. These requirements go beyond what is required by law and are typically complemented by a mandatory Schedule of Facilities and Services. These set out, for example, minimum storage accommodation, the sizes of waste outlets, central heating temperatures for rooms, the number of electrical sockets, and so on.

Leaving aside any warranty claim which you may have under these schemes, you may find that if your house does not comply with the Technical Requirements applying at the time, you will have a case for asking the insurer to review whether the housebuilder should remain on the Register. Even if not struck off, the builder may find that the insurer increases the premium it charges to provide insurance.

The certificate which the insurer provides for warranty cover probably does not state that your house complies absolutely with its Technical Requirements. What it means is that the inspector considers the house to be adequate, knowing that the builder is registered and has accepted the membership undertakings and is, in short, worth the risk of insuring. You, as the owner need to do the final checking! Many thousands of homeowners make building guarantee claims each year and this leaves aside the "snagging" problems which have been raised directly with the builder under the builder's initial warranty.

The warranty schemes operate in such a way that the developer has the responsibility for doing any reported repairs within the first two years from the date of completion of the building. The insurer does not pay out unless the building firm goes into liquidation.

Only if there is a serious problem, will the insurer become involved during this period. The insurer may therefore not know what faults are reported to registered builders in the first two years and will not be able to gauge whether a particular builder on its register is doing a good or bad job.

Once the property has been passed, the insurance inspector will probably not return to your property unless a warranty claim is made. You may even have to pay for the visit.

**Remember, this two-year scheme may run from the date of complet-ion of the property. That is likely to be the date of final building control inspection, not the date of occupancy, so watch your dates** – you may have much less than two years in which to submit initial claims. This problem has recently been recognised and one insurer at least is providing a six-month extension, for a fee.

If you claim even one day too late, the limited warranty may have expired in part. Remember that even if you do not know what the cause of a problem is, you can still report the symptom – for example, a damp patch on the north wall of the hall. If in doubt, or if the deadline is near, put something in writing and send it by recorded delivery. You then have evidence that your claim has been received.

You should not assume that because an insurer has given you a pass certificate for your home that it has been checked in great detail and that it complies with the insurer's technical standards. Quite possibly, apart from reading this book, you would never have been told about such standards.

Inspection for compliance under Building Regulations can be undertaken by a building control officer from the local authority or an inspector from NHBC Building Control Services Limited (which is an "Approved Inspector" for England and Wales). Other organisations or individuals have also become Approved Inspectors.

Clearly an Approved Inspector who manifestly ignores the statutory duties as set out under Building (Approved Inspectors) Regulations 1985, or as amended, will have approval withdrawn by the Department of Environment.

Not all properties have construction insurance cover. In those cases the purchaser may have alternative warranty cover, or indeed no cover. If alternative cover has been obtained, it is important that the homeowner understands its limitations.

If you are having a house built for you without NHBC cover, you could specify in the contract that the house must comply with certain minimum technical requirements and refer to the current NHBC or other insurance company's Technical Requirements (a copy of which can be bought).

## Who Builds?

Although the term "builder" is widely used in connection with newly built property, this really means the site developer. It is the developer who funds the house building, usually with a view to making a profit. Non-profit-making housing associations are an exception.

The developer might or might not be a registered building company. As the developer finances the building of the property, it controls those who physically build the structure and fit it out with services.

It is the developer who takes the risk of paying for a property to be built on a site and then sold or rented. The developer usually applies for planning permission or buys land for which planning consent has been granted.

It is the responsibility of the developer, often through the site manager (the clerk of works) to make sure that everything on site is done properly, on time, safely and to budget in accordance with the development plans.

Many developers rely heavily on subcontractors to undertake specific tasks. Often the final quality of a house will depend on how good the site manager is and what restraints are imposed – perhaps a sudden cut in the budget. If a number of houses on the estate are behind schedule, the subcontractors may be told to hurry up and encouraged to cut corners. Even the best site manager can be fooled by a devious subcontractor, since much of the work is concealed behind ceilings, walls and floors.

Some developers build houses on a speculative basis – 'Spec-built houses'. These developments are the most common. Other houses may be specially commissioned by a housing association.

Yet other houses are built on a self-build basis. Here the owner can either do everything as the developer, or more commonly obtain a prepared set of house plans and materials – a kit – from a specialist company.

# Inspecting the Property

The property which you have bought will include an area of land as well as the house built on it.

The plot of land has a boundary. It is important that you know where that boundary is. Legally, it is as shown on the plans with the title deeds. If there is any doubt about the boundary it is important that the matter is sorted out as quickly as possible.

As a general rule, the deeds will assign maintenance responsibility for a fence or wall on the boundary or there will be a shared responsibility. As a rule, the dividing line between properties sharing a wall is midway along the wall unless otherwise agreed. If you have a wall which borders the public highway, then responsibility for the wall will probably be yours, unless otherwise agreed. If it is still not clear who owns a boundary wall or fence, this can sometimes be determined by examining who has been maintaining it.

It is possible that official orders may apply to the land – for example, a Tree Preservation Order issued by the local council. This should have been revealed to you before you signed the contract. Any rights-of-way across your land should be shown in local large-scale maps of the area.

Converted buildings may have been listed and have required consent before being altered. Converted or refurbished buildings in Conservation Areas or other protected areas need approval before building work has started.

## Roadways

Your plot of land needs to have access to the public highway. If it does not, you may have bought a land "island" and could be prosecuted for trespass if you do not have permission before crossing someone's private land to reach the highway. Some house owners have discovered their houses are behind such "ransom" strips.

The public highway may be next to your plot. If so, this is obviously ideal. However, on a new estate your property may border a pavement and a roadway, but the land on which those sit may very well be in the hands of the developer.

The roadway may remain in private hands or be adopted by the local council and become a public highway. If it is in private hands, it is important that you know who owns it and that you are given the right to pass over it for access to your property.

## Installation of Service

The house on the plot must comply with the plans approved when the application for planning consent was given. It should also comply with Building Regulations, as well as regulations which apply to the installation of services. These plans will have been submitted to a Building Control inspector for approval. The builder should then build the property in strict accordance with the plans passed and do so within any time limit set.

The building inspector should ensure compliance by conducting frequent inspections, passing the work in stages. The inspector's powers are, however, limited to the statutory obligations (that is, those set out in the appropriate Building Regulations and the Act). The powers do not extend to many minor items which the builder may be including as features. Questions have been raised about the adequacy of inspections undertaken by one "approved" inspecting organisation. If "approved" inspectors don't inspect properly their approval can be withdrawn by the Department of the Environment.

Any garage or other built structure, such as large earth-retaining walls or bridges, must also conform with Building Regulations and planning consent. The garage and garden walls might not be covered by building construction insurance.

Services are laid on to the house and installed. These services are also subject to regulation. Should there be a breach of the regulations, enforcement action can be taken by the relevant statutory authority. Remember, any enforcement notices will be served on you as the owner, even though another may be culpable for the mistake.

How the garden is stocked with plants is not really a matter for regulation or for insurers but bear in mind that deeply rooted trees can cause serious foundation and wall stability problems.

There are various elements to the property: the site, the dwelling house or flat, and any garage, outbuildings and garden. You will need to look closely at each of these in turn, and they will be covered in the following sections. These notes are not intended to be fully comprehensive or definitive, just a guide. Not all need apply to your home. Add others which occur to you and undertake your own research if necessary.

## First Impressions

When you first look round a property, you will tend to take in the general impression rather than detail. During your second and subsequent visits you will start noticing details. Clearly anything grossly wrong should have been repaired or will have been covered up in case you lose confidence. So it is unlikely that you will find anything that is glaringly faulty before you buy. Partly this is because of the limited time you have to inspect the property before deciding whether to purchase.

If you do, try to have the fault rectified immediately before you commit to purchase. If this is not possible, insist on a letter from the vendors saying that the repair will be done immediately after you move in.

If you do find something wrong before purchase, you may wish to offer a lower price and accept it that way, or have the builder repair it, ideally before you take occupancy. You need to have this in writing. Promises by an estate agent that the builder will effect repairs before you move in, may be broken. You will find that out only once you move in.

Once you have purchased the property, you have more time to examine everything closely.

The developer or agent may unexpectedly present you with a form when you are given the keys to the property. This is likely to be a "Satisfaction and Fault Report" form or something similar. You may wish to take your solicitor's advice about what you should do if presented with such a form, and perhaps agree with the vendor in advance that you will not be asked to sign anything of this nature. Your solicitor may advise you to write "Unexamined" on it and to keep a copy for yourself.

The builder wants to know immediately whether there are any damaged items – broken mirrors, chipped sinks or scratched worktops. You need to make an early inspection for such problems and report them

## Fault Finding

Various kinds of faults can occur in a property. These can be roughly grouped under the following headings:

- accidental damage
- bad design
- biological damage
- deliberate damage
- ground contamination
- ground failure
- material failure
- incomplete work
- omitted items
- poor workmanship
- use of wrong material
- wrong building method

Sometimes it is not clear whether there is a real problem: you may just have a suspicion, since you are unlikely to know exactly what the law says or what the insurer's mandatory technical requirements are.

Even if you do a very thorough inspection, there may be some underlying problems which you will not see until the fault manifests itself. You should keep a record of all suspected faults, numbering each one sequentially, dating it, noting the location and describing the fault. When you make a claim, note the date and the action agreed, with starting and completion dates.

without undue delay. The greater the delay, the more likely it is that the builder will accuse you of causing the damage and refuse to repair it. So check carefully and quickly whether the worktops, ceramic fitments, glass, fitted appliances and doors have bumps, chips, scrapes or scratches.

One way of inspecting is to identify an area in the property which you are going to examine and then to give yourself, say, 10 minutes so that you can examine every constructional detail and fitting. Play the detective and ask yourself questions. For example, is this door handle firm? Are all of the screws there, properly driven home? Are there any sharp edges? Does the door shut properly? Are all the hinges there with a full complement of screws? Are the finger plates secure? Does the door swing properly? Is the door properly planed and painted? Does it clear the carpet? Does the door fit? Is the frame secure? Is the frame sealed? Similarly, examine and test all appliances, referring to the manufacturer's instructions. You should inspect the property at least twice. This way you might well see things which you missed the first time around, and will also be learning about your new home.

Apart from what your own senses tell you, you may need a spirit level, a plumb bob, a ruler, and perhaps even a metal and cable detector, a circuit polarity tester, a camera and a note pad.

A dated photographic record can provide invaluable evidence of a fault. Each photo or video which you take should have a card in the frame showing the date, perhaps the location if not clear, and a measurement scale. When you record possible faults, give each fault a unique number, a date, a location and note the nature of the fault.

Repeat this throughout the property, taking your time and making notes. Ask another member of your family or a friend to do a similar check, then compare notes.

At this stage, you should note anything which may be suspect and could be the basis for a claim. The cause of any problems may not be clear, only the effect, so just note that – for example, dampness on ceiling.

All this will, of course, take time. **If you decide not to inspect, then you must accept the consequences.**

# Surveying the Site

### Boundaries

When you survey the site, you will need to be clear about the boundaries. Sometimes these will be clearly marked, otherwise not. The boundaries on the site must correspond with the legal plans.

❒ Check your deeds. In open-plan front garden areas, boundaries are less clear. For surveying reasons, there is a tendency to open-plan design in new developments. The planning consent for the development may also prohibit the erection of fences or hedges.

❒ Check, too, that the boundary with the highway margin is clearly defined.

❒ Are there any public footpaths crossing your plot? If so, are they safe and marked?

### Paths and Driveways

Depending on the nature of the site, the builder may have left it somewhat rough or had gardens laid. The NHBC sets some basic standards for land around the building. These require the builder to smooth the topsoil and take some very basic action, such as clearing up building rubbish.

❒ Check the paths and driveways for evenness and for a gentle slope away from the building. Are there rainwater collection drains provided? Look at the site to establish whether there is any problem of flooding. Water should not be allowed to accumulate against dwelling house walls, but should drain away.

**Drains** There will be various drain chambers and service access housings.

❒ Are these all capped?

❒ What land drains are there and do they work?

### Steps, Walls and Fences

❒ Are the garden steps, walls, fences and gates properly built?

❒ Check for uneven or badly finished brickwork.

❒ Check for uneven or tilting paving.

❒ Do walls have waterproof tops such as coping stones?

❒ Are any steps in the garden or to the front or back doors safe?

### Gardens

❒ Do the outside and garden lights work?

❒ Are there trees present and are they safe?

❒ Have any roots been cut?

❒ Check which way the trees lean.

❒ Is the soil waterlogged?

❒ Is there any obvious sign of soil contamination?

❒ Is the site flat or sloping?

❒ Is there any possibility of a landslip?

❒ Is there any possibility of the land moving to weaken foundations?

❒ Is there evidence of any underground streams, tunnels or mineworkings?

### Pipework

❒ Does the house have vent pipes going from the underfloor void to the roof to vent underfloor gas? Do the vent pipes reach roof ridge height and are they capped?

❒ Are rainwater fittings sound?

### Foundations

❒ Where is the damp-proof course on the building? Is it at least 150 mm above ground level? If any loose soil is piled up against the building reducing this to less than 150 mm, the soil will have to be removed.

❒ Are the foundations showing?

## Surveying the House

Once you have surveyed the site, you can turn your attention to the building itself. Start with the front-door steps (are they too high?) and then inspect the outside of the building, partly for security.

If you live in a flat or apartment block, you will need to know what parts belong to your flat and what parts are common parts, which the management company or landlord would deal with in the event of a fault.

**Doors**

❒ Do the doors fit?
❒ Are the frames secure?
❒ Do the locks actually lock, and bolts bolt?
❒ Do you have the keys?
❒ Are the locks of a minimum security standard?
❒ Does the doorbell work?

**Windows**

❒ Are the windows properly installed?
❒ Are there window keys?
❒ Are the window frame edges sealed with sealant?

**Exterior Work**

❒ Is the external cladding – whether brick, tile, wood or UPVC – sound and uncracked?
❒ Are the air bricks unobstructed?
❒ Are external rainwater pipes and flues firmly attached?
❒ Do the gutters slope downward to the outlets? What happens during a heavy rain fall?
❒ Are all roof tiles, ridgings and flashings present and apparently in good condition?
❒ Is the chimney covered with a cowl?
❒ Is the TV aerial straight and secure?
❒ Is there any evidence of undue dampness on any exterior wall?
❒ Is there any evidence of serious efflorescence on brick or porous stonework?
❒ Is any render coat uncracked?
❒ Is the mortar holding bricks and blocks good?
❒ Are exterior lights properly weatherproofed and firmly attached?
❒ Are there any external fixing screws which are rusting?

**The Interior** Inside, check each room, hall and cupboard. Check doors, floor, walls, skirtings and ceilings and all fittings.

❒ Are the carpets in good condition?
❒ Is the paintwork good?
❒ Is any hardwood good?
❒ Check the position of the electrical consumer unit. Are the circuits marked?
❒ Where is the meter? If the unit is in a cabinet, do you have the meter key? Is there a low tariff meter?
❒ Do all light switches and sockets work?
❒ Are all electrical fitments securely attached to the wall or ceiling?
❒ Do the electrical appliances work?
❒ Do you have instruction and guarantee forms?
❒ Where is the gas meter? Does the main isolating valve have a key? If the unit is in a cabinet, do you have the key to it?
❒ Do all gas appliances work? Do you have instructions and guarantee forms?
❒ Where is the main water stopcock and do all water supply services work?
❒ Is there an immersion heater?
❒ Does the central heating system work? Do you have the operating instructions and guarantee?
❒ Are all fireplaces securely built and and do open fires have firebricks?

❒ Do electrical storage or space heaters work? Where are the instructions?
❒ For solid fuel and oil-fired heating systems, are all parts present with any instructions and guarantees?
❒ Rooms have functions and the services must be installed appropriate to the function. For example, the electrical fittings in toilets, bathrooms and shower rooms should be such that there is no danger of electrocution. Washbasins, lavatory bowls, bidets and shower trays should all be screwed down and not move when in use. Do all the sinks, basins and baths drain properly? Does water drain out of the washbasin, shower tray, bidet and bath correctly and reasonably quickly?

**Loft Space**

The loft should also be inspected, but with care.
❒ Is the hatch accessible and does it have a cover?
❒ Is the hatch area strongly built? Is the roof fully insulated?
❒ Is there a service walkway to the tanks?
❒ Are the water tanks and the overflows sound?
❒ Are the tanks and pipes fully insulated?
❒ Can air circulate in the loft space?
❒ Are the roof trusses stable or bowing?
❒ Is there any evidence of water penetration?

**Basement**

❒ Is there a basement? If so, is it intended to be habitable? It must be completely dry.
❒ Is any water accumulating?

**Apartments**

❒ Check halls and stairways for access, cleanliness, safety.
❒ Check lifts with care.
❒ Check refuse shutes.
❒ Check communal lights. Are they on a time switch? Do they work?
❒ Check entry doors, locks and entry phones.

## Checking the Garage and Other Outbuildings

❒ Check the walls and roof.
❒ Is the garage door lock strong or weak?
❒ Do the doors open?
❒ Is the floor smooth?
❒ During heavy rain, does rain water drain away without wetting the garage floor?
❒ If the garage is integral with the dwelling, it must be built to retain fire in the event that the car goes on fire. Check any doors to the dwelling. Are they fire proof? Will they prevent fumes entering the dwelling?
❒ Check whether your construction insurance covers the garage.

On the plot, there may be other outbuildings present. If so, they may need to comply with building regulations.

Wooden huts and movable greenhouses are unlikely to be covered by a warranty scheme or building regulations. Check the wording of your warranty.

The local authority can tell you what kinds of structures are exempted from building control and planning regulations.

# Basic Construction

Many people know little about basic house construction until they are faced with problems. This diagram is a quick, layman's guide to the principal elements of an average house, so that when a carpenter chats to you about "soffits" or "joist hangers" you will not be completely thrown. It will also help you if you need to explain a fault, as you can refer to that part of the building and use the correct terminology.

**Barge board** Timber used to neaten the edge of a roof at the gable ends of the house.

**Coping** Flat or ridged stones used to weatherproof the top of masonry walls. A coping can also be formed by a course of engineering grade, non-porous bricks laid on edge.

**Damp proof course** (DPC) The damp proof course is a layer of impervious material built into the brick structure to prevent damp rising into it from the ground.

**Eaves** the overhanging portion of the roof.

**Fascia** Timber used to neaten the back and front of buildings at the ends of the rafters. Gutters are usually affixed to the fascia.

**Flashing** Waterproofing strip - often lead - which seals the joins between the roof and surrounding protrusions.

**Foundations** the base for the property. Type varies according to land eg strip, stepped strip, deep strip, bored piles, and raft.

**Flaunching** A sloping layer of mortar around the base of the chimney pot at the top of the chimney stack.

**Joist hanger** A galanvanised steel bracket for supporting joists and fixing them to the walls.

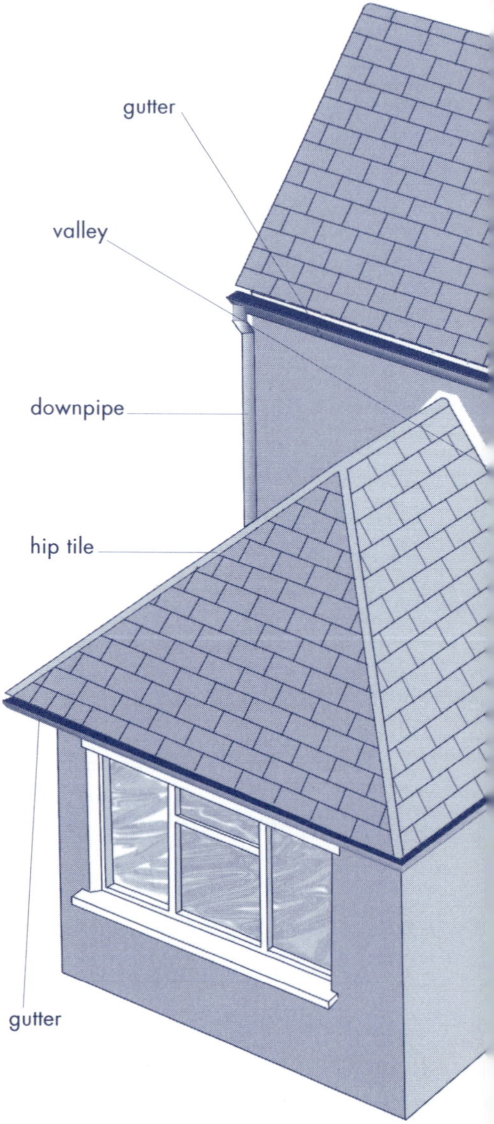


**Roof batten** Lengths of timber used in constructing the roof.

**Soffit** A length of timber that is fitted between the wall and the fascia board.

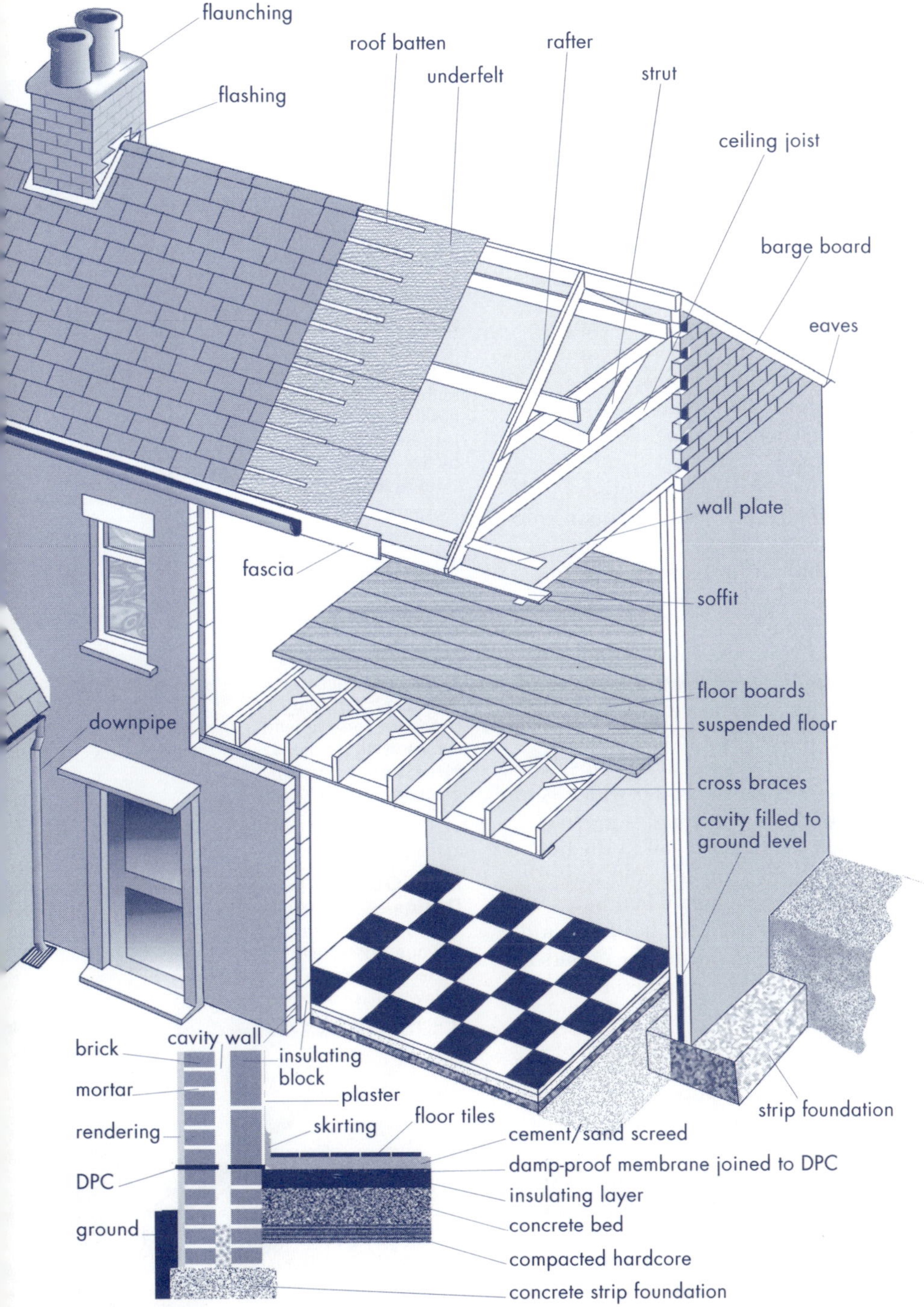
flaunching
roof batten
rafter
underfelt
strut
flashing
ceiling joist
barge board
eaves
wall plate
fascia
soffit
floor boards
downpipe
suspended floor
cross braces
cavity filled to ground level
brick
cavity wall
insulating block
mortar
plaster
strip foundation
floor tiles
rendering
skirting
cement/sand screed
damp-proof membrane joined to DPC
DPC
insulating layer
ground
concrete bed
compacted hardcore
concrete strip foundation

# The Water System

Your new home will supply you with both hot and cold running water. Basically, most plumbing systems are similar, however central heating systems can vary.

The cold water to your kitchen and sometimes outside taps will come directly from the mains supply and this water is pure and safe to drink. Basically, the mains supply will run to your kitchen tap and up to the main storage tank (and header tank, if you have one) in the loft. This pipe is called the rising main.

The rest of the water supply might then come from the main cold water storage tank. So the water in the bathroom for bathing, washing and flushing the toilet will come from this tank.

Water from the storage tank will also supply the hot water system. The water will run into the hot water cylinder where it will be heated and then fed to hot taps. The hot water from the boiler which is in a separate set of piping, is passed through the heating coil in the hot water cylinder causing cold water there to become hot. When hot water is used from the hot taps, and therefore emptied from the cylinder, cold water will be supplied back into the cylinder automatically, directly from the main cold water storage tank. For a description of unvented hot water supply systems refer, for example, to Seeley's *Building Technology*.

Waste water from the sink, bath, etc and from the toilet will flow out through downpipes and into the main drains which eventually connect with the main sewer.

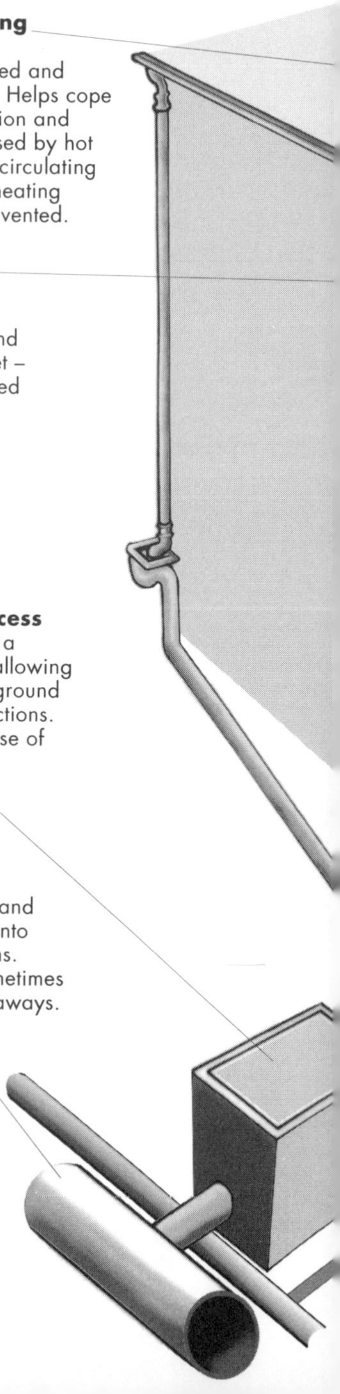

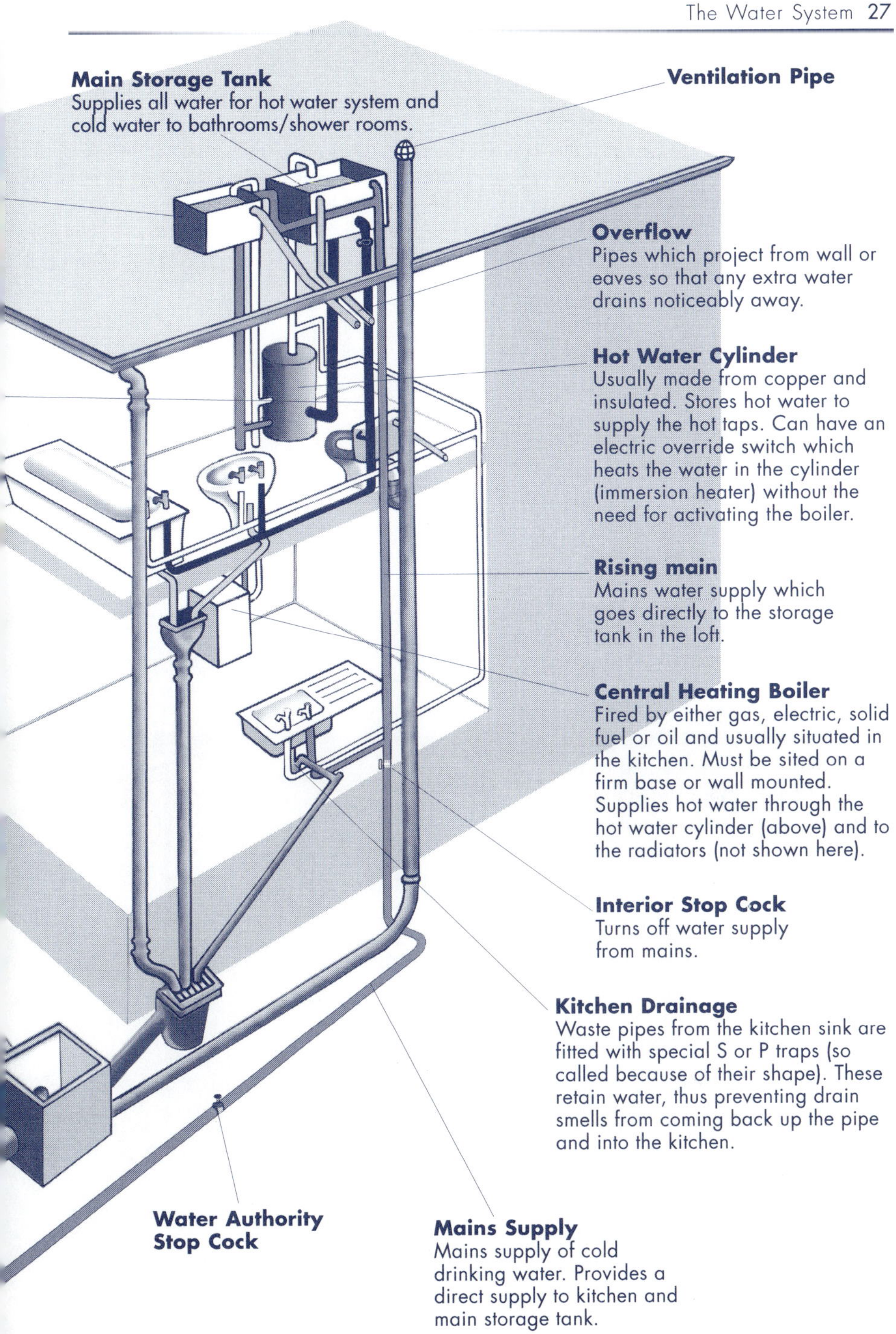
**Main Storage Tank**
Supplies all water for hot water system and cold water to bathrooms/shower rooms.
**Ventilation Pipe**
**Overflow**
Pipes which project from wall or eaves so that any extra water drains noticeably away.
**Hot Water Cylinder**
Usually made from copper and insulated. Stores hot water to supply the hot taps. Can have an electric override switch which heats the water in the cylinder (immersion heater) without the need for activating the boiler.
**Rising main**
Mains water supply which goes directly to the storage tank in the loft.
**Central Heating Boiler**
Fired by either gas, electric, solid fuel or oil and usually situated in the kitchen. Must be sited on a firm base or wall mounted. Supplies hot water through the hot water cylinder (above) and to the radiators (not shown here).
**Interior Stop Cock**
Turns off water supply from mains.
**Kitchen Drainage**
Waste pipes from the kitchen sink are fitted with special S or P traps (so called because of their shape). These retain water, thus preventing drain smells from coming back up the pipe and into the kitchen.
**Water Authority Stop Cock**
**Mains Supply**
Mains supply of cold drinking water. Provides a direct supply to kitchen and main storage tank.

# The basic Central Heating System (hot water type)

Most new homes are fitted with full central heating. Gas and electricity are the most common choices, although the system may be generated by solid fuel or oil. The system will provide a specified internal air temperature in the house, which is controlled thermostatically.

The most popular systems pump hot water through the radiators from a wall-mounted or floor standing boiler usually located in a kitchen. Other systems include underfloor electric heating and warm air systems.

Newly built homes are required to be well insulated (see Insulation, A-Z section) to keep heat loss to a minimum.

Opposite is a very simplified layout of a hot water central heating system. The radiators are connected to the boiler by pipes. With a suspended floor, the pipes can run beneath the floorboards. The pipe runs should take the shortest route. Sometimes the bathroom radiator is on a gravity circuit which means that hot water rises and returns from the system by gravity and is not pumped through the boiler. This is to provide heat to the bathroom when the pumped system is shut off.

Radiators come in various types, the most popular being steel panels which are bracketed to the wall. They should be sited in the coldest part of the room. Each radiator will have two valves, one as an on-off, the other to adjust the flow of hot water. There should also be a key-operated valve for bleeding off air trapped in each radiator.

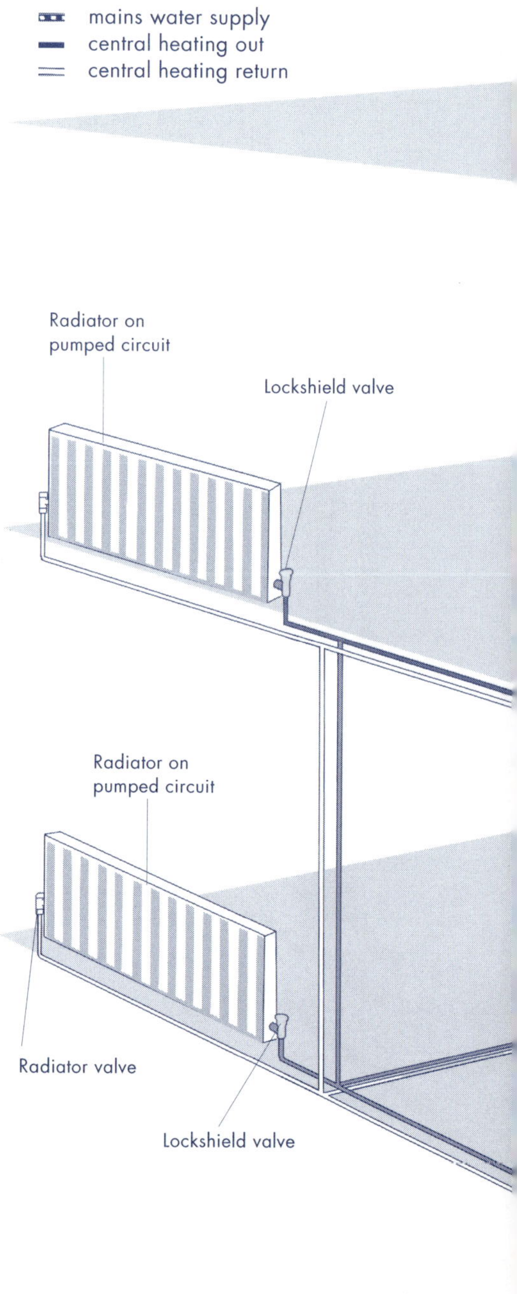

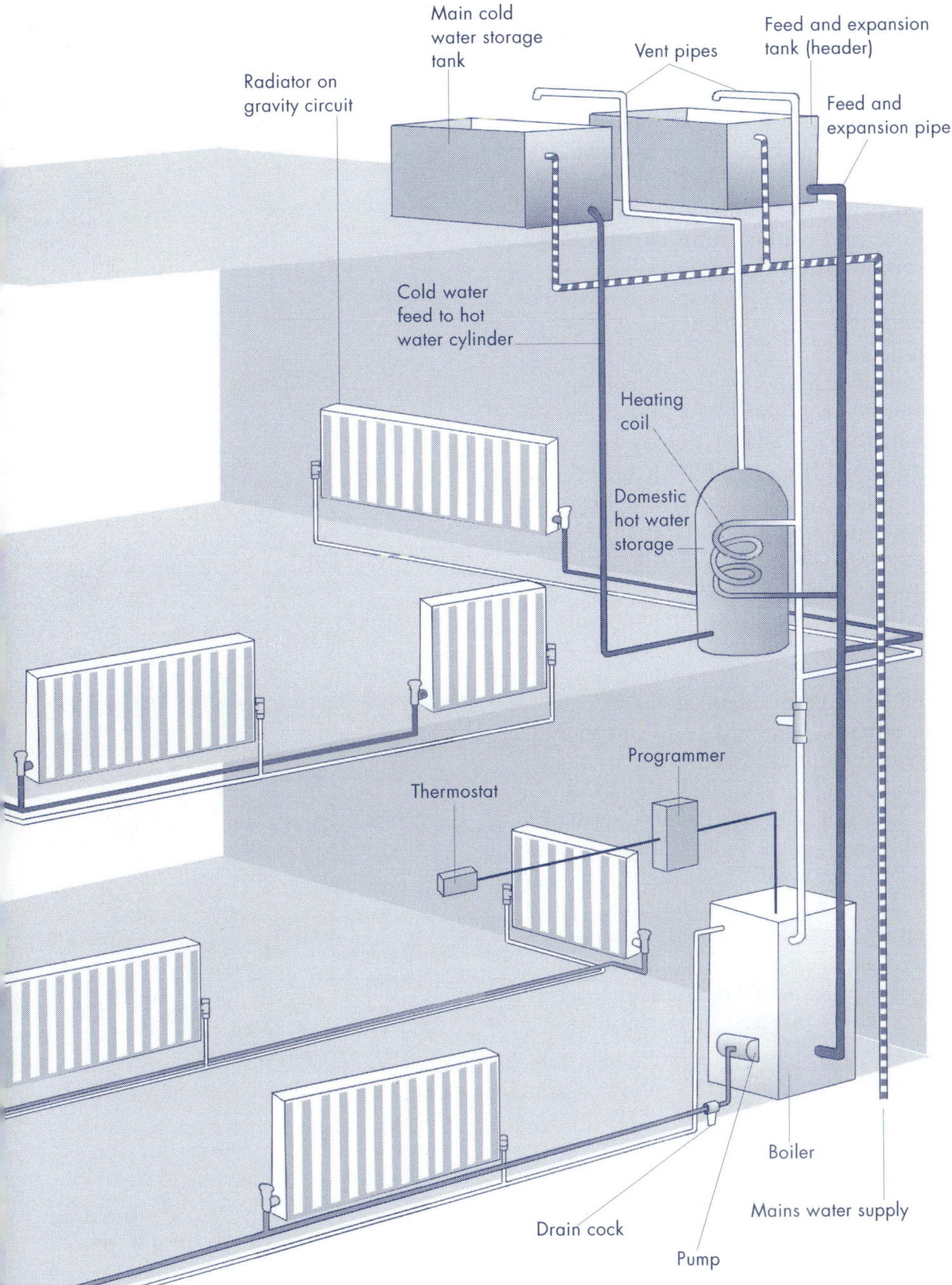
Main cold water storage tank
Vent pipes
Feed and expansion tank (header)
Radiator on gravity circuit
Feed and expansion pipe
Cold water feed to hot water cylinder
Heating coil
Domestic hot water storage
Programmer
Thermostat
Boiler
Mains water supply
Drain cock
Pump

## The Electrical System

Everyone knows the dangers of electricity and the guide here is simply to help you understand the basic electrical supply and how it works in your new home. **If you think there are any problems whatsoever, leave well alone and contact your site developer or a qualified electrician.**

Electricity will be supplied to your home through a thickly armoured underground cable which will pass through a sealed fuse and meter. In your home you will find a consumer unit (fuse box) which houses individual fuses or circuit breakers for the different electrical circuits in your home and a mains switch to turn off the electricity to the whole house or flat. If a particular circuit is overloaded, the circuit breaker will flick off and will need to be reset. If a circuit regularly "blows" there is a fundamental problem (perhaps insufficient amperage) and you should contact the main builder, the after-sales team or a qualified electrician.

From the consumer unit, electrical cables run either under a suspended floor or, for a solid ground floor, along the inside walls. The main ring circuits supply power to the electrical sockets. Lighting is on a separate circuit and cooker or heating cables are on yet another circuit. No ring circuit may serve more than 100 sq metres of floor area, so most homes will have at least two ring circuits. You can have as many sockets as you like, but they should be regularly spaced around the ring. The fuse controlling a ring circuit must be 30 amp. The ring circuit will take seven kilowatts of power.

**Remember: never take chances with electricity. Bad wiring could start a fire or electrocute someone!**

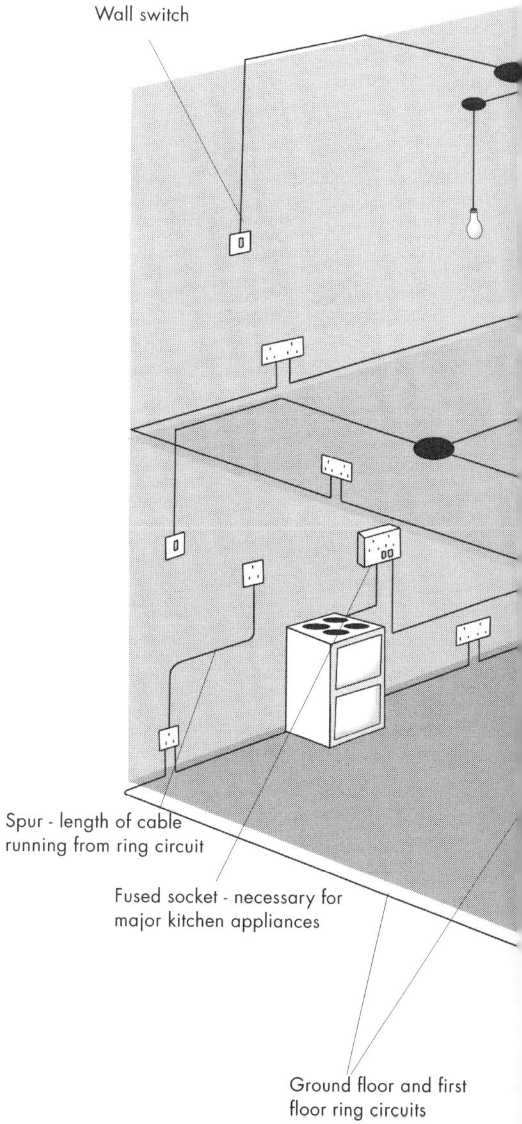


Today, all electrical cables incorporate earthing wire.

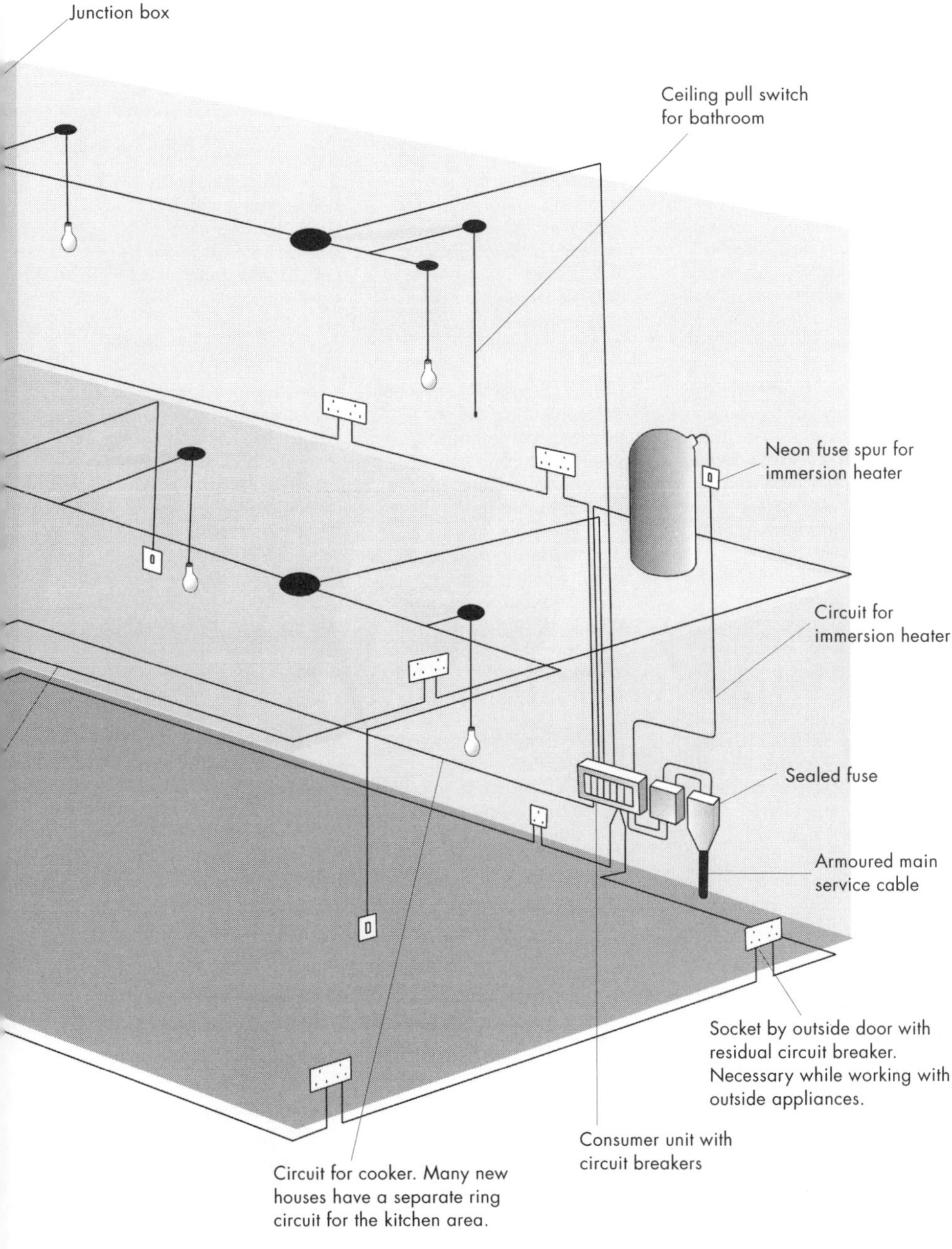
Junction box
Ceiling pull switch for bathroom
Neon fuse spur for immersion heater
Circuit for immersion heater
Sealed fuse
Armoured main service cable
Socket by outside door with residual circuit breaker. Necessary while working with outside appliances.
Consumer unit with circuit breakers
Circuit for cooker. Many new houses have a separate ring circuit for the kitchen area.

## Before Purchase

❒ Be aware that the vendor will naturally highlight the best points about the property and will not want anything to put you off buying.

❒ Read the small print on any brochures from estate agents or salespeople employed by the vendor. The small print is actually very important. It has been put there by their solicitor for a purpose, usually to the advantage of the producers of the brochure. It will probably include several disclaimers which means that you usually cannot rely on the information being accurate.

There will probably be an idealised "artist's impression" of your prospective home, if it is yet to be completed. This may be somewhat illusory and quite possibly will include non-existent trees and shrubs. If you want to see what is actually being built, ask to see the builder's plans.

❒ It is probable that most, maybe all, of the potentially negative things which apply to the plot will be only be disclosed to you later in the leasing or purchasing process, when you go over the details of the proposed contract with your solicitor. These will be discovered by means of questions put to and answers given by the vendor and from enquiries and searches which your solicitor has made.

Sometimes negative information will put you off buying so it is often the case that this is revealed many weeks after you have made an initial offer and had it accepted subject to contract. This may mean that just when you thought your search for a home was over, bad news may make you withdraw.

❒ You may wish to ask the salesperson at the start whether the plot has planning permission, whether it is on contaminated land, whether there is a motorway planned next door, whether a theme park is about to be built next to it, and so on. You may, however, be given only vague replies or even incorrect information.

❒ If the house has not yet been started or is only partly constructed, you could ask to see the site and have a look at the standard of workmanship.

❒ If the property is completed and you happen to notice faults when you are thinking about buying it, you may be told that the after-sales team will deal with these after you move in. Is the sales person giving a formal assurance to you that this will definitely happen? You may wish to ask precisely when, and ask for a confirmation in writing in case the builder later tries to disclaim responsibility.

If the fault is other than minor, you may wish to insist that the builder undertakes the repair work before you move in, to save you the later disruption. This could be part of your purchase agreement.

❒ Ask who is undertaking building control inspection – an Approved Inspector or the district council. You can try to see the building control plans. Any Approved Inspector is commissioned by the developer and there is some question about whether you will be shown plans. If refused, you could ask the district council building control department. The district council is always formally notified if an Approved Inspector is being used and the person's name may even be given.

❒ Even though the plot and the property seem very attractive, it is wise to look up the local planning file to see what conditions apply to the development. You can also purchase a copy of the planning application from the district council.

❒ If other people have bought adjacent properties from the same developer, you might wish to contact them and ask about their experiences.

## Fault Finding – and What to do

Once you have completed your first inspection, you may well have a numbered list of suspected faults. This list is part of your **"Fault Identification System"**. For each entry, put the date on which you noticed the fault, the area in the property (say, the front bedroom), and also where the problem is evident (say, the north wall). It is important to be very specific about the nature of the fault and its location. For vague or intermittent faults, note as much information as possible so that the cause can be tracked down.

Each potential fault should be given a unique number, starting at "1". Don't worry if you see further faults in a room which you have inspected. Just give the fault the next number in your list and let the list grow.

Examine the list and try to analyse the faults. You may see some repeated faults – for example, brass electrical sockets in direct contact with plaster may have become corroded and this may be a problem throughout the property if no gaskets have been installed or were improperly installed. You should be able to conclude if there are likely to be further problems which you have missed first time around.

Form a view as to the potential seriousness of each fault and the degree of urgency of the repair required. For an urgent problem, you should phone the builder straight away. If the builder is unavailable or cannot do the work quickly, you may need to arrange for a repair yourself, but send the bills to the builder (if the builder has a warranty obligation), with a note stating why the situation arose. Normally builders will want to give approval first, before any work is done, and if they do not they might refuse to pay.

Form a view as to the skill of each of the tradespeople employed. You may find an abnormal number of plumbing faults, indicating sloppy workmanship. If so, inspect all of the plumbing work more thoroughly.

You will be able to rate each fault and decide whether you wish to raise it with the warranty provider. If there are trivial ones, then you mark your list "No action". Then write out a fresh list, but don't change your numbering system, since each suspected fault has a unique identification number and a change may cause confusion. If you must change the numbering, make your secondary list numbers start with "B" to distinguish them from the "A" list.

**It is really very important for you that you do take time to check what you have bought.** In its advice to solicitors, the NHBC says that it inspects every home but the interval is often every three or four weeks. It will also sometimes use the same inspector to carry out both building control inspection as well as warranty insurance. It also states that the inspections "cannot be comprehensive" and that it leaves the finished work to be inspected by the purchaser.

NHBC may have since changed its arrangements; you should make enquiries to establish the current position.

*To use your "Fault Identification System" to make a claim, see page 36.*

### Rules and Regulations

Some faults may breach the law. Legislation sets certain minimum standards which developers, builders and owners must obey to avoid prosecution by the district council or other statutory authorities. Local authorities have the power to make bye-laws and some of these can affect buildings. The developer may also be open to a civil action by the purchaser.

There are many laws which apply to building structures (whether buildings or just large walls), and to the installation of services. If the law is breached, there could be an accident or other consequence which leaves the developer open to prosecution by the regulatory authority or perhaps even by The Health and Safety Executive. The laws and regulations may differ throughout the UK.

Other faults may result from a breach of a Code of Practice. This is not to say that something outside a code is necessarily illegal. It may not be. Sometimes Codes of Practice are 'Approved Codes' within the meaning of a particular law.

Many manufactured components, such as structural timber, are required to carry a British, European or International Standard number to show that the item complies with the Standard. This standard mark gives some surety.

Other faults may not be a statutory matter but a breach of a manufacturer's installation instructions. If you have the installation instructions, read them. If not, ask the manufacturer to send you a copy.

For insured properties, faults may breach the insurer's Technical Standards which were applicable at the time of construction and are 'faults' insofar as warranty claims are considered.

Other faults may be a consequence of a breach of planning permission. In this context, erecting a building without planning permission is a fault (and the building may have to be demolished if retrospective approval is not given).

As owner, you have the responsibility for the property. So if there were breaches of, say, the electrical supply installation regulations, then enforcement notices would be served on you, the owner, even though you were an innocent party in the creation of the fault.

It is probable that even if you do not have a construction fault insurance scheme, the builder will have stated in your purchase agreement that the property is built in a workmanlike manner with proper materials and that it is fit for habitation. Even if not stated, this is normally implied as a condition of sale.

**Thus there are different ways of tackling the builder – the construction insurance warranty scheme, your rights under common and statutory law, and your contract with the builder.**

Clearly, if the builder has gone out of business since you have bought the property, you will not be able to sue the builder for common law breaches. Construction fault insurance may be able to pay.

It is important that claims are made promptly. Not only do insurance warranty terms set time limits but Limitation Acts and other Acts may also set limits after which the taking of action – even with the strongest of cases – is legally barred.

If you have been insured for construction fault claims, it is important that you keep your notes on the property problems for ten or more years (or the period covered by the insurance).

Builders who are registered members of a construction insurance scheme need to comply with the membership demands. If not their membership can be challenged.

Any problems with an 'Approved' building control officer can be referred to the Department of the Environment (in England and Wales) or the appropriate offices in Scotland or Northern Ireland. Refer to the latest edition of *Whitaker's Almanack* for details of government departments.

Any problems with an insurance company can be referred to the Insurance Ombudsman.

Estate agents need to comply with the Estate Agents Act and Property Misdescriptions Act. Complaints can be made to the Trading Standards Department of the local council.

Complaints about solicitors and barristers can be made to the appropriate registration body.

Professional misconduct complaints about registered architects, surveyors, plumbers, electricians, electrical engineers, building engineers,and so on, can be made to their registration body.

Many builders are members of trade organisations whose aim is to share information among members and to promote the industry. These trade organisations are usually toothless. For more information on Organisations, see page 169.

## Making a Claim

When you make a construction fault claim, you are doing so under a contract. This could be your purchase contract (for an implied or explicit warranty) or a warranty given by an organisation such as NHBC or Zurich Municipal.

If you are renting the property or hold a lease, the landlord or freeholder has a contract with you and they have a contract with the builder. It is important that you deal with the right person; the developer will not entertain claims from a person renting the property unless the owner has granted permission.

Remember that warranties are always limited. You probably have no grounds for claiming against an organisation if the contract has expired.

The warranty policy document will set out the terms and may also establish a complaints procedure to which you have agreed. This may set out what action to take if the developer refuses the claim. This could involve conciliation, arbitration or court action.

Broadly, you will need to state in writing to the party against whom you are making the insurance claim: who you are; your policy number; the insured property; the suspected faults; and the fact that you are making a warranty claim so that there is no doubt. This note also needs to be dated and received by the other party before any time limit expires.

**The onus is on you to do everything required to make the claim.** Clearly, any claim for breach of contract should be handled by your solicitor unless you are competent in such matters. You may wish to send the claim by recorded delivery so that the other party cannot deny receipt. You must keep an exact copy.

It is important that you are clear about what the faults are. If there are any which are major and pressing, you may wish to emphasise the need to have them done promptly.

If there has been a sudden failure, such as a burst pipe, which you have had to repair privately, make sure that the plumber states in writing what the problem was, keep any removed parts, and hand these with the bill (which you have probably paid already) to the

## Fault Identification System

By using a clear fault identification numbering system, you can easily spot anything which the warranty provider is trying to drop on the quiet "Sorry, we forgot about it" should not be an excuse if you manage and review your list properly.

Suppose item 7 gives problems. It is easy then for you to write back to the warranty provider and refer to Item 7. Using numbers makes the description simple and comprehensible.

If you find any new faults, add them to your master list using the next available number, and advise the warranty provider of your new claim which will obviously have a new date.

For each claim, record the date you first reported it to the warranty provider; this must, of course, be within the warranty time limits. If you are making a so-called 'Two-Year' claim under the NHBC scheme, check your dates, since the clock may have started when the property was completed, not your later date of occupancy.

For each claim, make sure that you establish whether it is agreed to be done, agreed not to be done or is in dispute. Establish, too, the date when repairs will be undertaken, and which ones will be done on a given day. Once the repairs are completed, check the workmanship and materials. If these are satisfactory, enter a completion date on your list.

developer (if responsibility lies with the developer).

The developer or insurance company will take its own view as to whether each claim is going to be accepted. It is unfortunate that some builders and insurance companies have a reputation of apparently promising the earth and disputing many claims by resort to small print.

Claims which cost little are more likely to be passed, even with marginal justification. For goodwill, some claims which are not valid might be remedied nonetheless. More significant claims may be resisted even if justified – for example, if the building or insuring organisation is losing money. The claim may be delayed until the next financial year. Of course, you could take legal action for a valid claim that was not satisfied, but that is the last resort.

It is sometimes difficult for individual house purchasers to know exactly what the regulatory position is, and to establish whether a claim is valid or not. It may be helpful to ask neighbours whether the same fault has occurred in their property and has been reported and remedied. A professional adviser will also give an opinion and may even negotiate the matter with the warranty provider. This does, however, cost money and the warranty provider may be reluctant to provide recompense.

In the case of regulatory breaches, officers from statutory undertaking and other proper authorities could be commissioned to review the matter. These officers may issue prohibition orders and contact the builder or warranty provider.

For each item, you need to find out whether the warranty provider agrees to meet the repair claim, and if so, exactly when the work will be done. **Beware of less than clear agreement on each item. A mumbled reply might mean that the warranty provider's representative is just mumbling, not agreeing.** You may find out weeks later that the work you expected to have done is not being done.

It is important to submit only claims which you actually believe to be valid; otherwise, you could be guilty of fraud.

It is worth reviewing the condition of your property at intervals during the two-year period and the ten-year period in case there have been any changes requiring a claim.

Sometimes faults develop which are not sufficiently major in terms of the warranty to be covered. Insurers use a damage scale for cracks; if there are up to three cracks less than 15mm wide in brickwork, this may not be regarded as "severe" and therefore not covered. Check any insurance terms for your property in case they are different. The Building Research Establishment guidance note on cracks is commonly used as a basis for determining the seriousness: there is a scale used.

If the cracks are progressively opening but are not as yet covered by insurance, you should probably put the warranty provider on notice by writing a recorded delivery letter within the time limit of the policy so that the fault is on record. It is important that the claim itself is made in time even though remedial work might be undertaken beyond the time limit.

## Disputes

If possible, try to reach an amicable arrangement.

If you wish to dispute a construction matter, you may find that there is a dispute resolution procedure set down as part of the warranty cover, to which you have already agreed. It is important that this procedure is followed.

Alternatively, you may have contractually agreed to a dispute resolution procedure with the developer if you have no third party warranty cover. Your purchase contract should give the details.

Sometimes a dispute can concern a matter of fact. For example, the property may not be provided with a flue, though the plans show that a flue is mandatory. Here the facts speak for themselves and yet you may still be faced with a refusal.

In a dispute over a matter of opinion rather than fact, make reference to what happened in a parallel situation. This is because both sides can genuinely have different opinions, and it may not be clear who is right.

**For example, the developer may have repaired something in a neighbour's house on the site but now be refusing to make the same repair in yours. You could point out this discrepancy.**

Apart from warranty claims, you may wish to determine whether a fault is a statutory breach (i.e. an illegal construction method) or not.

There are time limits for taking certain courses of action and you will probably need to obtain the advice of a solicitor in such matters. The A–Z section of this book, which starts on page 43, gives hints on how to choose professional advisers and how to keep litigation costs under control.

If a dispute occurs with a warranty provider or builder, at a lower management level, raise the matter with the directors.

In some cases, the insurer might override the builder and send another builder in to do the work, a process called "sub-rogation".

The NHBC provides a conciliation service. Here the registered builder agrees to do work if the NHBC thinks it should be done. Arbitration is a further option but costs can be higher.

Finally, there is court action. **Sometimes the possibility of court action may concentrate the builder's mind, and a letter from your solicitor may be sufficient. Court action should always be regarded as a last resort.** Even if you have a cast-iron case, the hassle, expense and uncertainty may just not be worth the fight. And you might lose.

Different laws apply in the component parts of the United Kingdom; it is important that only the applicable law is cited.

Building firms are quite often forced into liquidation; if so, the party with whom you are in dispute may simply cease to exist.

## Keeping Records

In addition to your lists, keep copies of all letters sent or received. A chronological file is often the simplest.

Make notes of any telephone calls: the name of the person you spoke to, the company concerned, the date and time, the points discussed and the outcome. You might want to ask the builder to confirm the discussion in writing. Alternatively, you might want to write to the builder summarising what was agreed.

Keep the initial advertisements and sales literature, any photographs which you have taken and the receipts of any expenses which you incur.

### Useful Contacts

Use whatever system – manual or electronic – you prefer to record details regarding your new home such as site name and plot number, as well as information about services and suppliers. Obviously the latter will vary from person to person but the following list may be a useful reference in preparing such a record.

- After-sales service
- Builder
- Burglar alarm company
- Electrician
- Electricity supplier
- Freeholder
- Gas (mains/bottled) supplier
- Insurance:
  - Building
  - Construction warranty
  - Contents
  - Mortgage protection
- Landlord
- Liquid fuel supplier
- Local council
- Neighbourhood watch
- Plumber
- Police station
- Septic tank emptying
- Sewerage service
- Solicitor
- Solid fuel supplier
- Telephone company
- Water services

You will find it helpful to note the company name, address, telephone and fax numbers, contact person and his or her position; where relevant, the account number, date opened and the name on the account; and the numbers of all insurance policies. Such information may be needed quickly and it is best to keep it all in one place.

**Despite being a new house and still smelling of fresh paint and plaster, there is a pervading unpleasant odour of rotting vegetation or something similar. What could it be? And what can I do?**

Begin by detecting whether the smell comes from inside the house or outside. If it is inside, the problem is likely to be poor drainage. Check the U bends under sinks, wash-hand basins, electric waste disposal units, baths, shower trays, and washing machines, bidets, baths, toilets and external drain traps. These should hold water to prevent bad smells coming back into the house. Flush all waste outlets with a proprietary cleaner.

If the smell is localised to one room, it could be a dead rodent or something similar (and equally unpleasant, unfortunately) under the floorboards). Contact the public health department of the local council if you feel this is the problem.

If it is outside, it could be the drains. Does water run freely into them? If not, you may need to check the main drainage under the nearest manhole cover. A drain cleaning liquid or washing soda crystals in hot water may solve the problem. If the drains are becoming blocked frequently, contact the developer, as there may be a fundamental problem. If the blockage is further along the sewerage system and off your property boundaries, it will be the responsibility of the local council.

*Further help: See Smells, Rot, Ventilation.*

**Although the garden has been landscaped reasonably well, it never seems to drain adequately after a spell of rain. In fact, large patches of the grass never seem to dry out and are soggy most of the time.**

Check with the developer's office what sort of drainage has been laid in the garden. It may be inadequate. If this is not the case, it could be that the water is seeping in from somewhere else, eg a leaking main or small underground stream. Check with the local water authority. Also look at the soil quality; it may need sand or humus added to help drainage or in major cases a French (rubble) drain.

*Further help: Drainage, Gardens, Soils.*

### One of the electrical sockets in the bedroom becomes very hot when in use. Obviously, it is unsafe, but to whom should I complain? The property developer has promised to come and check it out, but I have been waiting for several weeks now to no avail.

A warm or hot electrical socket indicates a resistance fault and represents a potential fire danger as well as an electrical hazard. Insist the developer's office gives you a date when a qualified electrician can come to check the wiring. Insist that it is a fire hazard and must be dealt with promptly. In the meantime, do not use the socket until it has been overhauled. Otherwise contact the electricity authority or a qualified electrician.

*Further help: Electrical installations, Electrical supply.*

### I understand that my new home has a ten-year warranty. But what does this actually cover?

A warranty is a limited guarantee made by a party as a result of a direct or indirect payment made to it, to repair or rectify something supplied that is faulty. A warranty is always limited by a lapse of time and it may have quite a number of clauses which 'limit' its issuers' liability. The party giving the warranty also has to agree with you that your claim is valid and this can give rise to disputes if there is a disagreement. The purchaser or owner has a duty to report the fault in the correct manner if repair is sought, and to make the property available for repair at such a time as the person giving the warranty gets round to it.

While giving some peace of mind, the purchaser of the property still has to put up with the inconvenience of there being a fault.

Study the warranty in detail. Obtain help from your solicitor if you have a major problem. However, you may need to be persistent when making a claim.

*Further help: Complaints Numbering System page 36; HAPM; NHBC; Shield; Warranties; Zurich Municipal.*

### How do I find out where the legal boundaries of my property are?

Look at your deeds or contact the Land Registry.

### I think the land might be contaminated: how can I check?

Try the Environment Agency's contaminated land database or find a company which provides a database service. Be aware of the small print as the data is not always reliable. There are also specialist surveying companies which can undertake contamination audits and this may involve sampling the soil.

Your local authority might also have information about contamination Even if the land turns out to have been contaminated, there are now many methods of remediation which can render sites safe for habitation. Some builders specialise in reclaiming used land and they lead the way in new methods of treatment.

### Is my home in a radioactive radon hotspot area?

It might be if near granite or some other kinds of igneous rocks. Ask the local authority or try the National Radiological Protection Board which is mapping the country.

### The Builder claims to be registered with a construction fault guarantee organisation; how can I check?

Contact the registrar and ask for confirmation that the builder is on the register. If a builder has been on the register but has been struck off, the builder's publicity might still improperly have the insurer's logo on it. You could also ask for a reference from the insurer. Insurers tend to assign insurance ratings to the builders but they might be reluctant to reveal which builders are suspect. If you are having an extension built by a builder who is properly registered with an insurer, this can indicate that the builder is trying to maintain high standards - but it is likely that the extension's structure will not itself be insurable. Erecting an extension on a new house can also invalidate the main building guarantee.

### What does my construction insurance policy cover?

Locate your policy document, contacting the insurer if you cannot find it. You will also need to know what dates apply to the policy. Be sure to read what the policy covers and, importantly, what it does not cover. Sometimes these policies are sold on the basis that you need no longer worry - that is until you make a claim and find the insurers have a clause which exempts them from paying out if you have normal building structure insurance!

### Does my insurance policy cover land contamination?

Check what the policy says but it appears that construction warranty insurers have yet to get to grip with this, and to provide cover. Land contamination risks seem to be exactly the thing that insurance is supposed to cover, it is of public concern, yet the insurers seem not to have taken this on board.

The whole construction warranty business is becoming increasingly competitive and NHBC no longer has it all its own way. Quite likely one company will see a competitive advantage in offering land contamination cover for a reasonable premium, then the others will break ranks.

### Surely if my new home has been passed by the local authority planning department, been built by a well known builder, inspected for building regulation compliance and further inspected by the construction warranty provider which has technical standards and Type Approved the building, I need not worry?

In theory, no – but why do you think the author decided that this guide was needed? It started with the heavy glass shower door detaching, nearly lacerating someone's leg. Keep your eyes open for reports in the press of horrendous problems which some people have encountered. In some cases, the mortar holding the brick together was apparently far too weak. These properties were apparently "passed" and certified.

You can also read some of the problems in some trade publications such as *Building Homes* (perhaps the article called "Out of control" in the February 1997 edition for starters), and *Building Control.*

Sometimes home owners with clearly legitimate complaints find themselves fobbed off by builders and insurers. Quite often it seems that the home owner is dismissed as being in an insignificant minority of "problems". To the new home owner who has been sold an expensive home with back-up insurance but finds its value zero, it is a 100% problem. And it appears that, annually, well over ten thousand people who have bought new homes end up having to send claims to the insurer. This number takes no account of the innumerable "snagging" claims which most new homes appear to have and which the new home owner has to take up with the builder.

# A–Z

THE FOLLOWING SECTION TACKLES SUBJECTS OF CONCERN TO EVERY OWNER OF A NEWLY BUILT HOME. SO WHETHER YOU ARE TROUBLED BY BATS OR BALL VALVES; DAMP OR DRAINS – YOU'LL FIND HELPFUL ADVICE RELATING TO THESE AND MANY MORE TOPICS ON THE FOLLOWING PAGES.

KEY TO SYMBOLS

- Basic construction problems
- Environmental concerns
- Exterior problems
- Legal matters
- Interior problems
- Administrative matters

**The Land Registry** will provide ownership details of your site directly to you. These will include a plan of the land which should show the precise boundaries. There is a fee for this service but it should be less expensive than using a solicitor, and also faster.

**Access to buildings** by disabled people is governed by the Building Regulations.

**If the road** is not adopted by the council, there may be a private owner, who will be listed in either local council or Land Registry records. Equally, the land could be common land or government-owned land.

# A

## Access

The plot of land on which your property is built ought to have access to the public highway. Ideally the plot will share a boundary with the public highway or the highway margin.

If vehicles need access to the plot from the road, there must be a low, properly constructed kerb at that point.

Sometimes access from a plot to the public highway is across privately owned land. In this case, the land may be crossed only with the permission of the landowner, who will normally agree in a contract with the plot owner never to obstruct access and to keep the crossing point in good condition. The landowner will also usually agree that the land will not be sold without the next owner agreeing to these points.

Such contracts, which should be stored with the deeds of the property, set out in clear terms the rights and obligations of all parties. If, for example, there is any obstruction of the crossing, the owner of the plot of land can take civil legal action for breach of contract.

It is also possible that services such as electricity, water, sewerage, gas, telephone or cable will have to pass over or under the privately owned land. In this case, provisions allowing for service access must also be made.

Narrow margins of privately owned land sometimes exist between the plots and the highway margins. But, in several well publicized cases, the owner of the strip has refused either to sell or to allow the land to be crossed.

These strips are often called "ransom strips", for obvious reasons – the owner of the strip can demand a very high payment to allow access, even if the strip is narrow. Sometimes, of course, the strip owner might sell you the relevant land, thereby extending your plot to the public highway.

Free access to your plot is a vital issue and it is essential to ascertain, before purchase, precisely where the legally defined boundaries are.

Sometimes what is on site does not correspond with the legal boundary position. Your gateway, for example, may have been installed on land which is outside the plot.

If the property is on a new development where new roadways have been constructed, the roadway itself may be privately owned by the developer. Only when the roadway is constructed to a minimum technical standard will the local council consider taking it over.

For information on the exact legal position, contact the solicitors of both the local council and the developer. Other people in these organisations may be less acquainted with the facts and could give wrong information.

Delivery lorries will commonly deliver goods to a property only from the public highway; this avoids the need for vehicles to stand on private land where they may be outside the delivering company's insurance cover.

FURTHER INFORMATION: *See* **B**oundaries, **D**riveways, **R**oads

## Aerials

A television aerial may be supplied with the property; if so, check that it has been properly installed. The developer may, however, have provided only coaxial cabling and socket outlets.

If there is no aerial, it is quite possible that the coaxial cable may not actually be connected to the wall-plate socket outlet. A connection in the loft may also be needed. If there are a number of television outlets, fed from one aerial, a signal booster may be needed should the picture quality be poor. The orientation and type of aerial needed can usually be seen from neighbouring properties.

Sometimes aerials are also required for good radio reception. It may be possible to use a multiplexer to send both radio and TV signals down one length of coaxial cable to a dual outlet.

Satellite broadcast dishes are normally supplied by a specialist company. Before the satellite dish is installed, look at others in the neighbourhood so that you know the direction in which yours will need to point. You can then decide the best and most unobtrusive location on the exterior of your new home.

Optical fibre cable services can also be connected to the coaxial cable within your home, although you will need an adaptor and a supply contract. This usually avoids the use of TV aerials and satellite dishes.

## After-sales service

The developer will usually provide after-sales service. In large building companies, this may be run by a separate specialist department. If you have bought a new house from a small builder, it may be the builder who returns to do the work and there may be no formal department.

The after-sales department should look after all problems of construction except for faulty consumer electrical equipment, such as washing machines, where the manufacturers have probably provided their own guarantee.

Some developers subcontract this post-construction work to specialist organisations but the work to be done first has to be agreed with the developer so that one or more subcontractors can be instructed to effect repairs. This may take some time and you may be left wondering whether the repairs will be made. If there is, say, a plumbing fault, the developer may arrange for the subcontractor who initially did the installation work to attend to the fault.

Some faults will be apparent immediately on entry. Others may take time to emerge. Construction insurance schemes require the developer to attend to faults in the first year or two. It is, however, a limited warranty in terms of time and what it covers. A period of two years is common, but beware - the small print might reveal that you have only one year, in the event, say, of the house being completed but unsold for a year! It is important that you know the start date of your cover and that you understand what time limits apply.

Once the period of teething troubles has passed, only major faults will be

**If you have moved** from one television area to another, the channels on your television set will need to be adjusted. Your television manual will tell you how to do it.

**If the local** signal strength is sufficiently strong, you may be able to use a loft aerial. Of course, some portable televisions have their own aerials which may be sufficient.

**If the site developing** company folds, you will have no after-sales repair service unless you have a warranty underwritten by an organisation such as NHBC or Zurich Municipal.

**If you have** no insurance cover, then your repair rights are in accordance with the contract from the builder and common law.

**If you are about** to buy a house from a builder who is not registered with NHBC or any other insurance company, then it is desirable that your purchase contract includes details of technical standards to be met, and after-sales service arrangements in the event of closure of the vendor company.

**If a building material** does not have a certificate, then it may or may not be legal to use it. The onus is on the user or supplier to prove the point.

remedied as explained in your warranty arrangements.

Perhaps the developer will agree that your property will be built to comply with Zurich Municipal or NHBC published technical standards, a copy of which can be bought from these organisations, and that the after-sales service will be modelled on the NHBC or ZM insurance format.

As mentioned, this agreement should take account of what is to happen in cases of liquidation, bankruptcy or takeover of the developer. These events are commonplace in the building industry and the advantage of being in an insurance scheme is that the insurer should arrange for another building company to do the work in accordance with your insurance cover.

If the insurance company fails to do this and you have exhausted its complaint procedure, you could consider contacting the Insurance Ombudsman.

FURTHER INFORMATION: *See* **C**omplaints, **C**onciliation, **I**nsurance, **W**arranties

## Agrément Board

The British Board of Agrément (BBA) tests new materials and methods which are used in the construction industry and will also certify them. If a builder uses a certified material or method in accordance with its instructions and for an intended purpose, it is deemed to comply with Building Regulations. For example, it will approve certain brands of cavity-filling material and their installation codes.

FURTHER INFORMATION: *See* **B**uilding Regulations

## Air-bricks

Air-bricks are generally found just above the damp-proof course level in houses which have suspended floors. Their purpose is to allow ventilation of the underfloor space. Failure to ventilate allows humidity to rise. High humidity encourages the spread of dry rot in wooden floors.

Underfloor voids nowadays have an oversite covering of concrete laid on a heavy damp-proof membrane (usually heavy-gauge polythene sheeting), which is laid on sand. To provide a complete barrier, the damp-proof membrane must be continuous. If the barrier is breached, there may be rising damp. The surface of the oversite is usually higher than ground level to prevent water coming in and pooling.

Air-bricks are slatted in appearance. The slats should be unbroken and face downwards to shed rain.

In cavity walls, pairs of air bricks are placed opposite one another in both wall skins, installed in such a way that any condensation landing on the cavity bridge between the bricks does not run on to the inner skin and cause a patch of dampness.

The purpose underlying all of this is to ensure that variations in wind pressure between one side of the building and the other will cause the underfloor air to be continuously ventilated. This will, however, mean that the void will be cold during winter. Any underfloor copper pipes carrying water should be fully insulated to prevent bursts during freezing weather. It is worth running the downstairs taps at intervals during frosty weather to make sure pipes don't freeze.

Air bricks should not be covered, even in winter, as it is important to maintain ventilation.

Ventilation bricks or ports are used to provide fresh air to gas-fired appliances which draw air in from the room. Restricting the air to gas appliances can lead to a fatal build-up of carbon monoxide which is odourless and colourless. This applies both to mains gas and portable gas-fired appliances. Check the ventilators regularly to make sure they are not blocked. It is vitally important to make sure that fresh air can come into a room where one of these appliances is being used.

If methane or radon collection is a potential problem in the underfloor void, a ventilation stack is generally erected taking air from the underfloor void to the ridge of the roof. This stack should have a rain cowl which rotates or is designed to suck air in the void up the stack for expelling into the outside air. Check that the vent is securely fixed.

FURTHER INFORMATION: *See* **B**ricks, **M**ethane, **R**adon, **V**entilation

## Air quality

The inside of the building may be damp initially, as a result of all of the water in the plasterwork. Good constant ventilation is essential to avoid the growth of mould. If a foul or damp odour can be detected, the source should be investigated and identified.

One possibility is that it is sewer gas which is entering via a lavatory pan, sink or waste pipe because of the lack of a water seal in the important U-bend trap. This is more likely if the property has been unoccupied for a long time before sale or if there is a problem with the sewer which causes back flow. The solution may be simple – just fill the empty trap with water. Check shower trays and washing machine drain outlets, too. Outside drains may suffer from the trap drying in summer, which is why drains sometimes smell.

If the malodour still persists, there may be a gap in a sewer, even though this should have been tested before the building was passed fit for habitation, or a drain cover may be missing or loose. Sometimes vented fumes can enter from external flues or soil vents which are too low, relative to the ridge of the house, and which are not fan-assisted.

Cavity-wall insulation with urea formaldehyde can give rise to nasal irritation inside the building. It should have been installed according to the appropriate Code of Practice. Otherwise, unreacted formaldehyde vapour will penetrate the pores of the blockwork and plaster and enter your living space.

If you are downwind of a local restaurant, you can check the local authority's planning consent file for the establishment, then decide whether you believe the restaurant's ventilators are adequate. The local

**The plans** for the house as approved by Building Control will reveal how many air-bricks there should be and their location. It will also detail what gaps have been left (or are supposed to have been left) between any underfloor piers.

**Ventilation bricks** are sometimes used to facilitate ventilation in rooms and these should not be covered. They are located at the tops of rooms. Sometimes ventilation ducts will lead from a room up to the roof ridge or out through a wall.

**External pollution** can come from a variety of sources. If a neighbouring property is the problem, a polite word with your neighbour may be the solution.

**If you find** that aircraft are making certain items vibrate in your home, and causing the china to rattle, you may find that felt or rubber mats will reduce this.

**Flat surfaces,** such as plain brick walls, act as mirrors to sound. An important point to bear in mind if you are close to an airport or motorway. Plants and trees climbing up or covering these surfaces will help deaden the noise.

authority's environmental services department may also be able to help.

FURTHER INFORMATION: *See* **S**mells, **V**entilation

## Aircraft noise

Certain areas are under flight paths. Unfortunately you can do little about this.

Many airports are aware of noise problems and require incoming and outgoing planes to adopt procedures for noise abatement. The planning consent for airports may place restrictions on the hours during which an airport is open.

Double-glazing and sound-deadening insulation are a partial solution but do not help if you need to open windows in summer.

Noise can come into homes through the air, so any direct connections between the air inside and outside the house should be examined. But do nothing that will restrict good ventilation - without adequate ventilation, gas appliances can be fatal.

Sometimes sound-deflecting fences or sound-deadening trees (which have lots of leaves or fronds all year round) can help.

FURTHER INFORMATION: *See* **N**oise

## Airlocks

In any new plumbing system, airlocks can occur. This usually means that the pipes are not full of water and that air is caught in the system.

Clunking in the pipes when you run hot or cold water may mean there is an airlock. This is termed "water hammer" and is not good for the system. It should be remedied promptly. Once the air is discharged, the problem should disappear.

The area can sometimes be identified by tapping the pipe run at intervals or by running hot water and feeling whether there is a temperature differential to the touch.

Water hammer can also occur if a cistern valve does not operate smoothly or if there is an airlock causing water to surge or stop suddenly.

If the problem is caused by a cistern valve, it is possible either that the valve is faulty or that the incoming water pressure is too high for the valve's specification. Sometimes floats on cisterns have dampers to alleviate the problem.

It is good plumbing practice to install bleeding vents at the highest place in pipe runs. These vents may be found in built-in cupboards, in the loft, or under floorboards (which will hopefully have been marked by the plumber). Vents may require a spanner or special key to undo the screw so that the problem gas can be bled.

Gas in pumped central-heating systems can be due either to residual air or to hydrogen resulting from corrosion in the system. Trapped air is the more likely cause in a brand new house.

If radiators are warm at the base but cold at the top, the radiators need to be bled and a special key to fit the bleed screw will usually be needed.

Undo the vent nut slowly until you hear an hiss. Be patient. Soon a small jet of hot water will come out, indicating that the radiator is now full.

Air may also be present in some pipes when repair work has been done, so taps may splutter briefly when first used. This usually clears quickly but can be messy.

FURTHER INFORMATION: *See* the **B**asic central heating system on page 28

### Alterations

You may wish to have some alterations made to your home. These will usually be done at your own expense. When you are listing repairs for the builder, be sure not to include an alteration.

If you are having structural alterations whether to the building or to the supply of services, then check your warranty in case the work would invalidate it.

Also check the restrictive covenants on the property, because you may have agreed not to build an extension for a set number of years – or indeed ever - if the underlying land is contaminated.

### Anthropometric data

This is the data used by architects when designing homes. It purports to give dimensions of human beings and the space they need for sitting on chairs, getting out of bed, and so on.
It is accompanied by data showing "standard sizes" of tables, chairs, doors, beds and so on. There is now so much data that the published book version is the size of a telephone directory.

This data is used in architects' computer-aided design programmes to enable the dimensioning of rooms, offices, and so on.

### Ants

*See* **I**nfestation p.93

### Approved Inspectors

*See* **B**uilding Regulations p.55, **I**nspectors, Approved p.95

### Arbitration

*See* **C**onciliation p.64, **L**egislation p.102

### Architects

An architect may have been involved in drawing up the plans for your house or at least your house type. If the architect also oversees the construction, you should be provided with an architect's certificate on completion.

The site plans will be on the public record in the planning authority's public file, which you and anyone else can inspect.

There should also be plans lodged with Building Control. These reveal more details about the construction. The plans might not be on the public record but you can always ask. You will always have to pay for a copy.

The architect's plans are subject to copyright (except when on the public record) and there must be a copyright owner. This may be the architect but, as part of the architect's commission or employment, the copyright owner might be the developer.

If the developer is being evasive, do not let yourself be fobbed off with references to "confidentiality" or "company policy" or suggestions that the plans are full of technical detail – you can worry about that later.

Most architects are members of The Royal Institute of British Architects

**If you are venting** a heating system, then be sure to have an old towel ready to catch the inevitable spillage. Take care not to undo the vent screw too much otherwise it will come away in your hand and you may have a flood.

**Sometimes air** is present in the gas pipes in the building – for example a port may have been left open. In this case, it may take a few seconds longer than normal to ignite the gas but this should only be encountered in the first ever ignition.

**If the issue** of copyright is raised in an attempt to prevent you from seeing the plans "because they are subject to copyright", then just establish who the copyright owner is and ask to see the plans. The copyright owner can decide whether you can have a copy. Sometimes a mere sight of the plans is enough to answer a question.

**Plans** which are on the public record, such as in planning departments, can probably be copied without the permission of the copyright holder - but ask.

**Most architects** now use computer-aided design programmes: some of which go so far as to allow virtual reality simulations of new buildings.

**All valves** are rated by the manufacturer as to their water pressure range. If the water pressure is too high or too low, there can be problems.

(RIBA), Royal Incorporation of Architects in Scotland, or another professional organisation, and as such have to uphold certain standards. All architects in the UK have to be registered with the Architects Registration Board of the United Kingdom. Ask this board if you want to establish whether a person is presently registered or not. They will also be able to advise what procedure to follow if there is a suspected case of professional misconduct.

FURTHER INFORMATION: *See* **C**opyright, **P**lans

### Asbestos
Although the disposal of asbestos is now very strictly controlled and regulated, it used to be tipped into old landfill sites. If buried deeply there is no problem as particles cannot escape, but some asbestos deposits have been found near the top of rubbish tips. In this case the topsoil has to be removed and safely disposed.

Some nationally known builders have created new developments on landfill sites. They have taken measures to remove as much asbestos as they know about but there is always a possibility that there may be other deposits, fly-dumped, anywhere.

If you find asbestos in the soil, contact the local authority. An asbestos scare in a development can cause property blight.

The district planning authority may also not allow extensions to be erected onto houses to be built for fear of disturbing soil where asbestos might be present.

# B

### Ball valves
These are found in lavatory cisterns, and in storage tanks for cold water or for central-heating water. If set incorrectly, the ball valve may not close properly, which might result in an overflow. The washers on the valves have to be changed at intervals, like tap washers.

If a float valve gives a water hammer sound - investigate. Other valves can give a judder; this means that the valve is not closing cleanly or bouncing.

### Banisters
It is worth checking that these are firmly secured. The supports should be upright columns not more than 100 mm apart to stop children wedging their heads between the rails. If the supports were horizontally slatted children could use them as a ladder.

### Basements
If the underfloor area is to be habitable, the walls as well as the floor have to be watertight and special methods of tank construction may have been used. If water is coming in or if there is dampness, you should investigate this further as the problem can only worsen.

### Bathrooms
Any windows should have frosted glass – this may well be a planning condition. Frosted windows are, however, quite transparent at night, so a blind or curtain is well advised.

Some bathrooms are fully enclosed without any window. Adequate ventilation must be provided by an electric fan. This probably operates when the light is switched on and for a time afterwards. It is very important that you allow air to be drawn into the bathroom when not being used so that damp air can be sucked out: leave the door open to let air in.

BATHROOM SAFETY POINTERS:

- There must be no electrical plugs (other than shaver plugs) in a bathroom or immediately next to the bathroom door.
- All light switches should be of the pull-cord type or located outside the bathroom itself.
- Any electric shower or electrically heated towel rails must be properly connected so that no one can be electrocuted.
- All metal pipework must be earthed. If there are any earthing straps, they must be left in place, but make sure the wires are connected.
- It should not be possible to touch a light bulb when standing in the bath.

## Baths

AS SOON AS YOU HAVE MOVED INTO YOUR NEW HOME, CHECK:

- Does the bath have scrapes and scratches? Report any to the builder in case you are blamed.
- Is the seal around the bath intact?
- Are the outlets firmly fixed and not leaking?
- Does it have a plug?
- Do the taps or mixer tap work?
- Is the tap fitting wobbly?
- Is there a shower attachment and do the jets spray evenly?
- Are the bath handles secure?
- Does the bath settle when someone is bathing? If so, the supports under the bath may need to be adjusted. These can be accessed by removing the bath panel.
- Does the bath drain relatively quickly? If not, use a sink plunger to try to clear any blockage in the U-bend.
- Is there any evidence of back flow or gurgling when the wash-basin is emptied?
- Does the bath empty without leaving a pool of water at the opposite end from the drain? Use a spirit level to check the fall if there is a problem.

Hopefully the waste overflow is securely seated and actually connected to the waste pipe. If not, overflow water will flood under the bath and could bring down the ceiling below.

FURTHER INFORMATION: *See* Showers

## Bats

Bats are legally protected species. If they are nesting in a part of your property, it is illegal to remove the nesting site - even if you hate bats. Contact your local authority or the RSPCA for advice.

## Bird's nests

Birds like to build nests in the most imaginative places. Flues and chimneys should have cowls to prevent this happening. Birds which nest in lofts must use an entrance point. Close this after the

**Without good** ventilation, mould will start to grow and the bathroom will become musty. There are minimum standards set in Building Regulations. If you have a fan it will need to be cleaned at intervals. Check that you have the instructions.

**The bath** side panel can be removed for access to the waste traps and pipes. By seeing what sort of mess is behind the panel, you will have an idea of the level of care which has been taken during construction.

**Water overflow** 'inspection' pipes from lavatories and from the water storage tanks in the loft should be checked – before there is an emergency – by pouring water from a bottle and establishing whether they actually function. Some have been known to fall down when tested.

**Blockages** in sink wastes may be due to particles of plaster, sand, or whatever. The old-fashioned sink plunger is a useful and cheap remedy as a first resort. The plunger is useful for sucking out jammed sink plugs too.

**Gutter blockages** may be caused by leaves. Usually, there is a leaf guard which covers the downpipe exit from the gutter so that only rainwater and small particles go down.

**If your home** adjoins parkland, you may wish to ensure that your boundary fences are of a suitable nature. The planning authority may have placed restrictions on the type or height of fencing. If there is a fence, your conveyancing documents should reveal whether you, as owner, or the park owner is responsible for it. Do you have the name, address and telephone number of the park owner to hand in case it is needed?

fledglings and parents have left the nest.

The cisterns in the loft should have insulated covers otherwise you could end up with a dead bird in the cistern – this is bad both for the bird and for you!

## Blockages

Full or partial blockages can occur in waste systems, in pipes carrying water supplies, and in rainwater fixings such as gutters. In a newly built house it is possible that some debris may be the cause.

The foul waste pipes should have been checked for watertightness before being passed. A blockage may have been caused by someone flushing away something like plastic or newspaper. Sewer covers may have to be lifted to detect the blockage point and drain-clearing rods used. If you find any backflushing occurring, there may be a problem with the main sewer.

U-bend waste traps should be readily detachable as the flanges are tightened by hand. If you decide to remove the U-bend, first empty the sink as much as you can, then place a large bowl underneath to catch the remaining water. After cleaning, replace the U-bend carefully, making sure that the rubber seals are intact. Leave the bowl underneath and try some test water. If a gland leaks, the bowl will catch the dripping water.

If you cannot refit the U-bend and have to leave it, place a clear sign in the sink to stop it being used. Also, cover the pipe leading to the drain with polythene to stop foul drain smells coming into the house. You will need some disinfectant as the job is messy.

If a washing machine or dishwasher floods, this may be because the waste outlet pipes attached to the equipment have become blocked or kinked. In hard water areas the waste pipes can in time become blocked with scale and washing powder and this, rather than a washing machine malfunction, can be a cause of a flood.

Flues should be covered or they may become blocked with bird nests.

If a gas appliance flue becomes blocked, this could have fatal consequences.

## Boundaries

Your plot of land has a boundary – which should be clearly known to you. Refer to your deeds or the Land Registry plans or the plans kept by the local planning authority if you need confirmation. Hopefully these plans will be consistent with one another. The plans with your house deeds should be definitive and it is worth checking that they correspond to what is on the site. Perhaps a mystery fence shifter has been at work or perhaps the developer's landscaping team or site surveyor made a mistake. If there is a boundary problem, query it as soon as possible.

At the boundaries, there may be fences or walls. Your deeds should show who is legally responsible for the upkeep of each fence or wall, and may also determine whether repair costs have to be shared. Even though one party may have the responsibility for maintenance, the other party usually has to allow reasonable access for repairs. You may wish to check with your neighbours what their understanding about the boundary is.

In flats, shared walls are usually jointly owned – with the boundary being in the middle of the wall. You should have rights under the Party Wall Act.

FURTHER INFORMATION: *See* **A**ccess, **D**riveways **E**asements, **R**oads

## Bricks

These form the main structural element of many houses. Common bricks look unattractive and are used in places where they will not be seen. Facing bricks are attractive and varied but more expensive. Sometimes faulty bricks are produced which have an unacceptable level of cracks; these should not be used by the builders.

Most structural bricks are porous, meaning that they will soak up water. Engineering bricks are stronger and less porous. They are used in exposed situations, such as the top of a wall that is constantly wetted with rain and is possibly frozen in winter. In time a normal brick would splinter, crumble or flake.

Porous bricks allow dampness to penetrate. That is why, in cavity walls, the inner skin has to be isolated from the outer structure by damp-proof course. This will prevent rising damp, will stop rain soaking in from a chimney top and will prevent bridging of the cavity where there is a frame.

Many porous bricks contain a small quantity of soluble inorganic salts. In some cases if the brick is constantly wetted, the salts will be driven to the surface and form white efflorescences. These will gradually cause the surface of the brick to powder and crumble, although this may take some years.

A small amount of efflorescence can be tolerated but any larger amounts should be brushed off. Hosing off is unsatisfactory as the salts dissolve and are soaked back into the bricks. They will later reappear. A line of efflorescence indicates a line of dampness. You can sometimes tell if a wall is sodden by tapping the bricks with a hammer and listening for a dull thud. A damp brick will also feel colder and wetter.

Builders are supposed to keep bricks dry before using them.

FURTHER INFORMATION: *See* **A**ir bricks, **B**rick bond, **D**amp

## Brick bond

This is the way that bricks are laid and bonded together. There are a number of methods which are used, such as stretcher bond, English bond, Flemish bond and garden-wall bond. When done properly, bricklaying can become an art form.

It is important to have a good foundation and to use the correct mortar. As brick courses are laid one on the other, the vertical joints (the perpends) should be staggered from course to course. Usually courses are

**Although** most bricks are of the standard size, many special shapes are available. Ask your builder for the name and the maker of the bricks in your house. You will need this information if you ever want to buy identical ones for an extension.

**Bricks** are usually installed intact and should have properly pointed mortar joints. The mortar should be weaker than the bricks so that any cracks form in the mortar rather than the bricks.

**There should** be no structural cracks in the mortar courses or in any bricks. If there are, contact the builder immediately.

**Any manufactured part** used in the construction of your home which is not marked with a British Standard "kite symbol" might still comply with a standard – but it might not. So if there is a question about whether an unmarked fitting is up to the job, and a Standard applies, the onus lies on the installer and manufacturer to prove it.

**If you are** changing your door locks, be sure to buy locks which comply with the British Standard or equivalent as a minimum. This is necessary for insurance purposes.

**Building companies** sometimes open branch offices. This does not change the registered name or address. If possible, legal papers should always be served to a company at its registered address.

horizontal unless in an arch or controlled slope.

Stretcher bond is the most common. Here only the major sides of bricks show and the bricks in each course are halfway displaced from the lower and upper courses. This is common in cavity wall constructions: the width of the skin is the same as the width of a brick.

In cavity walls the two skins need to be parallel and joined by brick ties at regulation intervals. The wall ties are usually made of metal and should not be visible from the outside. They also have 'drips' so that water which condenses drops down the cavity to the area below the damp-proof course. This prevents the inner or outer skins from becoming wet.

Bricks are jointed with mortar which provides a levelling bed and holds the bricks together. The mortar can be made flush with the wall or weathered. In the weathered form, the tops of the horizontal mortar courses are recessed but slope to the edge of the lower brick, so throwing off rain. Sometimes – for decorative effects – the mortar is recessed. A bucket handle is used to level the surface.

Engineering bricks are used where water penetration is likely to be a problem. They are sometimes used to form damp-proof courses (two layers of bricks with staggered joins being needed) or placed on their sides along the tops of garden walls on a mortar bed to stop rain penetration.

FURTHER INFORMATION: *See* **Engineering bricks**

## British Standards Institution

Once a Standard is set, articles made to its requirements can be marked with the British Standard certification or "kite" mark.

If, for example, a plumbing fitting is marked with this or another certification mark, it means that the fitting has passed the test set in that standard. Overall it is a sign of quality and compliance. An item marked with a standard (whether British, European or International) or given an Agrement Board certificate, is deemed to satisfy the relevant regulation when used for its intended purpose and in accordance with the relevant instructions.

The BSI can provide details of British, European and International Standards which affect the UK, it publishes a long list. The SRIS section of the British Library has reference copies of many standards, which visitors can read. Beware – they are usually very technical documents.

## Brown land sites

*See* **Landfill**, p. 98

## Builder

The term 'builder' is commonly used to describe the organisation overseeing the construction of the property. A better term is 'developer', even though the developer and the organisation doing the building may be one and the same.

Building companies have suffered heavily during recent years; many have closed down for reasons of bankruptcy, others have gone into liquidation, perhaps as a result of a takeover. In the case of a limited company (and most major house builders *are* limited), a receiver or a liquidator will have been appointed and Companies House should have details about this. Changes in limited company ownership or name have to be immediately notified to the appropriate Registrar of Companies in England, Wales, Scotland or Northern Ireland.

Records for any limited UK company can be accessed by the public through any Companies House office. UK companies must submit their annual reports and accounts to the relevant Registrar every year; these are then made available to the public for inspection.

Public limited companies (PLCs) issue printed reports and account brochures to their shareholders and the public. As they are listed on the Stock Exchange, their share price and whether it is rising or falling, can be seen from the newspapers.

Usually if a company is taken over, the responsibilities of and undertakings by the company are also taken over. However, sometimes a company may have only its assets taken over, i.e. its assets are sold, and the company is then liquidated, thereby in practice ending its responsibilities.

Unless you have insurance cover such as that provided by NHBC, you may not have any fall-back if problems arise. If possible, negotiate something about this before you buy from an uninsured building company.

If you need to write formally to a builder or developer, then write to the Company Secretary at the registered office of the company. You may wish to send the letter by a recorded delivery service so that there is no doubt that a letter has been received from you on a particular date.

Remember, however, that a recorded delivery service does not provide any evidence about the contents of the letter. Remember, too, to keep your recorded delivery receipts and a copy of the letter.

FURTHER INFORMATION: *See* **D**evelopers

### Building line

This is a line defined by the local authority planning department which represents the nearest distance a building can be to the public highway.

### Building Regulations

If buildings are to be legal, they have to comply with building regulations.

The Building Regulations, popularly known as 'Building Regs'(a hard "g" as in kegs), arise from the Building Acts. There are different Acts covering England with Wales, Scotland and Northern Ireland.

The Building Act 1984 radically transformed building control in England and Wales. The Act is set out in very general terms and the Building Regulations 1985 (amended in 1991) result from this. Technical detail is contained in a set of Approved Documents covering structure; fire safety;

**If a different** form of construction not specifically described in the Approved Documents is intended, then the proposed user has to show that it does comply with Building Regulations. This may mean supplying engineering calculations to the inspector before the plans for the building are passed.

**Separate sets** of Building Regulations are issued by the Department of the Environment, the Welsh Office, the Scottish Office and the Northern Ireland Office.

**Statutory building** control does not extend to small garden walls, but large walls, perhaps those holding back a high embankment, are covered.

**If you need** to understand how Building Regulations work in greater detail than we have space for here, buy or borrow one of the latest textbooks which applies to your part of the UK. This will give the least painful introduction to the subject. Your local authority will provide you with a leaflet summarising the procedure in your area.

site preparation and resistance to moisture; toxic substances; resistance to passage of sound; ventilation; hygiene; drainage and waste disposal; heat-producing appliances; stairways, ramps and guards; conservation of heat and power; access and facilities for disabled people; glazing; and materials and workmanship. The Building Act also dovetails with certain other linked Acts, including the Water Acts of 1945 and 1973. Other non-statutory guidance is provided by British and European Standards and Codes of Practice.

Compliance with the standards set out in the Approved Documents for the relevant features in a new building means that the Regulations are deemed to be satisfied and thereby the statutory obligation also, as required under the Act. If a building is technically constructed in strict accordance with the Approved Documents, the provisions of the Act are therefore probably satisfied.

All building work is overseen by building control officers or Approved Inspectors. Their statutory activities are also governed by Acts of Parliament.

Until the new Building Act 1984 came in to effect, building control inspection in England and Wales was vested solely in departments of that name within local authorities. The local authority vetted the plans for the proposed building in accordance with the statutory obligations. Once those plans were passed by building control, the builder could then proceed to mark out the site. At various predetermined stages, construction had to stop until the work was inspected by a building control officer and passed. These stages included inspecting, the marking out of the site, the excavation of the foundations, the damp-proof membrane level and so on. Work which did not pass a stage was failed until it did pass. Anything built in contravention could potentially be demolished.

Under the new Act, in addition to local authority inspectors, there are Approved Inspectors who operate under The Building (Approved Inspectors) Regulations. They provide a private form of certification. NHBC Building Control Services Limited is an Approved Inspector.

**Note that building control inspection is, in law, quite different from the inspection made by NHBC or any other organisation for construction insurance purposes.**

All buildings must comply with the relevant building regulations unless exempted.

Building control is a complex subject; there are various textbooks which give further detail as well as a very interesting trade journal *"Building Control"*. You can refer to recent copies in The British Library Science Reference and Information Service holdings. The Institute of Building Control is the publisher.

If you have a question which could be asked of both the building control and planning departments, then ask both. If you are given an answer by one, you may still need to ask the other. For example, if you want to build a small extension and go to the planning department, you may be told that planning permission is not needed because the proposed extension is within an exempted class. However, you may not be told that you still have to submit plans for building control and that it must be inspected at various statutory stages of construction.

Building control is primarily concerned with securing the health, safety, welfare and convenience of people, including disabled people, in or around buildings. It is also concerned with conserving energy and preventing waste, misuse or contamination of water.

A number of English counties have supplementary local Acts, such as the Berkshire Act, which add further controls. There are also Inner London Building Regulations. Your local authority can tell you which Acts apply to your new home.

Building Regulations in Scotland and Northern Ireland are different, although the same overall objectives are set. Arm yourself with a current textbook and local authority leaflets if the need arises.

A builder who builds a property which is faulty and where the statutory requirements are broken can be prosecuted.

FURTHER INFORMATION: *See* **B**uilding services, **I**nspectors, Approved

## Burglar alarms

If one has been installed, ensure you are given the instructions, the keys or PIN number, any warranty details and the installer's information.

Some systems are hard-wired, meaning that wires run throughout the property connecting sensors to the control unit. More commonly, there are wireless systems in which the component modules are each electrically powered but which communicate by radio frequency.

Passive infra-red movement sensors are also often employed. They may be so sensitive that they can easily be triggered by heaters suddenly coming on, by pets wandering about or even by birthday cards falling down. These are frequently the causes of false alarms.

Your burglar alarm klaxon should automatically stop after a preset period to prevent neighbours and the police becoming annoyed by the incessant ringing if you are out.

# C

## Cables

Unseen electrical cables span the innards of any property. There are clear standards for cable sizes relative to their loading and lengths of run. Cables which are too small are likely to overheat, which represents a fire risk.

Cables running through a space 60 cm above the floor and 60 cm below the ceiling are supposed to be cased in metal or plastic conduit. They should run either horizontally or vertically from the switch or other device.

**'Buy back'** is acknowledged by Zurich Municipal as an option in some cases if the new building becomes unsound.

**Any cables** used outside should either be low voltage, or – if mains voltage – be properly installed in watertight fittings to comply with wiring regulations.

**All electrical terminal blocks** or connections such as switch outlets should be accessible. Any heat felt in plugs or sockets suggests a potential fire risk.

**Gas cookers** should be used only if the flame is blue. Although they are relatively safe, never ever block up the ventilation ports.

**Check the carpet's** joining strips at doorways. Are they secure? If a strip has been screwed down, press the strip down to see if a screw head protrudes. If it does, a bare foot might be cut by it. Do the doors close properly or do they catch on the carpet? Is there too much clearance between the carpet and the door? Try to remedy any of these problems by contacting the after- sales team or the developer immediately.

Any cables which pass across joists may be threaded through a hole in the joist or a metal-capped notch. There are strict standards in force about the positions of notches and holes, as drilling and cutting weakens the timber. The standards also take into account dangers from nailing.

All circuits run to a consumer unit and each circuit should have its own residual current device (RCD) switch.

In addition to the power wiring, there is also earth wiring. Part of this is run with the cables. Additionally all metal pipework in a property has to be bonded by earthing wires (which have a green and yellow casing), so that there is no danger of electrocution.

FURTHER INFORMATION: *See* the **E**lectrical system on page 30, **E**lectrical installations, **W**iring

## Carbon monoxide

Carbon monoxide is a colourless and odourless gas that is formed when fuel gas (either North Sea or bottled) is incompletely burned. Fuel gas should always burn with a clean blue flame, forming carbon dioxide which is relatively harmless.

Inhaled carbon monoxide can be a killer. Gas appliances — whether portable or fixed — should always burn with a clean blue flame. A yellow or sooty flame means danger – there is insufficient oxygen and carbon monoxide is being produced.

Even so, flame colour is not by itself a reliable indicator. The very greatest care must be taken to prevent any fumes from gas fires coming back into the room.

Symptoms of carbon monoxide poisoning include drowsiness, lassitude and mental confusion. It is possible to buy carbon monoxide detectors from hardware stores. There are two kinds. The first is an electronic sounder, rather like a smoke alarm. The second, which is cheaper, is a special patch that changes colour when carbon monoxide is present. If you suspect a carbon monoxide build-up indoors, quickly open all doors and windows to let in fresh air, turn off the gas appliance and leave the room. Anyone who has been affected may need urgent medical attention.

FURTHER INFORMATION: *See* **G**as leaks

## Carpets

Carpets are sometimes included with a property. This is not, of course, a statutory requirement.

The carpets may not be covered by the construction insurance. Inspect the carpet for stains, cuts and marks as soon as you move in and report any immediately to the developer.

Some carpets have a fault called "pile reversal" which makes the carpet appear blotchy.

## Cavity wall insulation

Cavity walls are only filled for thermal insulation purposes. If correctly done, the fill can provide a bridge from the outer (wet) skin to the inner (dry) skin. This can cause damp penetration.

Materials used for cavity fill must be approved by the Agrément Board or have similar certification. They must also be used correctly. The materials include glass mineral wool and foam. If you wish to have the cavity filled after the property is built, check that this does not invalidate your warranty. Also check that the installer is approved by the Agrément Board or equivalent.

Post-build cavity fill involves holes being drilled in the outer skin to allow a urea-formaldehyde or other approved foam to be injected into the cavity. Sometimes polystyrene beads are blown into the cavity, providing additional insulation. Note that formaldehyde vapour can adversely affect the indoor air quality if it penetrates into the house via pores or gaps.

FURTHER INFORMATION: *See* **E**nergy conservation, **I**nsulation

## Cavity walls

The exterior walls of new buildings are generally of the cavity type. This means that there are two skins. The outer is typically brick but could be insulating block either clad with tiles or rendered. The inner skin is usually insulating block. Timber-framed buildings have a slightly different construction with an outer skin of brick or block and then an inner wall of timber, protected by a barrier film.

In brick or blockwork walls, the two 'skins' are held together, but spaced apart, with wall ties. There is a set number of ties which is mandatory depending on the size of the building, but usually they are hard to detect after building. A wall may bow if not properly tied.

Wall ties should not protrude; this is a sign of bad workmanship. The wall ties have drip points so that any condensation falls down the cavity and runs to the outer wall, preventing dampness in the building.

The two skins are typically supported on two lines of bricks topped with a damp-proof membrane which must clear the external ground by at least 150 mm. The cavity must also be at least 150 mm deep below this.

Cavities are generally topped with wooden wall plates. They may have apertures for door openings and windows, and damp-proofing has to be provided to stop horizontal ingress of moisture.

It is important that the cavity is not accidentally bridged with falling mortar during construction since this could let rainwater penetrate from the outer skin. The cavity is supposed to remain dry; if water should accumulate, there may be a damp penetration problem. So establish the source, and as a stopgap, consider drilling a hole 150 mm below the damp-proof membrane level to let any accumulating water escape.

Usually no services are run within the cavity but occasionally it can be used as a route for a TV cable.

If the builder has installed cavity wall insulation, well and good. If you wish to have it done as an improvement, check the terms of your

**The cavity** in the wall itself is an unventilated airspace which means it also acts as a thermal insulation blanket.

**Not all walls** have cavity insulation. Certain types of exposed wall structures, such as timber or masonry walls, are not usually suitable for cavity fill.

**Many ceilings** are textured. Some are coved. Where there are joins or where there is a lamp fitting, check to see that the plasterboard is good.

**If there** is a bad flood above the ceiling, consider making a *small* hole in the ceiling with a screwdriver so that you can let the water out as quickly as possible. Do this where you want to collect it (perhaps over a bath or sink). Watch out for electrical cables and pipework.

**Ceilings** may be 'false'. Lift some squares to see what lies behind and to assess its condition. Beware of falling dust and debris.

construction insurance cover as you may unwittingly void your guarantee if you go ahead.

FURTHER INFORMATION: *See* **B**ricks, **E**nergy conservation, **I**nsulation

## Ceilings

Many ceilings are formed of plasterboard. The one nearest the roof space should be backed with the statutory thickness of thermal insulation whether glass mineral wool (glass fibre) or vermiculite. Ask the builder what the current minimum thickness is, probably 150 mm.

Any dampness on a ceiling should be investigated immediately. A pipe, a cistern or the roof may be leaking. If there is a burst pipe, water will run along the ceiling and the water level will rise until an outlet is found – often at a light fitting. This will usually cause some flickering and the electricity supply may then short. This is dangerous.

If there is a serious leak, turn off the main water supply stopcock. If you need to drain the cold water cistern in the loft, quickly turn on all taps. Be sure to turn off the immersion heater and also any other gas or electric water heaters to prevent the boiler being heated after it has run dry. If there is a coal fire (which means the heat cannot be extinguished immediately) you should not drain the back boiler.

If you act quickly, you may just stop the ceiling falling down, but it will take some days to dry out and you may have to remove the wet glass fibre insulation.

FURTHER INFORMATION: *See* **L**eaks

## Central heating

Central heating systems are common nowadays. Typically, they are heated water, hot air or storage heater systems.

The developer should have left you with operating instructions. If you have a question about the installation itself, the manufacturer should be able to supply a copy of the installation instructions for the boiler, pump and other main parts.

Hot air systems usually have adjustable louvres for each port. Some may be operated remotely by actuators. Hot air reaches the outlets via ducts.

In addition to heating room air, hot water units are used to heat water. The hot water cylinder may also provide heat for a drying cupboard.

If a central heating system appears not to be working and electrical power is being supplied to it, the pump may have jammed. In this case the pump may be humming and the casing quite hot. **Power to the pump should be turned off.**

An access port at the back of the pump motor (on the side furthest from the pipes) will allow you to gain access to turn the rotor which may have seized. The rotor will probably have a slot for a screwdriver at the end so you may be able to free the shaft. You will need a screwdriver and a towel to catch some water drips. **Make sure the power to the system is off before you start this procedure in case the pump suddenly starts when you are working on it!** This may save a call-out, but don't attempt this unless you are competent and confident. If the pump growls when operating, there may be a bearing or corrosion problem.

If the system has water radiators and they are all completely cold, the pump may have failed or may not be working because of the lack of a command signal.

If only some radiators are cold, check the hand valves on each radiator in the first instance to see if they are hot. If not, there may be a zone valve which is not operating or an airlock.

If warm only to partial height, there is air in the radiator and this will have to be bled out using a special radiator key available from a hardware store: look at the upper ends of the radiator to see the shape of key needed.

If the heating is uneven throughout the property, the radiators may have to be balanced. This is done by altering the flow, using the valve at the other end of the radiator from the hand valve.

If the heating level is low, this may be because the boiler water temperature is too low. There may be a thermostat on the boiler (behind a door or panel). Read the instructions first. It is possible that the boiler installed is too small for the house's needs. Check the building plans and compare the rating with what is marked on your boiler.

Corrosion and scale may accumulate in hot water systems. Consider using a proprietary preservative solution, but check the warranty first.

Usually there is a header tank cistern in the loft which supplies water to the heating system. This should be inspected. It must have an overflow and an expansion vent tube fitted. The float valve should also operate and the correct height of water be in the tank. The cistern itself should be on a stable base, free from rubbish, have a lid and be thermally insulated.

FURTHER INFORMATION: *See* the **B**asic central heating system on p.28

## Clerk of Works

This is the person who oversees the work on the site and who is responsible for the management.

The quality (or lack of it) can largely be attributed to the competence of the clerk of works, though financial constraints should also be taken into account.

## Coal fires

Many newly-built houses have a proper chimney to enable the resident to light a coal fire.

CHECK THAT:

- The fireplace is safely installed
- The flue is in good condition and has a cowl
- The fireplace is constructed from firebricks or fire-resistant materials rather than everyday concrete
- There is an instruction leaflet
- You have the proper kind of smokeless coal. (Who is your nearest coal or smokeless fuel merchant? What storage facilities are there?)
- You have somewhere to dispose of ash. Remember that hot ash can melt or even set fire to wheelie bins.

**Each home** will have a number of thermostats for regulating room air, circulating water temperature and storage water temperature. There may be additional radiator thermostats. The temperature sensor for the general house thermostat should not be situated near a heat source or in direct sunlight as this will cause the thermostat to sense a false temperature.

**Electric storage** heaters operate on a white-meter tariff and each unit has its own heat controls.

**A Residents Association** of a communal apartment block, for example, is a useful vehicle to ensure problems are addressed correctly and remedied properly. If you are involved in setting one up on a newly-built block, remember the Association should have a properly formed structure, including a treasurer. Any monies paid to the Association should be receipted.

**Take care** with management service agreements. You might find that you are giving the company permission to spend your money freely on 'repairs' which you think are either unnecessary or too expensive.

**Trade directories** such as "Kompass" are likely to be held by your local library. These will provide details of building and development companies, but remember that the latest directory is often out of date by the time it is published. Nevertheless, it can provide useful information.

- The smoke doesn't blow down the chimney in some winds. You may need a different cowl or a taller chimney.
- What your chimney should be like. The plans for your house should give some indication. It has been known, however, for houses to be built without chimney stacks, in spite of plans clearly showing that they were supposed to be there!
- The Solid Fuel Advisory Service can provide information on facilities.

### Cockroaches

*See* **I**nfestation p.93

### Common land

This is land which no one owns or can own. Refer to parish or local council records for its boundaries.

### Common parts

These are parts in a complex such as a block of flats. Each flat may be privately owned but each flat owner has rights and responsibilities in regard to electricity and other services, communal areas, communal gardens and driveways and so on. The details should be given in the deeds and in your lease.

Title to the commonhold parts may be held by the Commonhold Association which has as its members each flat owner. It is possible that this will be a limited company which is required to submit returns; alternatively, it may just be an Association with Articles setting out its existence, rights and duties.

### Communal facilities

If communal facilities are available, ascertain who is responsible for their maintenance and what rights and obligations you have. This should be found in your rental contract or other written agreement.

Sometimes flats have management companies to handle such matters. These companies may include the flat owners or be sub-contracted by a landlord or freeholder. Such companies will be registered with Companies House. Inspection of the register can provide details about the directors, the turnover and the business.

### Companies House

If you need to find out who are the directors of a limited liability company or wish to see the latest annual report and accounts, contact Companies House.

The office for England and Wales is based in Cardiff but there is a public search room in London, EC1. The Registrar for Scotland is in Edinburgh and for Northern Ireland in Belfast. Each office should have reasonably up-to-date records for the whole country although each Registrar registers only those companies in the local jurisdiction.

### Company structure

All limited liability companies have a hierarchy. It is important to establish what this is and to go ever higher up the structure if you have a complaint.

Commonly you will first encounter members of the company's workforce. They report to the relevant managers – typically there will be a sales and marketing manager, a technical manager, a site or production manager, a personnel manager and a finance manager. They in turn probably report to a general manager.

Above him or her, there may be one or more executive directors who have the authority to carry out the wishes of the board. The board may also include some directors who have no executive authority and are thus "non-executive" directors. Of the executive directors there may be marketing, technical, sales, production, personnel and finance directors as well as a managing director. Not all directors have main board positions.

So if you encounter a problem at one level in a company, you may wish either to remit it to the level immediately above or to write directly to the managing director.

Each board always has a Chairman; some are clearly more active than others. The Managing Director or Chief Executive has the highest executive authority (the ability to make decisions) and is therefore usually the highest level to which a complaint can be addressed.

Few companies publish their internal structures, so telephone the company and ask for the name of the director who has a particular function.

You may find that having written to a senior director you receive an answer from a lower level. Persist, copying correspondence to the managing director. The person lower in the hierarchy will then know that the MD or Chief Executive Officer is being informed by you of what is happening.

It is usually best to send a letter to a company marked 'For the attention of the (whoever)' as this means you are writing to the company itself rather than an individual.

### Compensation

Should you have had significant trouble with your new house, you may wish to discuss compensation with the builder. If you have incurred damage, then you may wish to discuss the matter with your solicitor, (but be aware of the high cost of legal fees).

If the property has been misrepresented to you before purchase, this is a matter for your solicitor.

FURTHER INFORMATION: *See* **C**omplaints

### Complaints

If you have faults to report, the after-sales service is, in effect, a complaints handling procedure. It is important that any suspected faults are reported quickly, clearly and that the developer, having recognised that there is a fault, agrees to do the remedial work.

A complaint numbering system is described on page 36; this makes it easy to discuss faults and ensures that none are 'accidentally' overlooked.

Once the repair is done, check the work to see whether the repair is good. If not, advise the developer or the after-sales service manager in writing – promptly.

The remedial work may still be unsatisfactory or the

**If the building** or development company is part of a group of companies and there is a holding company, perhaps a PLC (Public Limited Company), there will be a further set of 'Group' staff and directors and a main board.

**Any member** of the public can buy shares in publicly quoted companies. This enables the shareholder to receive annual reports and to attend the annual general meeting where questions may be asked of directors.

**Sometimes** companies will use the tactic of not replying to a letter. So write to ask if it was received and to request an acknowledgement, which after all is a basic courtesy. Alternatively, send the letter by a recorded delivery service.

**Before buying** a property from a builder you may wish to take up references – for example, from the construction insurance company.

**Construction insurers** set technical standards which are above statutory requirements and which extend to matters not subject to statutory control.

**If the ventilation** is bad, the house or a room within the house will have high humidity, which will promote the growth of mould. The room will start to smell musty, as may any clothes and books stored there.

builder may not accept your assessment. Then try the insurer and any dispute procedures if necessary. Exact details of the procedure should be found in any documents provided by the insurance company; otherwise ask the insurance company for details.

Ultimately, an organisation that is registered through such a scheme risks its membership if a valid complaint is made. The registrar of the scheme will be able to confirm to you whether any organisation is registered at a given time and will also provide you with details of what membership entails. Before being registered, a building company will have to have given certain membership undertakings, including compliance with technical standards laid down by the organisation membership. Breach of these undertakings can lead to the developer being struck off the register or being obliged (behind the scenes) to pay higher insurance premiums to the insurer.

Remember that the developer, and everyone else concerned, has no choice about fulfiling the statutory requirements for your new home. It is illegal not to satisfy these and the parties involved could be prosecuted for breach.

It is not clear to what extent some of these construction insurers actually know or want to know about initial 'teething trouble' faults.

The author hopes that builders and insurers will audit faults reported so that, in developments when it is clear that there has been an important fault in one property, other properties will also be checked automatically if the owners permit.

FURTHER INFORMATION: *See* **W**arranties

## Conciliation

You may find that your construction warranty scheme allows for the insurer to conciliate between you and the builder if you are in dispute about a fault. Usually the builder will do what the insurer requires. Check your policy for details.

## Condensation

In a new building the plasterwork has a high quantity of water in it, even though this may not be apparent. With thorough ventilation over several weeks, it will dry out. There is no point in heating the house without also ventilating it, otherwise the moisture will remain. Each room should be ventilated so that there are no stale corners.

If there is continuous condensation in one part of the house, you may see either a constant trickle of water (common with single glazing in cold weather) or mould patches growing on walls, ceilings or floors. If a patch is obviously localised, there may be a condensation problem; alternatively there may be another cause of dampness, such as a leak or rising damp. If the dampness is general, the room may be too cold or be badly ventilated.

The gradual drying out may also cause some timbers to contract just a little. This is quite normal, although in severe cases the timbers may split.

Temporary condensation is not serious – just make sure that the area dries out. This may mean remedial work if there is a construction fault.

FURTHER INFORMATION: *See* **D**amp, **V**entilation

### Conservation area

Certain developments are located adjacent to or in conservation areas such as protected woodlands. Trees on new developments are sometimes subject to Tree Preservation Orders, but may not be identified as such; even so, chopping them down would make you liable to prosecution. During the conveyancing of the property, do check any plans with the local authority to determine whether there are any such trees. The developer may have cut them down; this should be pointed out to your solicitor.
Conservation area consent is required for conversion of unlisted buildings in conservation areas and similar requirements and likely to apply in National Parks and Areas of Outstanding National Beauty.

### Contaminated land

The local environmental health department will be able to advise of any known problems and whether precautions need to be taken. The local building control officer may also know of any problems, as may the planning department or neighbours.

If you wish to check into matters yourself, you may discover additional sources of information from old maps, aerial photographs, town plans and local authority plans.

FURTHER INFORMATION: *See* **A**sbestos, **L**andfill, **M**ethane, **R**adon

### Contracts

Contracts can either be written or verbal. Written contracts are signed by all parties; each party should keep at least one copy, preferably an original.

A contract sets out the rights and obligations of each party. There is always a "consideration" (payment), in return for which property or goods are bought or services obtained.

It is important to understand exactly what a contract says before you sign it. If possible, obtain a copy in advance so that you can read it at leisure. If not, then read it at the time, perhaps twice, carefully. Do not be put off by small print that is difficult to read.

If you do not like or do not understand what is in the contract, then why sign it? Remember, you can always try to negotiate different terms.

Every clause in a contract is there for a reason. A simple way to check a contract is to go over the clauses one by one and mark by each whether it is (or is not) of benefit to you. You may find the contract has ten clauses, nine not in your favour.

Verbal contracts can also be made between two or more parties. These are equally as valid, although the law of the land sometimes requires certain types of contracts, such as licences, to be in writing. Verbal contracts can be difficult to prove if there are only two parties and no

**Metal-framed** windows can act as condensation points, despite the incorporation of thermal breaks. Single glazing is more likely to cause condensation than double glazing.

**If you are worried** that the land on which your home is built may be contaminated, have the site checked. There are organisations which hold data about sites. The Environment Agecy may also have data at its National Groundwater and Contamination Land Centre.

**Remember** that contracts include rights and obligations for all parties. If one party fails to deliver, the other can sue for breach of contract. In such an instance, it is essential to be able to prove both that there was a contract and also what it stated.

**Hesitate,** then hesitate again, before rushing into litigation. Many people have been driven to despair having initiated legal action without realising either where it would lead or the huge cost of legal bills. Sometimes you may have to decide to accept life's outrageous fortune; even though right is on your side. Try not to dwell on the matter – just regard it as a bad experience.

**It is very** important to check the title of the land and its history – the person purporting to sell may not be the owner!

**If you cannot** find a switch to isolate cooking appliances, some may be plugged into sockets accessible inside the built-in cupboards.

independent witnesses. The actions of both parties may, however, give weight to the existence of a contract.

FURTHER INFORMATION: *See* Legislation

## Conveyancing

This is the legal process of transferring ownership of a property from one party to another. It is usually carried out by solicitors but there are also licensed conveyancers. Some individuals handle their own conveyancing, but remember – the legal implications are enormous if a mistake is made. *The New Penguin Guide to the Law* (Penguin Books) gives a detailed overview.

## Cooker hood

IF YOUR NEW HOUSE HAS ONE, CHECK:

- Is it properly fitted?
- Where is the isolating switch?
- Does it work?
- Where are the instructions?
- Is there a warranty?
- Is the filter there?
- How do you change the filter?

## Cooking appliances

The main electrical cooking appliances are hobs, ovens, grills and microwave ovens.

Your kitchen should be fitted with equipment that is brand new. Check that you have the instruction manuals, guarantees and, if possible, have a demonstration of the equipment.

Gas cooking appliances may be provided. Usually there will be a spark igniter button present on the hob. Can you find where the sparker is connected to the mains? Is there a socket behind the oven below? The isolating socket should be accessible.

If the gas does not light after a few sparks, let the gas clear, then try again. If the unit has not been used before, there may be some air in the gas pipe from the meter that needs to be expelled; this usually takes only a few seconds.

If the unit does not spark, the power may not be switched on; if the igniter sparks poorly, it may be damp. If you can smell gas but the spark igniter is not operating, there may be contamination around the igniter. Turn off the gas. Lift away the flame rings, then dry out any water and remove any dirt.

## Copyright

All written works, drawings, plans and photographs are created by an individual and are protectable by copyright. Copyright exists in an original creation from the moment that work is expressed on paper or film or as data. The owner of a copyright work is usually the creator unless the work is done by someone in the normal course of employment.

The copyright owner has the right to decide whether copies can be made and whether a fee is to be paid in addition to that charged for making the reproduction. Usually, plans on a public register can be copied; otherwise, the copyright owner needs to be contacted.

## Corrosion

In heated-water central heating systems corrosion can

occur in either the steel radiators or the copper pipes. Proprietary preservatives can be added to the water used in a system as the circulation is usually closed, separate from the hot water piped to sinks, basins, showers and baths. There may also be scale-preventing additives, which is a benefit in hard water areas.

Corrosion is unlikely in a new system but tell-tale signs are gas bubbling in the pipes and gas accumulating at the top of radiators, which must then be bled frequently. When bleeding a corroded system, you may notice a slight smell of rotting eggs. The water will also be black. Unchecked corrosion can result in pinholes which allow fine jets of water to spray the floor or a wall.

Another form of corrosion is caused by the rusting of bright steel screws. These are appropriate for use in dry places indoors but should not be used in damp atmospheres or outdoors.

Check the downwater pipe brackets. Are the screws rusting? If they are, have them replaced. Remember to check the screws on the gutter brackets as well.

Corrosion can also occur in metal tanks or cisterns. Sacrificial anodes are sometimes used so that these, rather than the tank, corrode and can be inexpensively replaced.

Check the fittings in out-buildings for corrosion too.

FURTHER INFORMATION: *See* **E**fflorescence

## Council tax

The owner of each property is potentially liable to pay council tax and this is payable to the local council on demand. Remember, you are liable to pay from the moment you move in.

Houses are banded in value and you should establish from the local authority council tax office the band which your property is in and how much you have to pay annually. If you think your valuation is wrong, you can appeal to the valuation office. But have a good reason.

If you think you should be exempt from payment, you will need to fill in a form for the council giving your reasons. Keep copies of all correspondence and notes of all telephone calls or visits, including the name of the person to whom you spoke – even if the advice is to throw the form away. Bear in mind that local authorities do not always process exemptions quickly; the computer may send out bills because it has been incorrectly programmed.

## Cracks

Cracks appear in properties for different reasons – bad workmanship perhaps, or natural shrinkage or structural instability.

Minor splits in wood can usually be filled. Hairline cracks in plaster are usually of little consequence and are to be expected. However, cracks in external rendering may affect the water resistance of a wall. Insulating bricks may shrink more than other bricks when drying out or if left uncured; minor cracks may then appear which can be repaired by the after-sales team – if you report them.

**Sometimes,** you may be told that plans are copyright, suggesting that it is not possible to view them. However, if you wish to see the building control plans for your house, you can ask the developer and the local authority building control department. If the plans are Type Approved by the NHBC, then you can ask the NHBC to let you see the drawings.

**Council Tax Valuations** are done by external surveyors and are dependent on property values at the time of valuation. It may be possible to obtain details of the valuations of other properties by inspecting the council's records.

**Every new house** will develop some cracks. Usually most, if not all, are minor.

**Sometimes houses** under construction have been given foundations which are wrong for that particular site. In the worst cases, cracks extend across walls and ceilings. Professional help will be needed quickly, including an assessment as to whether the building is structurally fit for habitation.

**The local authority** building control department should be advised if a house develops severe cracks as it has a statutory obligation with regard to unsafe properties. Plans for rectification measures will also have to be given building control approval. Fortunately, severe problems are relatively rare.

**Once the house** has dried out, any further dampness will indicate faulty ventilation or heating, or a more serious problem.

Of more concern are cracks which have a structural origin. These can result from movement of the foundations, the walls (through bowing), the roof, the floor, or even an interior structure. Such cracks should be reported immediately to the developer or insurer and closely monitored to establish if they widen. A photograph may help: be sure to include a date and measurement card in the frame.

To measure the progress of a crack, mark two points on the wall, one on either side of the crack, and measure the distance. Record the date, and repeat the measurement at various intervals. Alternatively, bond a microscope slide across the crack with epoxy adhesive. Do not cover the crack with adhesive. Then wait to see whether the glass splits.

The Building Research Establishment has produced clear guidelines which give a rating method for assessing the severity of cracks. If you have a construction warranty scheme, the insurer may be using this *de facto* standard; you may be able to obtain a copy.

Do also check the ceramic ware and glass (windows, doors and mirrors) when you first inspect your property. If you delay reporting cracks or chips, the developer may rightly question whether the damage occurred after handover.

### Curtains

If you have yet to move in, be sure to measure the size of the windows with your own measuring tape.

If you need to install curtain rails, it is usually easier to attach a wooden batten to the wall and the curtain rail to the wood. You will probably need a hammer power drill to drill into any concrete lintel above the window; a metal lintel may, however, have been used. If the curtain rail is not securely mounted, the weight of the curtains will loosen it.

# D

### Damp

When a house is newly built, the water used to mix both the mortar and plaster makes it damp inside. The whole house needs to be ventilated until it has dried out. This may take some weeks, though the house will be quite habitable. Check that your heating and ventilation is even throughout the property. Otherwise, damp will condense in the coldest room leaving it musty.

Damp patches on the inner surface of exterior walls can be caused by bridging of the damp-proof course. Check where the damp-proof course level is and establish that it is at least 150 mm clear of ground level. If garden soil is piled up, compromising the 150 mm minimum, it should be removed.

Dampness can result either from improper coping at the tops of chimneys or parapets or from the failure of roof flashing.

Problems can also occur because of horizontal bridging between two cavities – a result, perhaps, of mortar clogging the cavity or of an inadequate membrane at door and window frames where the cavity is closed. Check also for leaks caused by plumbing work or by faulty roofing, guttering or seals around doors and windows. It is a good idea also to examine the integrity of the silicone rubber seals which surround sinks, worktops, baths and shower cubicles.

Problems can also be caused by faulty electrical machinery (such as a washing machine), by radiators or pipes developing pinhole leaks.

Local mould on wallpaper indicates a dampness problem which could be due to poor ventilation.

FURTHER INFORMATION: *See* **M**ildew, **R**ot, **V**entilation

## Data Protection Act

As a result of your new home purchase, various organisations will hold personal data about you, and possibly your family, on databases.

Be cautious about answering marketing questionnaires. These are designed to elicit as much personal information about you as possible. Often they offer the prospect of a prize – do you know anyone who has actually won? – before asking questions about who you are, your family, the size of your house, your financial accounts, the newspapers you read, the cars you have, what pets you have. This data is then processed and may be passed on to other organisations - for a profit. Then the junk mail will arrive.

Once information about you has been compiled, you cannot legally have it deleted from the source, only corrected if wrong.

The Data Protection Registrar is based in Wilmslow, Cheshire. It publishes a list of those organisations which hold data, the categories of data and the purpose of the data. You may contact the Registrar for details of a registration, but you will need to give a clear name and address, probably the registered address of a limited company rather than that of a branch office.

There is a fundamental flaw in the Data Protection Act – an organisation which puts data about you on a computer does not have to notify you. Nor are you readily able to check the accuracy of that information, even for typographical errors, unless you apply formally to the organisation (which ought to be registered with the Registrar unless specifically exempted). Following your request, you must by law be provided with a copy of the data stored about you within 40 days. Legally, you can require any errors to be rectified. Any damage to you caused by errors may entitle you to compensation.

If necessary, you can require the estate agent, the developer, the after-sales company, any insurance company, the mortgage company, the utility companies, legal firms, building societies, banks and so on, to provide details. They must do this unless they are exempted. If you find they are not registered, but hold data about you, tell the Data Protection Registrar who might prosecute.

**There is always** a reason for dampness but it can sometimes be hard to establish as the water may run down rafters before contacting the wall where dampness shows.

**Surveyors** use damp-meters to record levels of dampness in walls. Feeling a wall with the palm of the hand can sometimes be a useful guide.

**The person** or company holding the data about you can require you to pay a fee, currently up to £10 for the information if you want to see what it says about you.

**There are** a number of books written for the trade about common building defects. Trade journals also feature articles on defects.

**It is more** difficult to spot something omitted than something broken. For example, a hot water central heating plumbing system should have a draincock. Also an outside water tap should have an anti-siphon valve, so that in the event of low pressure in the main, water from a garden hose cannot be sucked into the supply pipes contaminating potable mains water.

**Remember** that many delivery companies will not permit their vehicles to drive on to private land such as your new driveway.

**If you have** not examined goods which have just been delivered, then write 'not examined' on the delivery note before signing it.

## Defective Workmanship

Despite there being statutory obligations specifying minimum standards of facilities, and an Approved Document about workmanship which is part of the Building Regulations in England and Wales, there are still ongoing problems.

Defective workmanship, no matter what the excuse, is unacceptable.

Many tradespeople genuinely do strive to do a good job so that they can take pride in their work but everyone can make the occasional mistake.

Defective materials are outlawed by Building Regulations and service installation regulations.

FURTHER INFORMATION: *See* **B**uilding Regulations

## Defects

If you think there is a problem, do some research to establish whether there is or is not a fault.

Even if you decide that there is not, keep an eye on any changes. Remember, it is important to tell the builder or insurer within the time limit. So, even if you are uncertain, alert the builder or insurer in writing if the time limit is about to expire. Discussion and repair can follow, after the deadline if necessary.

FURTHER INFORMATION: *See* **B**uilding Regulations, **I**nsurance

## Deliveries

If you are in a new estate, you may find that the roads are not shown in most published maps of the area. This may remain the case for some years. Be sure to inform any company from which you order something where your house is, perhaps drawing a map to show where it is in relation to the nearest established road.

The small print on the delivery note may state that your signature indicates that goods are 'Received in good condition'. Even if they are delivered in what appears to be strong packing and the packing itself appears good, it is surprising what damage can be revealed when the packing is opened. If there is damage, report this to the vendor straight away as some carriers have time limitations for accepting damage claims.

## Developers

The developer is the organisation or person responsible for developing the plot of land and maintaining financial responsibility for the site until the property is sold. Some developers are small organisations, others are so large that they advertise heavily on national television.

Many companies have free general brochures and prospectuses. There is also a number of property magazines. Those aimed at private individuals, sold by newsagents, may sometimes have advertisements by developers giving details of other sites and any standard properties which the developer is building. You may, therefore, be able to see a showhouse on another site, but be prepared to travel.

## Disabled Access

The Approved Document M 'Access and Facilities for Disabled People' is part of the

Building Regulations for England and Wales 1991. The Technical Standards for Compliance with the Building Standards (Scotland) Regulations 1990 include a section entitled 'Facilities for Disabled People'.

The utilities and charities concerned with particular disabilities may be able to advise about special facilities and fittings appropriate for specific needs.

## Distortion survey

Plumb lines, spirit levels, water-level gauges and rulers will be used in a special distortion survey to establish what deviations the property is experiencing from normal. A plan of the building can also be made during the survey by taking measurements.

## Domestic appliances

Your new home will have a number of appliances which have been installed by the developer. Do you have the instructions, guarantees and know how to turn all appliances on and off?

All electrical appliances should be earthed unless a manufacturer says differently. Also, they must all have local isolating switches so that, in the event of a problem, each appliance can be isolated from the power supply, which can then be maintained for the rest of the property.

If you have a gas hob with an electrically operated igniter, do you know where the local switch to isolate the igniter is? It may be hidden on the wall behind your built-in oven. Heavy-duty electrical appliances such as cookers, grills and ovens should have their own heavy-duty isolating switches in proximity to the appliance.

Gas supplies to appliances should also have local isolating valves. Similarly, liquid fuel supplies to oil-fired boilers should have local isolating valves. Plumbed-in appliances, such as washing machines, should have isolating valves adjacent to the connection of the flexible hoses. If your washing machine is fed by hot and cold water, there should be a local shut-off valve on each pipe, with blue marking cold water and red marking hot.

- Does the appliance need to be connected to a drain or vent? Has it been connected?
- Does your tumble drier need to have a venting hose and is it connected to a vent or do you have to hang it out of a window?

## Doors

Exterior doors should be checked for security and general fit. Pay particular attention to the hinges (have they been supplied with the correct number of screws?), handles, latches, locks and the seals against wind and rain. Where a frame closes an external wall, there needs to be a good mastic seal to stop rain penetration.

New hardwood doors may warp. A minor amount of distortion is acceptable, but you might need to have the door replaced.

You may wish to add security features, such as chains, bolts and viewers. Where possible, use security furniture which complies with the British Standard or a similar European mark. You should then be assured of a quality product.

**Stay beside** each appliance when it is first used in case there is a malfunction. You may need to isolate the electrical, gas and water supplies quickly.

**Some appliances** are hard-wired to a connection socket and may have a replaceable fuse and neon light to show when power is supplied to the appliance. It is puzzling that some switches with neons are installed hidden in normally closed cupboards.

**Wooden doors** may start to bind on sills or frames as a result of minor movement and swelling of the timber. (This is particularly common in the damp seasons.) Eventually the door may stick, and as a result security bolts may no longer align with their housings. This is less likely with metal-framed doors and frames.

**Tree and shrub** roots can seek out field drains and grow into the drainpipes, eventually blocking the drain. Willow is a notorious offender for destroying field drains, its roots extending great distances.

**Drainage and waste** disposal are governed by the Building Regulations.

**You may** wish to find out how high your house is relative to a nearby river and whether there is any flood-warning scheme in existence.

Sometimes doors are fitted into frames on site but there is a trend towards factory-fitted door-plus-frame assemblies which can be slotted in.

Doors, when hung correctly, should not swing either way unless designed to do so. Some internal doors are hung with hinges which have removable pins making the removal and replacement of the door simple.

FURTHER INFORMATION: *See* **F**ire Doors, **L**ocks

## Drainage

The land around your house property should be properly drained. Drains may have been inserted by the developer, perhaps by the placement of rubble-filled 'French' drains which duct water away to soakaways, boreholes or ditches.

You may not be aware that these are present, but ask the developer or check the local planning authority records. Some drains may have been added without being marked on plans; it is not always necessary for French drains to be marked (although this is obviously helpful at a later stage).

If you come across a trench of deeply filled stones in your garden, you may have found a soakaway or French drain. Block this and you may cause water to accumulate rather than drain as intended.

It is important that your land drains properly and promptly. Watch what happens when there is a heavy rainfall. Is there any flooding?

Clay soils are impermeable and if water cannot drain, mud will form. If you are adjacent to high ground, you may even find that patches of sogginess in your garden are due to miniature canals in the clay channelling groundwater into your garden.

Unless there is a drain present, the land immediately around your house should be very slightly cambered so that any rain which does fall runs away from your house, rather than towards the walls.

Foul waste is always ducted away in sewers but rainwater can be led to soakaways or to a storm drain system. The local planning authority will tell you what official drainage arrangements have been made for your plot of land.

Rainwater gutters should be fitted with stop ends and the pipes properly connected. The gutters must have a slight fall to the outlet, otherwise water will accumulate and stagnate. Outlet ports should have leaf-guard cages. If there is no cage, leaves will collect in the gutter and cause blockages.

If there are drips from gutters, the seals or joints may be at fault, or there may be a break in the plastic. If you find that rainwater spills over gutters, unseen leaves and debris may be the problem.

Check to see that open drains have debris covers and that any inspection chambers have good covers with any necessary retaining bolts or fixings. Septic tanks also have covers and vents, which should be inspected.

If the cover of an inspection chamber is wobbly, it probably means that some soil or sand has gathered within the rim.

This can be easily cleared (though it is not the pleasantest of tasks). Any cracked covers should be replaced.

For obvious health reasons, any new connections to sewers have to be tested and approved. If you have an outhouse distant from any drains, then a soakaway for rainwater is probably the answer.

Rodding points are provided in foul waste drains. Manhole or inspection chamber covers should obviously be present and undamaged.

Inside the property check that water from sinks, waste-disposal units, basins, baths, showers, bidets, lavatory bowls and water-filled appliances drains away promptly and cleanly. These should be checked soon after you move in lest there are blockages or leaks.

The overflows from lavatory and storage cisterns in a loft should be checked, too. All cisterns must have an overflow; if there is none or if it is blocked or improperly connected, there is likely to be a flood. Check before it is too late.

FURTHER INFORMATION: *See* **F**lood plains, **S**oakaways

## Drain cocks

Your property will have a number of drain cocks to allow the water systems to be drained during servicing. Potable mains water comes into at least one tap and the supply cistern. Cold water and hot water are then drawn from the cistern to supply tap outlets and any plumbed-in washing machines. The hot water central heating system has a closed water circulatory system and this may contain preservatives. Each of these systems must have a drain cock so that water can be drained before servicing.

Make a note of where the drain cocks are. If you cannot find them, ask the developer's after-sales team - hopefully they will know from the service plans for your house what is supposed to be there.

Draining a system is always messy and a hose pipe is often useful to pipe water away. Before draining the hot water system or the central heating system, always turn off the central heating boiler and make sure any immersion heater is switched off too.

FURTHER INFORMATION: *See* the **B**asic heating system on page 28 and the **W**ater system on page 26

## Driveways

Driveways are preferably hard-surfaced and suitable for all weathers. Gravel is less desirable because of the effect on car tyres.

Concrete driveways should have a proper base and thickness of concrete. If the surface of the concrete is flaking, the mixture may have been improperly made, or the site frosted before the concrete had set.

Paving slabs and paving blocks are usually laid on a base of compacted sand, which may have been mixed with a small amount of cement. (Ants love this sort of arrangement: sand is excellent for tunnelling.) Paving bricks may easily be lifted out and replaced if they become stained or the drive needs to be excavated. The paving bricks are usually made of coloured concrete and laid in place on the sand

**Drain covers** are not attractive to look at but it is important that they are not permanently covered over with soil and hidden. A paving slab or pot plant can disguise the cover while providing easy access for servicing.

**Sometimes** there are planning restrictions about what can be left on a driveway – for example, a caravan or boat trailer.

**As the primary** route of access to the property, the design should take into account factors such as security and lighting.

**During a drought,** try to reduce the evaporation from the soil immediately around the foundations by covering it with some water-vapour barriers – perhaps heavy-duty polythene covered with slabs.

**If shelves** have been erected on a dry-lined wall, be aware that the plasterboard on its own may not have sufficient strength to support the shelves. Anchors which project into the blockwork are needed and these should be placed where there are battens or dabs to ensure a stronger mounting.

bed. The gaps are then filled with dry sand.

The driveway should be provided with a suitable slope so that rainwater can run off, if necessary to a drain.

Driveways usually access the public highway directly. Any alteration to the highway margin which is needed when widening the driveway should therefore be done only with the consent of the highways section of the local authority (or the Department of Transport if access is to a trunk road).

FURTHER INFORMATION: *See* **R**oads, **P**arking, **P**aths

### Drought

A prolonged period without rain can mean that the groundwater level below your property will fall and the soil dry out. Depending on the foundations and the nature of the soil, this can have serious implications for your property.

Clay soil, in particular, can shrink. As it does so in a drought, the walls of your property may crack. Once the drought is over, the clay then expands causing the ground to heave.

As a result, your house may need its foundations underpinned. This requires building control consent and is a difficult operation.

The problem can be exacerbated by the presence of nearby trees which extract large volumes of water from the soil and can therefore cause problems even in normal weather. Before removing an established tree, however, bear in mind that the drier soil will rehydrate and the resulting soil heave may still affect foundations.

The foundations for swimming pools can also be affected by soil collapse and heave.

Building control officers and builders go to a great deal of trouble to make suitable foundations. Sometimes, however, problems do arise.

For more information, consult the technical manuals issued by the construction insurance companies.

FURTHER INFORMATION: *See* **F**oundations, **S**oil heave

### Dry-lining

Dry-lining is a fast and effective form of plastering. To dry-line a wall, plasterboard sheets are applied to the underlying blockwork. Plasterboard is an inexpensive fabricated product, with a flat and even surface. The blockwork is lined with battens and the plasterboard nailed to that. This is how many ceilings are formed. Alternatively, the plasterer may apply dabs of bonding compound directly to the blockwork and then place a plasterboard sheet against these. The dabs set, holding the sheet in place. The joints are then sealed.

Where there are no dabs or battens, there is an air gap behind the plasterboard. This adds to the thermal insulation of exterior walls. Service cables may be run behind plasterboard before it is put in place.

You can find where dabs or battens are by tapping with your knuckles along the wall at different levels, perhaps at 10–15 cm intervals. Listen to the sound. Where the plasterboard drums least is where the blobs or battens are to be found. This is a simple and very effective method which will allow you to map the back of the plasterboard.

Dry-lining is used on interior block walls but not on timber-framed partition walls which have a void between the two skins of plasterboard. By tapping, you can locate supporting timbers in partition walls and ceilings.

Remember that there may be cables, pipes or nails lying behind the plasterboard. Metal and electric-current detecting devices are available in hardware stores or DIY stores. These can be used to trace underlying metal or cables but care is still needed in case there is a plastic pipe or deeply buried metalwork.

### Dry rot

*See* **R**ot p.131

### Duty of care

As a new homeowner, you have a duty of care in regard to the safety of others who visit your home whether for work or play. You could be held negligent if you fail in this duty.

Check for potential dangers. If there is a danger, erect warning signs or restrict access.

# E

### Easements

An easement is a legally enforceable permission given by a landowner to allow another party to cross the landowner's property, such as a utility company with service pipes or cables. The landowner may be required to give this permission as part of the purchase undertakings. Once granted, the utility can lay and service the supplies without seeking further permission from the landowner.

Whether a charge is made by the landowner for granting access is a matter between the landowner and the party requiring access.

If a property is built without direct connection to the public highway, then services have to cross over another person's land. This requires permission.

FURTHER INFORMATION: *See* **A**ccess, **B**oundaries

### Efflorescence

Efflorescence is a white deposit which occurs on the surface of external brickwork. It is caused by small amounts of water-soluble inorganic salts which are commonly present in the material from which bricks are made. The problem occurs with porous bricks rather than non-porous "engineering" bricks. Mortar may also be affected. Water evaporates from the facing surface of the bricks, bringing with it the salt, which crystallises on the surface of the brick – creating efflorescence. When it rains, the salt dissolves and moves back into the pores. As the bricks dry out, the process starts all over again. This is why efflorescences seem to come and go.

A fine layer of efflorescence probably does little harm. But crystalline, snowy deposits should be brushed off onto a collecting mat (perhaps a damp newspaper) to prevent them

**Usually the** utility provider – such as the gas company – will agree with the land-owner to undertake to reinstate the land affected to its original condition after their work is finished. This is important as it means that paths will be properly reinstated.

**Brick manufacturers** do try to reduce the amount of salt present in their bricks but salts may also come from the soil, or from additives used in the mortar to control its setting properties. Sea water contains salts and must not be used for making mortar.

**Electrical regulations** are difficult for a lay person to understand but there are a number of guides available, some of them written for use by electricians on site. Alternatively, consult your local library or a technical bookshop. Page 30 gives a general layout of electrical circuits.

**The full title of** the NICEIC is the National Inspection Council for Electrical Installation Contracting.

**Work carried out** by electricians should comply with the Wiring Regulations in force at the time of the installation.

falling into the soil and possibly affecting the porous brickwork below the level of the damp-proof course.

Hosing with water is not usually suitable because the salts will dissolve and re-enter the pores. But it might just work if you are quick and direct the hose jet at a shallow angle.

Because the physical forces involved in the creation of the salt crystals are much stronger than the bonds holding together the material around the pores, efflorescence causes bricks to crumble. It is a major cause of porous brick and stone decay, though this process may take some years. Impermeable stones and bricks are not, of course, affected.

Efflorescences are quite difficult to remove: it may take some years of brushing off deposits to clear a wall. Badly affected, crumbling brick-work or stonework has to be cut out and replaced.

Efflorescences are most destructive in walls which are constantly exposed to wind and rain.

FURTHER INFORMATION: *See* **B**ricks, **S**tonework

## Electrical installations

Electrical supplies and installations are governed by Acts of Parliament. As a rule, most domestic installations have to comply with the standards laid down by the Institute of Electrical Engineers in 'The Wiring Regulations'.

Developers who subcontract electricians are likely to use those belonging to a trade body. Electricians who have qualified for entry on a register (rather than merely paid to join an organisation) are obliged to comply with membership requirements. Breach of these can lead to a member being struck off the register. Many electricians are registered with the NICEIC.

Safety is of paramount importance. Faulty electrical installations are potentially dangerous; an installer could be liable to prosecution. If the construction of the property is subject to a warranty, the insurer probably has technical standards which set minimum numbers of sockets per room, etc. When you check your home's installation, check that all sockets are securely mounted, that there are no loose wires and that nothing is obviously unsafe.

For example, mains voltage socket outlets should never be located immediately beside a sink. Similarly, a high level of electrical safety is required in bathrooms, shower rooms and toilets; to avoid electrocution, there should be no power socket outlets (other than shaver outlets).

Raise any queries with the developer. If you suspect something is potentially unsafe, call in the electricity supplier or a registered electrician to inspect the installation.

Residual current breakers are provided on all consumer units and these have test facilities. The consumer unit should be accessible in the event of a power failure. All of the circuits supplied by the consumer unit should be written on the consumer unit. If a problem occurs with one circuit, it may be possible to switch that circuit off and use the remaining circuits.

You may find that you have two metered supplies, one for cheap-rate electricity.

Find out what each switch does. They are all there for a purpose. Similarly if there are any blanking-off plates which have cartridge fuses, these are present for a reason.

The earthing connections in your new home are very important. All service metalwork should be earthed. You may find green and yellow plastic-covered wire behind sinks, linking copper pipes. Never remove these links as they are there to prevent electrocution.

Any lamp fittings which are attached to the ceiling should be fitted to the wooden rafters which support the plasterboard. Plasterboard itself is a weak material and while lightweight lamp fittings can be attached, anything heavier must be securely fixed to stop it falling down.

FURTHER INFORMATION: *See* **P**lugs

## Electrical supply

Have you arranged an account with the supply company? If not, do so without delay, preferably before you move in. Otherwise, you may have no supply.

Does your previous supplier have your new address?

Always read the meter when you move in. If possible, have the reading witnessed and signed off on paper.

If you do not have a key to open the outside meter cabinet, then ask a neighbour to lend you one and contact the developer or the electricity supplier for a replacement. The cabinet should be lockable with the special key. If it does not lock contact the developer who will probably contact the supplier whose property the cabinet is likely to be.

The meter is connected to the consumer unit, your main control for the house. You may have a second meter operated by a timer for supply when demand is low at night.

You are responsible for the wiring on your side of the meter.

## Energy conservation

Because of the importance of energy conservation, Building Regulations now lay down certain requirements. Broadly, this means that new houses have to be much better insulated than before. This should result in lower fuel bills for you.

The outer walls will typically be built from thermally insulating blocks in an air-cavity construction. In timber-framed houses, the outer brick or blockwork is usually accompanied by an inner layer of glass fibre wadding.

Double-glazing tends to be the norm as building control consent will not be given unless certain technical requirements for the thermal insulation of windows are passed.

FURTHER INFORMATION: *See* **B**uilding Regulations, **I**nsulation

## Energy rating

A government approved SAP (Standard Assessment Procedure) rating is now required for building control

**Keep an eye** out for any sockets or electrical cables which become warm or hot. This indicates a resistance fault and represents both a potential fire danger and an electrical hazard.

**Brass switchplates** will corrode if mounted directly onto plaster; a black edge forms. These plates should be separated from the plasterwork by a rubber or transparent plastic film gasket made especially for the purpose. If you find corrosion on one brass socket or switchplate, inspect all of the others as the problem may not be isolated.

**The National** Home Energy Rating (NHER) is a further non-statutory rating which can be applied. It is often used as a marketing tool by builders. This NHER figure is plot specific and takes additional factors into account, such as geographical location, exposure to sunlight or shading, and so on.

**Meter cabinets** seem to be installed in a variety of places. Each service undertaking will have rules about installation of meter cabinets. Check that you have a key.

**Loft spaces** are now heavily insulated with glass fibre or vermiculite insulation. Cisterns and pipes in lofts should also be properly insulated. Insulation is often omitted immediately beneath the cistern to provide some local heat to the cistern, and thereby inhibit the water freezing. However, in really cold weather you might want open the loft hatch to allow heat to rise and reduce the likelihood of pipes freezing.

**Estate agents** often try to dig into your reasons for buying and may try to find out what pressures you are under to buy and your financial limit. This may weaken your negotiary position.

purposes for most new dwellings.

This is a figure calculated to indicate the energy efficiency of the proposed dwelling. The rating scale is from 1 to 100, and it assesses the overall way your home uses energy - eg, is it highly insulated or not? New homes should have a rating of at least 60; very old homes have a rating of less than 40.

The ratings indicate for a given kind of property whether the relative running costs will be high (low score) or low (high score). The difference in running cost between the best and the worst can be as much as a factor of six.

Bear in mind that the ratings are meaningless if the builder has decided not to build exactly according to specification. For instance, the loft insulation may be too thin; the calculated figures will therefore mislead prospective buyers and the building may not in fact comply with building regulations. Whether the building control officer will pick this up is open to question.

Remember that building control certificates are not a guarantee of absolute compliance with building regulations, despite what you might expect of the certification process.

Organisations such as NHBC and Zurich Municipal can calculate National Home Energy Rating Values as they are qualified assessors under the SAP scheme.

## Engineering bricks

These are bricks which are non-porous and therefore prevent the passage of water. They are very strong and are much more durable than common or facing bricks.

They can be used to cap walls. Since they are less prone to crumbling than normal porous bricks, two or more courses are often used as a damp-proof course. They are also used in situations where bricks need to have an higher than average load-bearing capacity.

FURTHER INFORMATION: *See* **B**ricks

## Escape routes

Approved Document B 'Fire Safety' governs the escape requirements in England and Wales under Building Regulations. There are similar regulations in Scotland and Northern Ireland.

## Estate agents

The activity of estate agents is partly controlled by the Estate Agents Act, introduced to reduce malpractice in the trade, and the Property Misdescriptions Act introduced later to regulate further unacceptable excesses. Action can be taken against estate agents if any part of the Acts is breached.

There is no statutory registration process for estate agents, so any "Jack-the-lad" can set up and start giving property valuations. However, some agents are personal or corporate members of a trade association. If you have concerns about a particular person, you can find out from that trade organisation what undertakings members make when joining and whether there is a disciplinary procedure in the event of a complaint. The local Trading

Standards Office may also act if there is a problem with the improper conduct of an estate agent. Remember, too, the Advertising Standards Authority has responsibility for upholding standards in advertisements and will investigate complaints.

As an agent or salesperson does not wish to lose the sale (and perhaps will receive a commission payment or be on a profit-sharing scheme), it is possible that incorrect or incomplete answers may occasionally be given.

Hopefully the instances when such problems occur are rare. You may encounter an agent who is thoroughly professional, open and honest with you. Nonetheless, what you might do once you have been given answers to key questions which you have asked, is to summarise the key questions and answers to confirm your understanding with the agent. Ask the agent or salesperson to put the answers in writing to you so that you have a record. These answers can then be passed to your solicitor who may append them to the sales contract as representations made by the vendor's agent to you.

The effect of having answers written down is twofold. Firstly, it should immediately smoke out any obvious mistruths or invented answers. Secondly, if there are misrepresentations, you have a legal handle on the vendor.

If the salesperson becomes evasive or tries to pass the buck onto solicitors, you may wish to say that this is not acceptable and that you want in writing the answers which you have just been given. If the salesperson still refuses, then you may wish to take a view as to whether the information you have been given is accurate.

Estate agents are skilled negotiators and are likely to follow up enquiries to establish whether you wish to buy or not. If you do not, you will probably be asked for reasons. The estate agent will then try to satisfy the reason and close the sale. Objection handling is one of the key aspects of securing a sale. It is very hard for an estate agent to argue against vague objections.

You may also find that the agent tries to bounce you into a sale by emphasising deadlines, other interest or the prospect of a price increase. Despite what you may be led to believe, the value of the property is not the asking price but what someone like you is actually prepared to pay.

If one solicitor or licensed conveyancer is acting for both the builder and you, there may be a conflict of interest (to your detriment). Will a conveyancer (who is probably receiving a lot of work from the builder) really advise you against accepting certain terms in the builder's contract?

## Estimates and quotations

If a written quotation is given for works to be done to your property, the quotation should hold whether the work has proved easier or more difficult than expected. Work in addition to the quotation, or variations from the quoted work, can involve additional charges.

Cost estimates are looser

**Sales literature** about new housing estates may have small print saying that the literature is not to be taken to comply with the Property Misdescriptions Act, nor should it be taken to be part of any purchase contract. In other words, the literature may be glossy but unreliable in some respects.

**When you** are enquiring about a property,you rightly expect to be given unequivocal and truthful answers and for your time not to be wasted. After all, you are about to spend a considerable sum on the property.

**When asking** for a quotation for building or maintenance works, it is also important to establish whether the quoted figure includes VAT (and indeed all materials and labour), or will that be added mysteriously at the end?

**Care must be** taken about extensions to new properties. New work, particularly on the existing foundations, could affect the building. This, in turn, could invalidate any warranties which you have.

**There** is a tendency in modern estate design to reduce fencing at the front of properties. This may be for security reasons or because the local planning authority issued planning consent requiring no fences. Anyone who erects a fence or even a hedge in contra-vention of the planning consent will be required to pull it down. Sometimes fences are required to be a certain height.

**Any door** from a garage leading into a dwelling must be properly constructed and comply with the relevant building regulations, including having adequate fire resistance.

but they should not exceed 10% more than the figure given to you.

Builders who do not want to do work may put in a very high quote to purposefully discourage you from hiring them.

Time estimates are notoriously vague in the building trades. This can be avoided by agreeing before work starts, and in writing, financial penalty clauses for late finishing.

### Extensions

Depending on the size, position and nature of an extension to a property, it may or may not require planning permission from the council through the local authority's planning department. Any extension must also comply with Building Regulations unless specifically exempted. Both departments can supply you with information leaflets.

If you wish to have a new extension and your property has a construction warranty, contact the insurer, who may allow you to proceed, albeit with some restrictions.

Extensions are sometimes not permitted on new estates for a specified period, or indefinitely if the planning authority has decided so. Contact your planning department. You may also have covenanted with the previous landowner when you bought the property not to build any extensions. Check your deeds. Permanent restrictions against extensions may be in force on contam-inated land. You could always ask the planning department if the prohibition can be lifted in any circumstances.

Treat conservatories as extensions. The salesperson may tell you they are exempt, but if the sales person is accidentally or deliberately wrong, you will be legally liable. Your construction warranty may be voided and the local planning authority may force you to take down the conservatory.

FURTHER INFORMATION: *See* **P**ermitted development, **P**lanning permission

# F

### Faults *See* **D**efects

### Fencing

Your plot may be marked out by boundary fencing or walls. Usually the land plan with your deeds will show who is responsible for the upkeep of the fencing and walls.

Check fences and walls for constructional stability and general performance. Does each gate close?

Fencing sometimes can be useful for deflecting noise.

FURTHER INFORMATION: *See* **B**oundaries, **R**ights of way

### Fire doors

For preventing the spread of fire, it is legally required that certain doors are fire-resistant. Usually these are rated to withstand a normal fire for half an hour.

### Fire escapes

Check the exit route, any signing and emergency lighting. Who is responsible in blocks of flats?

### Fitted units

Fitted kitchens and bedrooms are common sales features.

Sometimes the units are supplied in knock-down kit form for assembling on site. Others may have the carcasses supplied from a factory, with just doors and drawer fronts to be added. Others may be completely made in the factory, requiring only delivery and erection.

Fitted kitchens also integrate sinks, washing machines, dishwashers, cooking hobs, ovens, refrigerators and freezers. This involves plumbing and electrical fixtures.

- Check that doors and drawers operate properly.
- Do the carcasses have a backing board or are they fixed straight onto a wall?
- Are all the shelves present?
- Are the door handles securely mounted?
- Do the electrical fittings look safe and are they properly located so that you can access them safely?
- Are there any leaks?
- Is the sink sealed?
- Are the taps working and are they properly sealed onto the sink?
- Is there a mirror? Is it marked or cracked?

## Flat roofs

*See* **R**oofs p.130

## Flats

Flats may be owned, leased or rented. The contractual arrangements will set out what rights and obligations each party has. They should also set out what obligations the builder has and to whom, and also what obligations the warranty provider has and to whom.

The situation is further complicated by the presence of common parts which are associated with flats. These are the halls, stairways and gardens, as well as piped or cabled services.

In newly built, newly converted or newly refurbished flats it is important for there to be clear lines of communication with the builder. To this end, it is worth forming a Residents or Commonhold Association. Each flat owner can probably complain about faults in their private flat, but developers may respond more quickly to a joint complaint than a single complaint. A fault in one flat may be repeated in others and this should be noted.

Complaints about faults in common parts may have to be channelled through the chairperson of the Association. Common parts should be inspected by someone on behalf of the Commonhold Association.

Some landlords put in seemingly innocuous clauses insisting that tenants clean windows every six weeks. This is done not just to keep the windows clean but to provide a way of evicting tenants they do not like if the windows are not regularly cleaned - ie, if there is a breach of contract.

Housing association Property Mutual Ltd provides 20- and 35-year insurance policies for defects to housing associations and social landlords. It provides design audits and site inspections.

FURTHER INFORMATION: *See* **C**ommon parts, **H**APM

## Flood plain

Establish if your new home is on a flood plain by asking

**Check** that kitchen units are properly installed and are not loose. Coving and cornicing should be properly cut; there should be no "bird's mouth" gaps where the edges join. Clearly, the plinth and cornicing should not fall off their supports.

**The relationship** between landlords and tenants is complicated and subject to much legislation. Refer to specialist books on the subject, perhaps in the local public library, or contact your nearest Citizens Advice Bureau.

**Low-lying** property near the sea can be at risk from high tides, especially if the sea walls are not intact. It is worth making local enquiries about this from neighbouring residents.

**Services** are sometimes run immediately under floor coverings but the installer should have marked this on the covering floorboards. A metal or voltage detector can be used to detect cables or pipes before nailing. Carpets can be stapled in place. Staples are usually shallower than tacks and less likely to penetrate under-floor cables.

**The timber** used in some floors may have knots which fall out as the timber dries. This leaves holes in the floor.

**Check for** loose floorboards.

locally, and by checking the level of the land through OS maps. The relevant river authority or waterways board will also provide details.

In certain areas there may be a flood-warning system in operation, perhaps operated by the Environment Agency.

## Floors

Floors are generally made of concrete (whether floated or in beam form), timber, or chipboard. A lower floor can be solid or suspended.

A solid floor does not have a void underneath it. The floor is laid on compacted ground, which is covered with hardcore. An oversite layer of concrete is then laid and covered with sheets of damp-proof membrane, often heavy-gauge polythene. The membrane is lapped over the damp-proof course, providing a continuous barrier to rising damp. The membrane is then covered with one or more layers of concrete, and a levelling coat applied.

Sometimes differential movement of the ground directly under the floor occurs. As a result, the floor sags. This may be due to improperly compacted subsoil or a subterranean cavity and is potentially serious. It is possible to measure the displacement and monitor it over time. Brick sleeper walls for supporting joists in suspended floors can also sink differentially.

Concrete floors can generate dust and while they may be left untreated in the garage or in other non-habitable rooms, they are usually treated with a floor levelling and sealing compound inside a dwelling house. The floor surface is then covered with a synthetic floor covering.

Timber floors are made from tongued and grooved timber nailed to joists. The timber used for joists should be of the stress-graded type and marked accordingly. If the nails are not firmly embedded or if the timber dries, the floorboards may start to squeak. The timber used for floors is usually white pine, which though kiln-dried, may continue to dry and shrink a little after the house becomes occupied.

Hardwood floors are usually supported on softwood. Parquet flooring needs a good base and must be properly sanded and sealed.

Another form of construction is floor decking. Flooring-grade chipboard is laid in large sheets, usually tongued and grooved, and nailed to joists. Chipboard is relatively cheap but suffers from the disadvantage that it is likely to deteriorate quickly with prolonged soaking. It is therefore important to keep chipboard dry.

There may be drain cocks or vents underneath floorboards. These should be marked on the floorboard surface and a note kept so that their existence is known after carpets are laid.

Floorboards that bow as they dry may have to be flattened by an industrial planer. In some cases, it might be possible to use a proprietary levelling compound.

## Flues

Flues allow combustion fumes to escape, for example, from a

gas- or liquid fuel-fired heating system. A faulty flue can be life-threatening. Flues should be checked to ensure that they are not blocked and are of adequate size.

In a balanced flue system, a fan draws fresh air into the combustion chamber; and the pressure then forces the combustion gases out into the open air. This has the great advantage that it does not draw air in from the room. As the electric fan pressurises the air, the exhaust flue pipe can be very short indeed and may be just long enough to go through a cavity wall.

If there is no fan assistance, hot gases will rise up the flue, then exit into outdoor air. The flue should be positioned so that it reaches to the very top of the building.

In cold weather, you should be able to see the steam from gas combustion emanating from the top of the flue stack when the appliance is working. This shows you where the flue gases are going. They should be dispersing and not re-entering the building. A smoke test will also show you where the exhaust gases are drifting.

Does the flue present a hazard to passers-by? Remember that the flue will become hot and that it should not expel gases into people's faces or be able to be touched. If so, it may have to be guarded or repositioned.

It is illegal for an unqualified person to work on gas appliances. Gas appliance contractors might not work on vertical flues and chimneys, other than to test that they function as designed. If a gas inspector places a prohibition notice on an appliance because of a faulty flue, you may have to arrange for the developer to bring in a builder to do remedial work on the flue. Only when the system has passed the test will the prohibition be lifted.

The house construction insurance company inspectors should also be informed as they may wish to ensure that similarly built properties do not have faulty flues.

Heat-generating appliances installed in buildings must comply with the Building Regulations.

FURTHER INFORMATION: *See* **G**as

## Flushing

Building hygiene is covered by the Building Regulations, water supply laws and the insurer's technical requirements.

Check that every lavatory flushes cleanly.

Do the flushing handles operate correctly or do they feel loose? If loose, remove the cistern lid and tighten the flange nut by hand.

There is also an adjustment inside the cistern where the handle spindle connects to the siphon lever. This is usually a small metal cage with securing screws which should be done up tightly. Some of these cages are however made of plastic – which can break much more readily than metal.

Is there any rubble lying at the bottom of the cistern which would stop it working? Does the cistern fill up relatively quickly after flushing? If slowly, there may be a pipe blockage or the valve or stopcock beside the cistern may not be fully open.

**If a gas installer** fails to comply with gas installation regulations, inform the developer, the gas board and CORGI, the Confederation of Registered Gas Installers – the installer may be struck off the register after due enquiry.

**There are two** kinds of flues – fan operated and non-fan-operated. The latter always has a long flue stack.

**For builders,** there are guidelines aimed at reducing noise from lavatories in dwellings. Building regulations also set minimum construction standards for the passage of sound.

**If the water** level in the toilet cistern is too high, it will overflow into the pipe; too low and the cistern will not flush properly.

**Every water-filled** appliance is supposed to have a local isolating valve. Some require a screwdriver to turn the valve. When the slot in the valve is in line with the pipe run, the valve is open; when across, it is closed.

**If there is** a problem with a footpath, the builder may disclaim responsibility as it may not be covered by your warranty arrangements. Major site flooding is, however, a different issue and the builder is probably liable.

**The building** control inspector should have inspected what the builder was doing on site and indeed approved the foundations of your new home.

Does the filling water stop just a little below the overflow (warning) pipe? There must be an overflow pipe. Does it work? Empty a glass of water down it. The warning pipe sometimes drains into the toilet bowl.

The ball on the float level should be tight and not have any water in it. The level of the float can be adjusted either by a screw provided or, if metal, by careful bending.

Put some toilet paper in the pan. Does it flush away or swirl around? Is the flushing water evenly dispersed around the bowl? Is there any evidence of back flow? If the cistern does not close after flushing and trickles water into the bowl, either the levers have jammed or something is making the seal faulty. If the water does not stop, the valve may be faulty. It may need a new washer or to have swarf removed.

Some lavatories have electrically operated macerators which homogenise and expel waste along narrow pipes. Does this work? If the motor has jammed, you will hear a humming sound; the unit should be isolated at the isolating switch immediately. Anything which cannot be easily macerated will cause the motor to jam; you should have a warning above the lavatory to remind people.

FURTHER INFORMATION: *See* **L**avatory

## Footpaths

Footpaths should be properly laid out so that they are stable and present no trip hazard. They should also drain properly.

A right-of-way footpath may cross property. This should have been disclosed to you in advance of purchase. If you suspect the path has moved, OS maps and local planning authority maps will show where paths truly lie.

Those walking along the path have the right for it to be safe but they are obliged to keep to the path and not trespass onto your land.

Remember - service pipes or cables may run underneath footpaths.

Steps in gardens should also be examined for security and drainage.

FURTHER INFORMATION: *See* **B**oundaries, **P**aths, **L**and, **R**ights of way

## Foundations

There are various forms of foundations used in houses – strip, raft, trench fill, piled and reinforced beam. Special methods of making foundations are used on landfill sites.

If you can see the plans for the house which are lodged with the planning authority or, better, the building control or builder's plans, you will know what foundations are – at least in theory! If the property is 'Type Approved' by the NHBC for insurance purposes, it too will have a copy of the plans though on site, different foundations may have been used.

If foundations fail, the stability of the whole property is at risk. Sometimes the remedy is to underpin the foundations, and the building control officer will again be involved.

In the worst cases, the whole property may have to be demolished and rebuilt with new foundations.

If you intend to do any external work to your new home, check whether the foundations will be affected. You may need to have the approval of the building construction insurance company before proceeding if you wish to keep your warranty intact.

It is quite common for the soil on a site to settle gradually for a year or two after the disturbance caused by the building works.

A potentially big problem for the stability of foundations is nearby trees, and to a lesser extent large shrubs. These relentlessly extract water from the soil and this can affect foundations on shrinkable soils such as clays, especially if there is a drought. The mechanical forces of root systems can also have a devastating effect. We have all seen the effect of large roots on garden walls – they crack and, in the worst cases, fall over.

The depth of roots is greatest under the trunk; this is where the ground is driest. If foundations are placed where there recently was a tree or hedgerow, the dryish soil will gradually re-wet and exert a considerable force on the foundations as it expands. This is called 'soil heave'.

Some trees have mature heights of twenty or more metres. Tree roots spread out a similar amount to the height, usually within the top layer of soil.

This is a matter which is not often fully appreciated. If you want to know more, refer to the insurer's technical manuals. The Building Research Establishment has issued guidance on the effect of trees on buildings; this may be incorporated in insurer's guidance. Your local building control office may be able to give general advice.

FURTHER INFORMATION: *See* **G**round settlement, **S**oil, **T**rees, **U**nderground springs

## Freehold

Owners of freehold property should ensure that they know where the boundaries are and check the site against legal plans.

A dwelling built on any plot of land must have local authority planning permission for its construction. Lack of planning permission could mean that an enforcement notice is served and the property has to be pulled down. If no planning permission has been obtained, an application could be made late in the day. There is, however, no guarantee that the local authority will give permission just because an house has been built.

FURTHER INFORMATION: *See* **B**oundaries, **P**lanning permission

## Freezers

If the freezer compressor is causing vibrations in the backing wall, the wall may have to be insulated against noise transmission. As an alternative, it might be possible to stand the freezer on rubber plates and place a rubber gasket between it and any timber or plasterboard.

## Frost

The main damage from frost occurs to water-carrying metal pipes, though plastic

**Foundations** for paths, patios, boundary and garden walls and garden steps are also important. Poor foundations will lead to problems – for example, slabs cracking, puddles forming and walls toppling.

**Trees** are most likely to damage foundations on shrinkable soils like clay. Different trees take up moisture to different extents; as a rule of thumb, the softer and larger the leaves, the more water which the tree will extract from the soil.

**The freehold** of land is generally provided, in the purchase contract, with a number of covenants, usually restrictive. The deeds to the property will state what these are.

**Pipes** which are out of your sight (for example, underneath suspended floors) should have been properly insulated. Whether they have been is another question. Cold air via airbricks can cause underfloor pipes to freeze even in a brand new property, especially if the pipes supply water only infrequently.

**In properties** which are vacant for a short time, set the central heating system to a minimum level, perhaps 8°C, to keep the house from freezing. In properties which are to be left for a time, all pipes may have to be drained. Take care when refilling the system in case bursts have occurred.

**In the UK,** frost heave is usually confined to the upper layers of soil; rarely does the soil freeze more than 15 cm deep. Foundation design should take account of this factor.

pipes may also be affected. Within the property all water pipes should be insulated if there is a danger of frost exposure. This especially applies to pipes under a suspended, wooden, ground floor; to pipes which are in loft spaces; and to pipes which are out of doors or in unheated porches.

Insulation simply slows down the cooling process but it does not eliminate the possibility of a frozen pipe. Indeed, once the temperature rises, it will take longer for the insulated pipes to warm up!

Check that the insulation is properly wrapped onto the pipes. Even if there is a short stretch which is uninsulated, the pipe may freeze and burst there.

Here is a rough and ready test which can be useful to find out where cold points are in a water pipe. It is best done with a hot water pipe, perhaps paired with a cold water pipe. As you know, hot water takes some time to reach a tap from the hot-water cylinder. Suppose it takes ten seconds. Run the tap so that the water coming out is hot. Then let it cool for ten minutes and run the tap again, feeling, or, better, measuring the water temperature as it flows out of the tap.

If, say, after two seconds and seven seconds, the water briefly feels colder, then there are cooling spots two tenths and seven tenths along the pipe run to the cylinder. If the water cools evenly but quite quickly, there may be a general lack of insulation. Compare the results with a pipe which you know to be insulated (or, indeed, uninsulated).

Hot-water cylinders usually have an insulating foam cover applied by the manufacturer but glass fibre blankets are available if more insulation is required.

In normally heated dwellings, some of the pipes in the airing cupboards can be left uninsulated to provide heat for airing clothes.

Around 200,000 properties are affected by pipe bursts each year. Those in Scotland, the north of England and Northern Ireland are worst affected.

FURTHER INFORMATION: *See* Insulation

## Frost heave

Frost heave on soil occurs when the ground is frozen hard. The sideways and upward forces resulting from the formation of ice crystals are very powerful and can displace or break both fragile and seemingly strong items.

This is what breaks plant containers in winter and what causes damp, porous brickwork and stonework to start spalling or crumbling. Porous brickwork and stonework which can be kept dry will survive frosting much better.

## Fuel bunkers

Solid-fuel bunkers and liquid-fuel tanks should be checked for structural stability, weatherproofing, dampness and leaks.

For liquid fuel systems, what precautions are there for leaks? There should be a readily accessible isolating valve and a breather tube.

Tanks should be checked for rust and in case there is

any water inside. Liquid fuel vent pipes should be inspected. Check that the fuel gauge operates.

Liquefied gas cylinders should be kept in a dry, ventilated area.

### Fuses

Most plugs use standard fuses of the following ratings: 3, 5, 10 and 13 amp.

There are also fuses present in fused spur outlets and some sockets. If the fuse is not there, the electrical circuit will not work.

Always use the correct fuse as the replacement. If you find that an appliance is fusing constantly, check the fuse rating labelled on the appliance in case the one in use is too low. Do not be tempted to use a higher-rated fuse, which could damage the appliance or even start a fire.

Some appliances, such as kitchen waste disposal units are designed to have overload cut-out switches which operate if the unit overloads or heats up too much. Resettable thermal cutouts take several minutes to cool, during which time the item cannot be used. Resettable cut-outs are found on the casings: see the user instructions for the units. Some electrical appliances have tilt switches to stop current flowing should the appliance be accidentally tipped over.

Instead of fusible links, Residual Current Devices are now used in consumer units. These immediately trip if there is an electrical imbalance. Some plug sockets also have RCD circuit breakers. If a fault occurs in an appliance, the breaker next to the socket cuts off the power. This type of socket protection is highly desirable in garages and outhouses.

FURTHER INFORMATION: *See* Electrical installations

# G

### Garages

Garages have to be constructed in accordance with the Building Regulations.

Check the stability of the structure and the general condition of everything. Do the lights work? Do the doors work? Do you have all the keys? Are any of the doors broken or chipped; are they affected by damp, mould or warping?

Commonly, garage floors comprise compacted hardcore over which a layer of sand is laid. On top of this, a membrane of thick polythene sheeting is placed and concrete is then deposited. The garage floor may be rough and, depending on your arrangements with the developer and insurers, may or may not have had a smoothing layer provided.

If there are damp patches on the floor or walls, there may be a damp penetration problem.

Check what the construction warranty says to establish whether a garage is covered under the scheme.

### Garden electricity

There are legal requirements setting minimum standards for mains electricity supplied to outbuildings. These exist to reduce the risk of electrocution.

**Sometimes** just the local circuit switch automatically cuts out, sometimes it is the main supply switch. Unless you know where the fault lies, try turning the switches on again; the problem may be over. A light bulb blowing is sometimes enough to trigger the switches to cut off the power. If the power goes off again, then leave the individual circuit switch off and try the mains switch. Having isolated the circuit, you should still be able to use electricity elsewhere in the house.

**Is there** appropriate ground clearance outside your garage? If the floor of the garage is below ground level, is there a drain to prevent flooding?

**Because** concrete attracts dusts, you may wish to have the garage floor sealed with a proprietary composition at your own expense.

**There should** be an electrical circuit isolator inside the house so that you can cut off all outside power. The outside circuit should also be protected by a residual current circuit-breaking device. Check that there is one.

**Climbing plants** will break up bare walls and fences visually. For security, heavily thorned hedges and roses may deter intruders. Plants and trees which do not provide hiding places are also preferable. For example, thinly trunked trees with no lower foliage offer little concealment. Your local crime prevention officer can probably recommend particular plants.

**Some sheds,** wooden gazebos or summerhouses may not be watertight or heated. Anything inside will therefore become damp.

Power to outbuildings is supplied either by an overhead weather-resistant cable suspended from a wire catenary or by deeply buried armoured cable.

FURTHER INFORMATION: *See* **Electrical installations**

## Gardens

Tree and heavy shrub roots can affect foundations and underlying service pipes. It does not take many years for some of these plants to become established, so take care to site heavy-rooted items as far as possible from the house. Consider planting a less damaging alternative.

Willow is a tree that takes an enormous quantity of water from the soil, and is best planted in open parkland. You are asking for trouble if you plant one near your house. Willow roots will also find and block drains.

Establish what kind of soil you have – is it acid or alkaline, does it contain sand, clay or chalk? The orientation of your garden will also be an important factor in deciding what to plant. Remember, good drainage and proper soil are the keys to successful gardening.

FURTHER INFORMATION: *See* **Soil**, **Trees**

## Garden sheds

Wooden sheds should be situated off the soil on piers or supports. Use a damp-proof membrane to provide ventilating air underneath and so prevent rot, even in timbers which have been soaked in preservative.

Your construction warranty may or may not cover the shed. If there are problems, you may have to rely on your contract with the builder.

## Gas

Fuel gas supplied by the mains is methane to which odour has been added. Sometimes the odour will remain in the soil for a short time after a leak has been repaired.

Gas flames should burn blue. A yellow flame means that insufficient oxygen is reaching the fuel gas and that potentially deadly carbon monoxide is being produced. If you are in doubt about a gas flue, stop using it and have the gas supplier check. The engineer may do a smoke test to see if smoke comes out of the top of the flue as it should or spills into a room.

Bottled fuel gas is mainly butane but builders sometimes use propane. Whatever the source of the fuel gas, it is very important that safety standards are met.

Installers must be "competent" in the legal sense of the word and should be registered with CORGI.

Each house which has mains gas will have a gas isolating valve and a meter. Both the valve and meter may be in a meter cabinet to which you must have a key.

FURTHER INFORMATION: *See* **Flues**

## Gas cylinders

If gas cylinders are being used to provide cooking gas and heat, they have to be stored safely and away from heat or sources of ignition.

The threads to engage flexible hose connections to cylinders may be left-handed, the opposite from normal. So do check carefully; you may think you are tightening a joint but in fact are slackening it. This could lead to an escape of gas. Read the instructions.

### Gas leak

IF YOU SMELL GAS...

- do not operate electrical switches – on or off
- do not smoke or use a naked flame
- open doors and windows to get rid of the gas
- check to see if the gas has been left on unlit or if the pilot light has gone out
- turn off the gas supply at the meter
- telephone the gas emergency service.

### Glass

Check how easy it will be to clean windows, inside and out. Check all glass – windows and mirrors – for chips, breaks and scratches. Glass doors should use toughened glass.

Double-glazing units should have been be sealed to stop water penetrating between the panes. Examine the windows, in case there is condensation between the panes.

Are all the glazing bars fitted?

### Greenbelt sites

Certain areas of the UK are designated as green-belt areas.

Given the pressure for new homes, some will be built on greenfield sites – ie on areas of land which are new to human use, other than agriculture or similar.

Land which has previously been used for housing, industry or landfill is also being used. This is termed "'brown land" and provides new life to older parts of towns and cities.

FURTHER INFORMATION: *See* **L**andfill

### Ground settlement

The soil on which a building is built will settle somewhat over time. Foundation design should be sufficient to cope with most eventualities but there can be unforeseen problems. A house may be built accidentally on ground which may give way because of underground springs or unknown mine shafts which have long been in existence but badly filled in.

Special compaction methods are used, for example, on some landfill sites, to consolidate ground before foundations are laid.

If the ground is weak and moves, this is likely to cause foundation problems. Land which becomes permanently waterlogged may lose its load-bearing capacity. The load-bearing capacity of soils differs depending on the type of soil and is a major factor in foundation design. Drainage is important.

Minor cracks in external walls could be the first indication of a problem. Contact the developer who may arrange for a structural surveyor to come in to make measurements and report. Ask to see the report.

FURTHER INFORMATION: *See* **C**racks, **F**oundations, **S**oil

### Groundwater

The groundwater level is very important and the design of the foundations will take this into account. The level depends on the geology of the area and prevailing

**Building** regulations and insurer's technical standards relate to the preparation of ground before foundations are laid and also to the type and detail of foundation design. If there is a foundation problem after construction, the building control officer will need to approve the remedial plans and the work itself. This might involve expensive under-pinning. Local authorities have powers to act if a building becomes unsafe.

**Land near you**, which is starting to bulge and ooze, is a sign of water which has not been drained away. Once the soil is softened, it can start to move sideways and in some cases may cause a landslip. This could be very serious if remedial measures are not taken quickly. Contact your local authority environmental services department in the first place, and inform the developer. If the structural stability of your property is threatened, inform the building control office and insurer too.

**Water companies** may have the right to extract water from the ground. It is not safe to assume that spring water which you find in your ground is safe to drink. It may be contaminated with pollutants, micro-organisms or both. Play safe.

**Binoculars** (used by many surveyors) will help you to see inaccessible gutters better.

**Plastic guttering** will tend to expand in direct sunlight and this can produce clicking noises.

meteorological conditions. It will be lower during drought.

Clearly hard rock will not drain but sandy soil will. A soil may have alternating layers of clay and sand. Clay acts as a barrier to drainage and becomes soggy when wet, shrinking when drying out. This can cause certain soils to move and in turn cause foundations to become unsupported. When the clay soil later re-hydrates, it will expand again but perhaps not quite to the previous position.

To counter this, some houses have 'raft' foundations, acting as a platform for the super-structure of the house. Sometimes piled foundations will be laid.

In well-drained soils, the groundwater will drain out to the extent of the local water table. The level of the water-table will depend on the season, being higher when wet.

Groundwater can break out of clay and similar poor drainage soil as a small rivulet. If the ground feels mushy, this may very well be due to miniature rivulets which are constantly soaking the clay. It is highly desirable to drain them away. This may mean major drainage work such as a French drain with a borehole or soakaway installation.

To trace the source of the rivulets, try taking out spadefuls of clay and making a hole in the ground. It will start to fill with water and from that you may be able to establish the direction of the source.

It is unlikely that you will be able to stop the water coming in; if you do stop it in one place, it may build up and emerge later elsewhere. Even a small rubble-filled soakaway a metre deep may solve the problem if the quantity of water is small.

The purity of groundwater can also be of concern. Rain draining through landfill sites will leach out certain materials, which may then find their way to water courses or to gardens.

## Guarantees

*See* **W**arranties p.159

## Gutters

Check that the gutters and downpipes are securely fixed, not bulging or hanging off.

Gutters are supposed to slope gently down to the outlets – but may have been installed in such a way that the water is supposed to run uphill! This will create a permanent lagoon at one end of the gutter. Use a spirit level to check or pour some water at one end of the gutter and see what happens.

The screws securing the brackets should also be there, none missing, and of a non-rusting kind.

Gutters must have stop ends. If you see a drip, it might be coming from a crack in the plastic, a joint that is faulty, or a clip which has not been engaged properly. Neoprene rubber seals are provided at gutter joints. Anything which compromises a seal, such as debris or a cut, is likely to cause a leak.

Look at the gutters when dry but also when it is raining hard. Are they coping with a normal downpour? If the water is spilling over, is it spilling over in the wrong place? If so, why? The width of gutter should be suitable for the volume of water to be removed. The gutter should also be positioned so that it catches water draining off the roof.

# H

## HAPM

HAPM, Housing Association Property Mutual Ltd, was created by a group of housing associations in 1990. Well over one hundred associations are members now. It is a not-for-profit mutual insurance club. It insures against both structural and non-structural defects. It oversees designs and construction whether on new buildings or renovations.

## Hard water

*See* **S**cale p.133

## Health and safety

The Health and Safety at Work Act applies in your home if people are there to work. If a workperson has a serious accident, the Heath and Safety Inspectorate may pay a visit to the site. If you are concerned about dangerous working practices, you may wish to contact the local Health and Safety Inspector's office.

The Construction (Design and Management) Regulations require builders doing significant work to prepare a site safety plan and have someone responsible for overseeing its implementation.

Hazardous materials used on site are regulated by the Committee on Substances Hazardous to Health (COSHH) regulations. All such hazardous materials must be identified. Each manufacturer must also produce a safety data sheet.

There are also Manual Handling Regulations.

FURTHER INFORMATION: *See* **D**uty of care

## Heating

Heating your new home is important in the early days of occupation as it has to be dried out. This will obviously mean that you have to ventilate the building (otherwise it will just be warm and damp).

Whether you have hot air central heating, hot water central heating or warm air storage heaters, there are recommended temperatures for each room in a dwelling house. The heat from the radiators or heaters must be balanced so that the living rooms and bathroom are warmer than the bedrooms.

If you think that a room is generally too cold, even when the heating system is working fully, it may be that the valve, louvre or thermostat for that room is set too low. In hot water central heating systems, the adjuster valve is at the other end of the panel from where the handwheel is.

Solid fuel fireplaces should be checked before use to make sure that the fireplace is properly built. The flue should also be working – can you feel air being drawn up? Coal-effect gas fires should also be checked and the flues inspected to make sure they work and are not blocked.

FURTHER INFORMATION: *See* **F**lues, **R**adiators

## Highway Authority

The Department of Transport is responsible for trunk roads,

**Radiators** in bedrooms may be cold, if the main thermostat is in, say, the hot lounge and is therefore keeping the rest of the house cold.

**Building Regulations** govern the installation of heat-producing appliances in the home. These and other regulations ensure that they are installed in such a way that the home will not be at risk of fire. Workmanship and materials standards are also part of building and other regulations.

**The district council** should have a map of all highways and rights of way. Rights of way may also be found on 1:50000 scale OS maps, which should also show national park boundaries and other such features.

**If there is** a unitary hot water heater for use with a shower or wash basin, do you have the instructions and guarantee? A heater in a shower cubicle must be properly sealed and electrically safe.

the county or local council for other public roads. If your land borders on the highway margin, one of these organisations is in effect one of your neighbours.

Your land needs to have access to the public highway. If you are completely surrounded by private land, you will need formal permission to cross the private land.

Your deeds should show who is responsible for any garden wall bordering the highway or public property.

FURTHER INFORMATION: *See* **A**ccess, **R**oads

## Highway margin

This is a strip of public land which is adjacent to the roadway. It may be paved, or may be grassed, in which case there should be a boundary marker stone placed there by the Highway Authority.

Any modifications to the margin can be undertaken only with the Authority's approval. It is an offence to interfere with a highway boundary marker.

People sometimes mistakenly assume ownership of strips of grass in the highway margin which borders their property. They may even threaten anyone who walks on it or parks beside it. However, this is illegal occupation of the land. More to the point, people who do this open themselves to legal claims for damage and prosecution if an accident is the result of their unauthorised modification to the public highway. The local council should be informed so that an enforcement order can be issued.

## Hose pipes

Water supply companies permit the use of hose pipes except when there is a drought order in force. You may have to pay extra for it, particularly if you use a sprinkler or need to fill a swimming pool.

Check whether the property has an external tap and whether it can be shut off from inside. Is the tap protected from frost? Does it leak? Is there a backflow preventer?

## Hot water supply

This is always thermostatically controlled. Check where the thermostats are (there may be a number) and if they are properly set.

For an electric immersion heater, the thermostat is usually located in the head of the immersion heater assembly. The electrical power must be switched off at the mains before attempting any adjustment.

If there is an off-peak electricity supply, the hot water cylinder may have two immersion heaters, one controlled by a clock. Remember, it can be expensive to leave an immersion heater running constantly. There should be a manual switch with a neon.

There may be a thermostat on the hot water cylinder itself if remote water heating is employed. There should be isolating valves near the hot water cylinder. Do they work and what circuits do they close? Be sure to reset the valves. Are there any leaks?

Gas, electric and oil-fired boilers also have thermostats to regulate the temperature of the heating water.

### House number

When you move in, put the number on the property if one is not already there. The number should be clearly visible from the road otherwise, it will be useless to visitors and emergency services.

FURTHER INFORMATION: *See* **P**lot number

### Housing associations

Housing associations are responsible for many new house developments. The association may either have sold or rented the property to you or there may be an initial period of shared ownership between it and you. Establish what the legal position is about ownership; it is the owner who must contact a separate developer in regard to repairs or poor quality work.

Sometimes housing associations may themselves be developers. If there is shared ownership with private individuals, this can lead to muddied responsibilities and perhaps even conflicts of interest.

### Hygiene

Food storage might not be covered by Building Regulations as most people have fridges and freezers.

However, hygiene in bathrooms and the provision of sanitary conveniences and washbasins is covered. So too is hot water storage.

## I

### Immersion heater

*See* **H**ot Water supply p.92

### Improvements

If you intend to carry out structural or installed service improvements to the property at your own expense, be sure to check your construction warranties. You may also need approval for building work from the building control department of the local authority and perhaps the planning authority as well. Major engineering works in gardens also need building control approval for structural stability.

Electrical, gas, plumbing and telecom services need to comply with the appropriate regulations.

FURTHER INFORMATION: *See* **W**arranties, **B**uilding Regulations

### Infestation

Ants, cockroaches, wasps, woodworm, death-watch beetle, dry rot fungus, mice and rats are all potential enemies.

- ANTS spread relentlessly. The sandy foundations used for brick driveways are almost perfect for their tunnels. Powder and poisoned ant food are the two usual remedies but it is a constant battle – control rather than elimination is the best you will achieve. Try to keep ants at bay in the garden: once established in the underfloor cracks and crevices of a dwelling house, they are very, very difficult to remove.

- COCKROACHES are disease carriers which can infest buildings. They thrive in warm atmospheres and are often found in the ducts of flats and multi-occupant buildings. They can be a

**Building Regulations** cover aspects of hot water provision and storage. Water supply regulations also apply.

**Hardware stores** and some garden centres will stock a range of remedies to deal with infestation.

**Take great care** when using insect-icides, rodenticides etc to keep the materials away from children, pets, ponds and rivers.

**Masonry bees** look different from bumble and honey bees. They scrape away at mortar and can invade cavity walls. The entrances and exits can be plugged – with care!

**You might need** specialist help with infestations. It is best to act immediately rather than let the infestation develop.

particular problem in kitchens as they may try to obtain food. Contact the environmental services department if there is a problem.

✸ WASP stings are painful and in some individuals can cause anaphylactic shock, an acute allergic response. A person's airways may start to close, making breathing difficult – treat such symptoms as a medical emergency. An adrenaline injection must be given – fast.

Wasp nests can be built anywhere (in attics, say, or under roof or wall tiles). The nests are difficult and dangerous to destroy. Because of the danger to life from a swarm of wasps, be very careful when trying to eliminate wasp nests yourself. You could ask the local authority's environmental service department to send an officer to visit.

✸ BEES are usually less harmful if left undisturbed. If bees swarm, keep away and ask a bee-keeper to collect the swarm. (Consult a local trade directory.)

✸ WOODWORM can be found in any natural timbers and can be identified by the presence of small round entrance and exit holes. Badly affected wood will crumble and may even turn to sawdust. It should be cut out and replaced.

Attacks take many years to develop, so be vigilant for early signs and consider treating timber before there is an attack.

Woodworm can be brought in to new homes in old furniture. So inspect and, if necessary, treat.

✸ DEATH-WATCH BEETLE is found in timber; the entrance and exit holes are much larger than the woodworm's. Real damage takes some years to develop so treat any affected areas quickly.

✸ DRY ROT thrives in conditions of high humidity, typically in damp timbers under the floor. It has a distinctive, musty odour, and takes some years to establish. The only solution is to cut away affected timber and to treat both the new and surrounding timber and brickwork.

✸ MICE AND RATS can be trapped humanely. Remove any sources of food and block up any entrances and exits. Consider using poisons, but beware that the poisoned animal may go into a crevice and rot, causing an offensive odour. Their saliva, urine and droppings may carry disease. If necessary, contact environmental services.

FURTHER INFORMATION: *See* **R**ot

### Inspection

You new home should have been inspected for building regulatory and optional insurance compliance before being sold to you. The utility services should also comply with the appropriate regulations but may not have been inspected independently.

Your own inspection is particularly important. It will allow you to become increasingly familiar with your new home and to monitor any adverse changes which occur to the construction or the services.

If your home has suspected faults, the developer should inspect these and then agree with you what faults are to be repaired. Items which you report but which are not agreed by the developer will not be repaired as the developer may not regard them as faults or be disclaiming liability.

If there is a dispute or if some faults are serious, it may be necessary for you to call in the construction insurance company, or other inspectors such as building control, water authority, electrical authority, or gas authority inspectors.

Registered surveyors, registered plumbers, registered electricians, registered builders, and registered gas installers should be able to provide an independent written report on your facilities if you are having problems, although you will be expected to pay.

You may be able to reclaim these inspection costs if the developer later agrees to repair the reported faults. You are unlikely to be able to obtain recompense if the builder becomes bankrupt or goes into liquidation.

Keep all copies of inspection reports – if you ever have to start legal proceedings, the dates and content of the reports will be germane.

Any inspection certificates which you have probably do not give you an absolute guarantee that the work inspected fully complies with statutory requirements. Beware that an inspection certificate may include the disclaimer 'As far as the inspector is aware, the work complies...'

FURTHER INFORMATION: *See* **B**uilding Regulations

## Inspectors, Approved

The Building Act 1994, which applies to England and Wales allows the use of Approved Inspectors for the purpose of building control inspection. Previously local authorities had to provide Building Control inspectors.

NHBC Building Control Services Limited is an Approved Inspector under the meaning of the Act. There are special regulations which govern the statutory activities and fees. Often the Approved Inspector will be competing for business against other Approved Inspectors and the local authority Building Control department.

If an Approved Inspector fails in its statutory duty, the local authority may be able to take action against it, as may the builder to which it has contracted itself. Note that the Approved Inspector is not, however, under a direct contractual arrangement with the first owner.

The private certification procedure in England and Wales is described in greater detail in *The Building Regulations* by Powell-Smith and Billington, (Blackwell's BSP Professional Books).

FURTHER INFORMATION: *See* **B**uilding Regulations

## Insulation

All properties have to be well insulated to comply with building regulation requirements. It is now mandatory that new buildings have an SAP energy

**Approved Inspectors** are paid by the builder or developer to inspect, not the homeowner. Approved Inspectors who do not inspect competently can have their approval withdrawn by the Department of the Environment.

**The local authority** is under a statutory obligation to be satisfied that a building complies with the law, but does not have to carry out the inspection itself if advised formally that an Approved Inspector is inspecting. In some cases, although the homeowner will have expected two different people to conduct the Approved Inspection and the building defect insurance acceptance, one person will inspect for both purposes, and then only every three or four weeks.

**There is a** monthly journal called *Building Control* which can be a useful source of background information since it covers specific topics and court cases. The periodical *Building Homes* is also a mine of information.

**Insurance policies** are probably sensible to have but the premiums can add up to a sizeable sum. You need to determine whether that particular insurance expenditure is worth the cover and peace of mind. Be aware of the limitations of the scheme: they don't always pay out.

**Insurance** companies may try to present their premiums to you as a daily or weekly cost. Be sure to determine what the annual cost will be.

assessment rating calculated before their construction. The building control officer will not pass the construction plans for the building unless the insulation is adequate.

Insulation must be provided on walls, windows and roof ceilings. Your house may also have lower-floor insulation.

Cavity walls offer some thermal insulation, which is supplemented by the use of insulating materials such as lightweight building blocks and mineral glass wool. The plans for your house should tell you what has been used.

The loft space must also be insulated with a minimum thickness of an insulator, typically 150 mm of glass mineral wool.

Heat loss through windows is also a critical factor. Nowadays double glazing is the norm. A single-glazed window in an otherwise double-glazed house will probably experience condensation. So it is worth asking why it is single-glazed.

Inner walls may be made either of insulating blocks or, sometimes, of stud partitioning. These partition walls may be filled with glass fibre for thermal insulation and also to deaden sound. The plans should indicate whether that insulation is supposed to be there.

FURTHER INFORMATION: *See* **C**avity walls, **E**nergy rating

## Insurance

Accidental damage can occur at any time, whether to property or to people (either occupants or visitors). It is common for people to insure themselves against foreseeable hazards with house structure insurance, house contents insurance, personal accident insurance and personal liability insurance.

Remember that even if you are insured, the cover is always limited. You, as the prospective policyholder, need to understand what is covered and what is not. If you do not take the time to understand, the insurance company will tell you when you make a claim!

If an insurance salesperson tells you something on which you rely when you take out a policy, insist on a letter confirming the point before you sign the proposal form, or attach a statement to the effect that you are relying on the relevant information, which you then specify. Keep a copy. Hopefully this will give you some protection against incompetent or unscrupulous salespeople. But remember – if you have been misinformed, the insurer may not accept a claim you make.

FURTHER INFORMATION: *See* **H**APM, **N**HBC, **Z**urich Municipal

# K

## Keys

Do you have all of the house keys, as well as the keys for any cupboards or wardrobes; for patio doors, the garage, the shed, the greenhouse, and any outbuildings; and for gates and padlocks? Do you have a key for the electricity and gas meter housings?

The main locks in your new home should be of high

quality, at least to the British Standard (look for the kite mark) or an equivalent. If not, ask the developer why not. The small print in your house contents insurance policy may require you to have British Standard or equivalent standard locks fitted.

If there is a burglar alarm or security access system, do you have instructions, the PIN numbers and any cards or keys?

Changing normal door locks is not very difficult. If you are reasonably competent, you may save yourself some money by buying replacements and fitting them yourself. Make sure you buy the correct kind of replacement lock. Buy the same make, if possible, to avoid problems.

Consider installing extra security measures on the doors such as security chains and viewers.

FURTHER INFORMATION: *See* **S**ecurity

# L

## Lagging

It is important to lag all water service pipes which are vulnerable to frost.

You should be able to check the lagging of the pipes in the loft. Checking whether pipes which run under a suspended floor have been insulated is more difficult, especially as there may be no inspection hatch.

FURTHER INFORMATION: *See* **F**rost

## Land

The land on which your property stands should be registered with the Land Registry. So also should any neighbouring land which has recently been built upon, but be aware that not all land is registered.

If a river or stream runs through your property, the ownership of the water-course should be known to the local council or the river authority.

If you live near an commercial airport, the Civil Aviation Authority can give details of the airport layout and flight corridors.

It is very important to know where the boundary of your land is. Check that your fences are where they are legally supposed to be.

The developer may have removed the topsoil from your site whilst building work was in progress, but this should have been reinstated. Topsoil supports plant life whereas underlying soil brought to the surface is devoid of nutrients.

FURTHER INFORMATION: *See* **B**oundaries, **F**reehold land, **R**estrictive covenants

## Land registry

HM Land Registry for England and Wales has its principal office in Lincoln's Inn Fields, London. However, there are about twenty regional offices. The land register of Scotland is maintained by the Registers of Scotland (Executive Agency) which is located in Edinburgh. This registers many other matters than property. The land register for Northern Ireland is based in Belfast.

Land is generally owned on a freehold basis in England and Wales. In

**You do not** know who has previously handled your house keys. They may have been hanging in the site clerk's office for many weeks. So consider acting quickly and changing all of the external locks. If someone has an unauthorised key and is intent on burglary, they will want to use the keys soon!

**If your lock** has a barrel, you can probably obtain a replacement barrel and save the expense of changing the rest of the lock.

**Fit a burglar alarm** if you are going to have to leave your new home unoccupied before you move in. It is not unknown for new houses to be stripped of their contents.

**People** usually contact Land Registries through their solicitors but there is no reason why you cannot make an enquiry yourself. It should be cheaper and may be quicker. Why not ask the Land Registry for details of its services and how to go about making an enquiry?

**The local authority** development plans will show your site and should also reveal whether your property is on a landfill site and what is buried there. The records should also show any rights-of-way across your land.

**Local** planning authorities may place special restrictions on the development of landfill sites. Extensions to properties may be prohibited if the land is contaminated.

Scotland it is called 'feudal tenure'. A leaseholder is given the exclusive right to hold the land for a certain amount of time or period of notice.

Title deeds are usually registered at the Land Registry. These documents may reveal "restrictive covenants" (England and Wales), or "real burdens and conditions" (Scotland). Where there is a long leasehold (of about 21 years or longer in England and Wales, 20 years in Scotland), the leaseholder has additional rights.

Land can be licensed by the freeholder. The licensee is allowed to use the land but the freeholder may also do so.

## Landfill

Solid waste from domestic, industrial and commercial activity is deposited in landfill sites. Although controls are now quite tight on what can go into landfill sites, it is questionable whether local authorities knew what was being dumped before registration of landfill sites became mandatory.

As sites are filled, the rubbish is compacted and covered with soil. The whole site is then covered with soil to a good thickness.

Because of the shortage of land, many houses have been (and are being) built on top of landfill sites – ie on "brown land". Some famous developers specialise in this. Special construction methods are used, including for the foundations.

Other "brown land" sites are where housing or industry previously existed.

If the site is above putrefying waste, there may be a problem with methane escaping from waste as it rots. Methane is better known to us as North Sea gas, and a surprising quantity of methane can be generated from such a site; some actually have flares to burn it. Methane accumulating in any underfloor void represents an explosion hazard and at least one house has blown up.

Gas-barrier films are sometimes placed on top of the waste before the soil is added. Pipes may then be installed in the waste layers specifically to duct away the methane to the atmosphere. These are like street lighting poles and are generally lit; the flare burns with a characteristic blue flame.

Fly-tipping may result in sites being illegally contaminated. Many companies conduct land audits to establish whether the land is contaminated. If you have not bought your new home, why not ask your surveyor to tell you what the position is. The surveyor should have local knowledge and will provide advice that is more reliable than that provided by an estate agent or developer, who could be economical with the truth.

Be aware, though, that some building surveyors do not wish to discuss land contamination as it is a subject outside their professional indemnity insurance cover.

There has been some confusion in local government as to which council – district or county – has the power to act when landfill problems arise. New legislation is planned which should mean that local authorities are required to investigate potentially dangerous sites. The environmental services department of your local authority should also be able to provide information.

FURTHER INFORMATION: *See* **M**ethane

## Landlord

The landlord of a property is either the owner or a lessee who is allowed by the freeholding landlord to sub-let the property.

There are many rules and regulations which apply to landlord-tenant arrangements. Tenants always have a contract, which imposes obligations on them and also on the landlord.

If you find the new property faulty, tell the landlord and insist it is repaired. If you suffer damage or unreasonable inconvenience during repairs, the landlord may be in breach of contract. Citizen's Advice Bureaux can give more details.

## Landscape

The local landscape may have been substantially altered by the developer prior to building and the topsoil around your property may have been brought in from elsewhere.

Once building work was completed, the developer may have engaged landscapers to complete the site, laying turf for lawns, laying driveways, and so on. It is important to check that this work has not altered the ground level to the extent that the minimum damp-proof course clearance of your house is breached. It is also important that land immediately adjacent to the building should slope away to prevent undue dampness on the brickwork or rendering below the level of the damp-proof course.

New trees and shrubs, which absorb large amounts of water, can also give rise to foundation and drain problems if planted too near houses.

FURTHER INFORMATION: *See* **T**rees

## Landslip

Landslip near a property is potentially serious as the soil supporting the foundations may be moving. In other circumstances soil, rocks or slurry may slide down a hill towards a house.

If land is slipping, then civil engineering work may be needed to remedy the problem. The local authority should be contacted as well as the developer and insurer.

Sometimes the problem can result from water which is accumulating above an impermeable layer of soil. Soil which was loadbearing may become soft and, at worst, non-loadbearing.

Landslip sometimes occurs suddenly like an avalanche. Usually there are tell-tale signs such as an unexpected bulging of the soil or perhaps rivulets. Not all such occurrences need be serious but clearly need to be properly investigated.

Taking photographs may help to record differences. The rate of slippage can also be determined by measuring the distance which a point moves over time.

FURTHER INFORMATION: *See* **D**rainage, **S**oil

**Some estates** on landfills may have computerised monitoring systems so that methane levels can be monitored and a warning given if there is a build up of gas. If there is such a system in operation beside your home, ask who runs it, who funds it (probably you contribute), and what exactly it does. The planning authority will have initial details of this scheme.

**Landlords** must have gas-fired appliances checked in their tenant's properties once a year or at intervals prescribed by government or statutory bodies.

**Building work** may have cut tree and hedge roots and it may take time before any damage is evident. If a tree or hedge has been removed, the shrinkable soil will expand on rehydration with rain water or ground water.

**A garden** or retaining wall which does not let water drain, may cause the soil behind the wall to become mushy. Lateral pressure from this may topple over a poorly built wall.

**If there** is algae growing in your garden, the ground is too wet – which may indicate a drainage problem. If the grass fails to grow, the land may be too wet or too dry or not have enough daylight.

**Check** your warranty to see if your lawn is guaranteed (though probably it will not be).

## Lavatory

Check that the cistern is properly fixed, including the bowl. Check the stability of the seat and that the connectors at the back are not leaking.

The flushing handle should operate with a smooth action and the cistern fill up without undue delay. Does the pan flush properly? Does the cistern have a lid? Is the ceramic ware scratched, marked or chipped?

Is the window glazed with opaque glass? This is probably a planning requirement. Opaque glass is not very opaque at night; a blind or curtain might be advisable.

The floor should be properly laid. Pay special attention to wobbly floorboards as the plumber may have been cutting joists.

FURTHER INFORMATION: *See* **F**lushing

## Lawns

The lawns laid initially may very well be from commercially supplied turf — builders like instant results.

The undersoil may not have been properly prepared, just raked flat and the turf then laid. New turf needs to be regularly watered to allow the roots to grow down into the subsoil. It is especially important to water the edges of turf as these dry out fast.

If there are gaps left between adjacent pieces of turf, fill them in with good quality soil and the right kind of seeds. If the turf borders concrete edging, remember that concrete is unfriendly to roots. Ask the builder what kind of turf has been laid, as there are many kinds.

For a good quality lawn the ground below the turf should be turned over, raked and fertilised. If the lawn is in bad condition, you may wish to redo it properly.

It is important to irrigate turf in its early months so that the roots can grow into the underlying soil. Ideally there should be no traffic on the newly laid turf for some months. If you find unexplained brown patches on your lawn in summer, the builder may have left behind a plank of wood or a broken pipe under the lawn which is depriving the grass of moisture.

Much commercial turf is made by growing grass seeds on a layer of soil which incorporates a nylon net of coarse mesh made of fine strands. The nylon net makes the turf easier to roll up for delivery. Do take care that babies and toddlers do not catch their fingers on this net. The nylon is very strong and can cut or stop blood supply. It is an unseen hazard for pets too, so do snip away any exposed strands.

## Lawyers

*See* **L**egal representation p.100, and **S**olicitors p.141

## Leaks

There can be leaks of gas, liquid fuel, or water.

✱ LEAKING GAS should be detectable by its odour. Do you know how to turn off the gas supply at the mains? Isolate the supply and extinguish all naked flames and cigarettes. Don't operate switches – on or off. Open the doors and windows. Summon the gas supplier if necessary.

❋ FUEL for liquid fuel systems should be contained within the pipes. If you see a leak, isolate the supply and if it is safe to do so, apply a temporary bandage until a repair is made.

❋ WATER SUPPLY PIPES can leak or burst from frost or corrosion. Leaks around compression joints are the most common. There can also be leaks from soldered joints if the solder has not quite sealed the joint. In this case the pipe will have to be drained before it can be resoldered.

The sealing flanges on tanks and cylinders, where they connect with water or overflow pipes, may also leak.

Taps may leak, often along the spindle. Here the solution is usually to tighten the gland nut. If the shaft of a tap seems wobbly, tighten the gland nut; beware, though that overtightening will cause the shaft to jam.

A dripping tap indicates a gap between the bed and the seal. If the bed is at fault, it can simply be reseated with a reamer. If the washer is at fault it may have to be replaced (or try turning it over to present a new surface). In a hard water area, the continual dripping of a tap will lead to a small channel being scored in the bed. It is more difficult to reseat the bed if the channel is deep.

Water-heated central heating systems have many joints – at radiators, valves and pumps, and with cisterns and tanks. Water can leak from the on-off valve of a radiator; take off the cap and tighten the gland, if necessary replacing the rubber "O" ring beneath the gland. To determine if there is still a leak, wrap a paper tissue around the pipe and see if it becomes wet over a few minutes.

Some hot water central heating systems are filled with preservations.

FURTHER INFORMATION: *See* **F**lues, **F**rost, **G**as leaks.

## Leasehold

Tenants of property have many rights under law. For details, contact the Citizen's Advice Bureau.

Read the proposed tenancy contract and query anything you do not like. If you consider some clauses to be unacceptable, attempt to have them struck out of the contract or negotiate additional clauses to balance them.

## Legal representation

By using this book, you will hopefully be better prepared if you do need legal advice. Extra research will also be useful – the latest annual edition of *Whitaker's Almanack* gives a good summary of the parts of law which affect the average person. If you have a general understanding of the points at issue, you should be able to give your solicitor (or other legal representative) a good briefing. Writing down the key points and handing them over with your verbal explanation should help you both.

Some estate agents now offer a package with a conveyancer or a solicitor. However, it has historically been the case that a prospective housebuyer seeks independent advice: the

**If you are** a tenant, you should not formally discuss repairs with the developer without the owner's permission. It is usually between the owner and developer to agree what is to be done, and for the landlord (or in some cases the long-term leaseholder) to satisfy contractual oblig-ations with the tenant.

**If there is a** continual leak around a pipe, a kitchen towel bandage can help soak up water which would otherwise stain the carpet.

**Water drainage** systems, sink wastes, waste overflow systems and toilet pipes can also leak. The water may trickle down and appear somewhere else.

**You might** appoint a solicitor to handle the conveyancing. A similar service is offered by Licensed Conveyancers, who do not, however, have such an extensive legal background. This can have consequences if other aspects of the law become involved.

**Legal trade** directories can tell you who's who in the larger practices and chambers. These directories include a few pages on the current fees being charged. See, in particular, 'The Chambers and Partners Directory' for the Legal Profession. You may be able to borrow a copy of such a directory from a library. Make sure that you are sitting down before you read the hourly rates!

buyer and vendor do not use the same solicitor because of a direct conflict of interest. If you were to ask a conveyancer who was acting for both you and the vendor, a question pertinent to you, how independent would you expect the advice to be?

If your solicitor needs to instruct a barrister, ask to see a copy of the barrister's practice brochure and fee sheet. If no fee sheet is produced, ask why. You should also ask for an undertaking that the barrister whom you are employing will be the one representing you in court and has proper experience.

Barristers in England and Wales are governed by the Bar Council for England and Wales. Barristers in Northern Ireland are regulated by The Honorable Society of the Inn of Court of Northern Ireland. Advocates in Scotland are regulated by The Faculty of Advocates.

Licensed conveyancers are registered by The Council for Licensed Conveyancer.

FURTHER INFORMATION: *See* Solicitors

## Legislation

Legislation is enacted through Acts of Parliament. These are sometimes worded vaguely – or, indeed, badly – which can create a problem with interpretation (which is then resolved through the courts).

A breach of the law means that an individual or body corporate (ie a company or other institution) is open to an action. Each law states what the penalties are.

In civil cases, action is mounted by another person and the matter is resolved between the two. In criminal cases, where the conduct has impact on society, the prosecution is mounted by the Crown as a statutory undertaking. It is sometimes possible for one individual to mount a private criminal prosecution against another, but this is rare.

Laws differ throughout the United Kingdom. Scottish legal practice and courts are separate from those in England and Wales; also separate are the legal practices and courts of Northern Ireland.

So, depending on where you buy a house, you will be subject to different laws. In Scotland, a contract usually exists once an offer is made and accepted. In England and Wales, offers are made "subject to contract". One party may therefore withdraw at any time before signing the contract. That is then the end of the matter. No reason need be given – the prospective buyer may not have liked the survey report; may have been unable to get a mortgage; either of the parties may have had a change of mind.

In Scotland, properties are usually surveyed, and mortgages and certain contract details arranged before any offer is made. The offer is sometimes made subject to a time limit so that it is automatically withdrawn if the vendor does not accept within the time limit. Under this system, two prospective purchasers may be vying for the same property at the same time. Neither will know what the other is offering. This can also lead to disappointment but has the advantage that the disappointment will happen sooner rather than later.

For certain legal actions there are time limits imposed. Unless legal action is commenced within a certain period of time, the complainant can do nothing. The time limits are not there to allow parties to delay taking action just because they cannot be bothered. So if a six-year time limit applies, and a fault comes to light after six months, the complainant should not wait five years before starting action. The courts will take a poor view of such conduct unless there is good cause. Refer, for example, to the Limitation Act and the Latent Damage Act.

A considerable number of Acts of Parliament relate to newly built homes in one way or another. There are acts which regulate the building of structures; Acts which govern electrical, water, gas and telecommunication services; and Acts relating to sewerage, waste disposal, health and safety, and so on.

Most people access Acts of Parliament through their solicitors but if you simply want to know what the law on a subject is you could look up that part of an Act yourself. There is a understandable tendency to overlook these as direct sources of reference. However, Acts of Parliament are never light reading. Beware, too, that Acts may use fairly vague wording, the intention being for the courts to interpret the meaning and this to evolve through judgements over time. In other cases, the wording of Acts may leave no doubt as to what is legal and what is illegal.

Bear in mind also that when an Act comes into force, there may be only some provisions which have immediate effect in law. Sometimes an Act allows the government scope to bring in new regulations or to bring into force dormant clauses. If the government of the day does this, another publication called a Statutory Instrument is published, usually by the order of the relevant Secretary of State. In Northern Ireland they are called "Statutory Rules". Details can be obtained from the Stationery Office.

The Building Act 1984, which applies to England and Wales, is relatively short but it is supplemented by a series of Building Regulations issued by the Secretary of State for the Department of the Environment. These are further supplemented by a series of Approved Documents issued from the same source, which carry technical detail too extensive to be written into the Act itself.

If a builder builds a structure which complies with the Approved Documents, then that part of the Regulations is satisfied and so nothing illegal is done within the meaning of the Act. If the builder does something outside the scope of the Regulations, it may not necessarily be illegal but it is for the builder to justify.

If a legal problem arises, it possibly only relates to a few paragraphs within an Act which should not be too difficult to understand.

Before you take legal action against anyone it is in

**There are time** limits imposed by law for taking certain classes of action.

**In addition to** your contracted rights, you might be able to take action for a wrong which does not arise out of the contract but for which there is a remedy by compensation or damages. In England and Wales a civil wrong is a 'tort'.

**Hopefully** it will not be necessary for you to take legal action against anyone but in the event that it is, make sure that you know precisely what the law actually says - and do so promptly because of legal time limits.

**Quite often** when an Act is given the Royal Assent and comes into force, explanatory books are published; these are aimed mainly at lawyers or at the practitioners in the industry, and describe the Act, giving explanations and commentaries. These too are never light reading but are quite often better to use in the first place than the Acts themselves. In particular there are some excellent books which describe Building Regulations, water bye-laws etc.

**Reports** of legal cases are published within the legal profession. Legal textbooks also exist which describe what is happening as a result of judgements. Some of these textbooks can be found in major libraries.

your interest to be clear about what the law says and why you think it has been broken by the other party.

Acts of Parliament may apply variously to England, Scotland, Wales and Northern Ireland. The law courts of England and Wales, Scotland and Northern Ireland have corresponding territorial jurisdiction. For example, Scottish Building Regulations are separate from those in England and Wales: Technical Standards are issued by the Scottish Office.

There is always an appointed day when an Act first comes into force, and this may be some time after the receipt of Royal Assent. Other provisions may come into force later, perhaps on dates set by the relevant Secretary of State. These are announced in the Statutory Instrument lists.

Failure to comply with the requirements of an Act leads to a breach and each Act will indicate the remedies possible under law. In some cases the matter may not just be a civil matter where two parties can go to court, but may be a criminal matter involving a prosecuting authority.

Do not be confused by your own perceptions about what is legally right or wrong in a given situation; what you hope the law might say is not necessarily the same as what the law does say. Remember that the Acts provide the definitive wording. Certain things may be outside the scope of the law, and may even be covered by the wording of an exclusion.

Although legal advice will be necessary if a serious problem arises with a property, owners may find it useful to do some background research as to the legal position so that they really understand the issues at law before speaking to the solicitor.

Solicitors are able to advise whether provisions of Acts are in force and whether there has been any litigation which has examined the wording.

It is important to understand your obligations once you become the owner of a property; if there is something illegal about the construction you, as the owner, are potentially liable under law even if you have a building construction warranty. Any enforcement notice will be served on you as the present owner, rather than on the developer. And you will then be legally responsible for rectifying the situation.

Although you may have warranty cover for this or a legal claim against the developer, it may take time for the developer to agree to do the work and then to arrange for the remedial work actually to be done. Remember that fines can be applied for each day during the time that the law is breached. In some cases authorities have powers to take action – for example, to shore up a dangerous wall, demolish a dangerous structure or to enter your property.

FURTHER INFORMATION: *See* **B**uilding Regulations, **H**MSO, **L**iability

## Liability

In civil law, you can be held liable to another party for breaching a contract or for being negligent and causing damage to the other party. Negligence can also give rise to criminal charges, for example, if someone is injured. Even if you think you are liable, it is worthwhile talking to your solicitor before you admit your liability to anyone else. Consider using your solicitor or your insurance company to do the talking with any other party.

Once you become the owner of your home, you are responsible for anything illegal in it, even if you did not have anything to do with it. You will therefore be responsible for any violation of building, gas, electrical, water and telecom regulations. You may have a limited warranty for rectification, but any enforcement notices will be sent to you if you are the owner.

If you are renting a flat and an enforcement notice arrives, inform the owner immediately.

### Lifts

Lifts are essential items of machinery in high-rise developments. Servicing must be done by qualified personnel.

If there is a lift near your flat, find out who is responsible for it and who pays for service calls. What is the procedure for summoning service calls and what is the name and telephone number of the servicing company?

### Lighting – indoor

Do you know how your consumer unit works and which sub-circuit controls which lights?

Check that all light switches are securely fixed and work. Dimmer switches are usually fitted with tungsten filament bulbs rather than fluorescent (including low energy lamps). Check the instructions, or ask.

Are all electrical fixtures safely mounted? Do any light pendants become engaged with doors when doors are opened, thus causing the bulbs to smash?

Is there any evidence of charring or overheating? If so, the fitting should be taken out of service, pending repair.

See if there are any potentially dangerous bare wires or unterminated insulated wires. Never touch any bare wires in case they are live. Any protruding wires should be safely terminated with an electrically insulating cover.

All structural metalwork in the building and any metal pipes should be electrically earthed. Metal lamp fittings should also be earthed using a three-core flex.

Are the earthing straps in place with their wires connected (look for the green-yellow insulation)? Make an immediate note if you see any earth wires not properly attached to the clamps.

With care, you might be able to reattach the earth wire yourself but be sure that it is securely reconnected. If in doubt, have someone competent double-check. Never remove any earthing straps: they are there for your safety.

Are there concealed lights fittings anywhere, perhaps in the bedroom, kitchen or bathroom? Do they work?

Do you know how to change all bulbs? Are there any time switches or photoelectric cells for operating lights when it is dark? Are there instruction leaflets?

**It may** be possible to borrow Acts and interpretative books by ordering them through your local library.

**Low wattage,** plug-in, night lights (available from hardware stores) use minimal electricity yet help to make unfamiliar layouts more visible at night. Children might like them, especially as you can buy ones shaped like animals or favourite characters. They plug into electrical sockets; some being just illuminated plugs.

**If you wish** to move a pendant lampholder off centre, extend the flex and loop it to a ceiling hook designed for supporting the new light fitting.

**Lampshades** can create very different effects. A translucent lampshade will illuminate the whole room. Dark lampshades will cut off light and cause shadows. While this can be used to good effect, it does mean that one part of the room is lighter and one darker. You will have to use a higher wattage bulb for the same level of illumination with a darker shade than a lighter one. Don't however exceed the appropriate wattage for the fitment.

**Lighting systems** which use low power are available for gardens and pools from garden centres or specialist suppliers. If these are installed already, check that they work.

**Energy saving** bulbs can provide useful illumination outside at low running cost. They may take a few minutes to build up to full intensity output.

To prevent electrocution, light fittings in the bathroom should be out of reach when someone is washing, bathing or showering. For similar reasons, it is dangerous to have plug sockets for powered appliances, except shaver appliances in a bathroom. The appliances should be permanently wired to connection sockets.

Do any lamp switches in the bathroom have pulls or are the switches outside the bathroom? Improperly located electrical fittings increase the risk of electrocution, so special rules apply to bathrooms, shower rooms and kitchens.

Do fluorescent light fittings work, including any in fitted kitchens/bedrooms?

Can you remove lamps from the lampholders, or are they jammed or skewed? Is the wattage of the lamps within the range for the fitting? Are lampshades properly fitted and not charring? Are there any "hot" smells?

If you have spotlights, can they be tilted? Are recessed lights working and not overheating? Can downlighters swivel if they are supposed to do that?

Energy-saving lamps are expensive, although the price is falling. As a rule, a low energy bulb offers the same light for about a fifth of the energy used by a tungsten filament bulb. Low energy lights tend to flicker when they first come on and may take a few minutes before producing full brightness. They also have a blue-white hue, which is cooler than the warmer hue of a tungsten filament lamp. Don't use a low energy bulb with a dimmer switch.

FURTHER INFORMATION: *See* **E**lectrical installation

## Lighting – outdoor

Electric lighting must be electrically safe when installed. For mains services this means using weatherproof fittings and cable runs in accordance with the Wiring Regulations.

Do the outdoor lights work, and are they properly mounted and installed to prevent water penetration? Do you know where all of the switches are? Is there any evidence of overheating?

FURTHER INFORMATION: *See* **G**arden electricity

## Lintels

Lintels are used to support the superstructure above doors and windows. They are usually made from folded metal or reinforced concrete. (The latter can be factory made or cast in place.)

The load-bearing demands of lintel fitments need to be carefully assessed before the correct one is selected. The plans for your house should indicate the kind of lintels used.

Factory-made lintels are always wider than the gap. It is essential that an adequate support area is provided at each load-bearing ledge on which the lintel sits. For a combined door and window fitment, the lintel will be the length of the gap plus ledge margins.

For a door and window separated by a short brick pier, both lintels have to be supported by the pier, which must therefore be sufficiently wide to support them. The pier is a critical load-bearing structure – if it were to be demolished unsupported, both lintels would be freed and the upper superstructure would therefore collapse.

Arches also provide load-bearing spans over openings. The arch has to be designed so that the load above the opening is spread evenly to the lateral piers. These piers must be supported because of the sideways thrust. In the most extreme cases, a buttress wall will be needed to stop the piers bulging.

## Listed buildings

Consent is required before any alterations are made. Contact the local planning office and English Heritage, etc.

## Load-bearing capacity

Load-bearing capacities have to be calculated for walls, floors, and roofs before Building Regulations approval can be given.

It is important that the timber used on site is actually that specified in the plans and not undersized. It is also extremely important that roof trusses should be exactly as designed. Roofs are very heavy and the roof trusses are made using stress-graded timber. There are also required methods of handling roof trusses so that they do not spring apart or distort on site.

The timber may be notched or drilled on the site to accommodate pipes and cables. Timber should never be notched underneath; any notch should be on the top. Even so, there are strict standards stipulating the positions of notches and holes. A notch or hole in the wrong place can seriously weaken the designed load-bearing capacity. There are clear Codes of Practice.

Walls and floors have maximum load-bearing capacities, too. In a property there are probably some internal load-bearing walls. No load-bearing wall should ever be removed without proper replacement supports as the structure will then be unsupported and may collapse. Lucky owners may see cracks first; unlucky ones experience the building suddenly falling down.

If you want to know more about load-bearing in houses, consult one of the building textbooks first (see Further Research and Reading on page 164). Building Regulations are harder to understand.

If in doubt, ask the builder for written confirmation that the part you are worried about is (or is not) all right.

FURTHER INFORMATION: *See* **Rot**

## Local authorities

Local authorities have powers given to them by Acts of Parliament; there may be by-laws which are applicable only in the local area.

In some cases local authorities may be involved in the enforcement of legally required standards. Councils can act only within their legal powers; they have certain obligations placed on them by Acts of Parliament.

As a new home owner your property renders you liable to pay Council Tax. The council should have a leaflet describing the departments, their locations

**Depending** on what the lintel is made from and how the plaster is finished you may have a greater or lesser difficulty in erecting a curtain rail. It is usually best to fix a board to take the curtain rail, rather than fix it onto the plaster.

**Although margins** are included, the price of timber and other materials is rising and there are more and more drives for builders to be efficient and to keep costs down. This may mean they use the minimum timber necessary.

**Roof trusses** should never be cut unless replacement load-bearing members are already connected. This is a task for specialists. A timber truss or roof joist should never be cut to accommodate a loft hatch unless there are alternative load-bearing timbers in place.

**All councils** are statutory bodies, with a form and functions dictated by Acts of Parliament. They all include elected representatives and their officials.

**You should** have one or more local area councillors. Lists of councillors are kept by the councils and are probably also listed in your local public library. As an elector, you can attend council meetings which are open to the public. The press also attends many of these meetings. Each council meeting produces Minutes.

**Check the roof** timbers and covers for signs of damage or rainwater penetration. Check the woodwork for signs of woodworm.

and how to contact them. As an elector you can raise matters with councillors or directly at council meetings. You also have a vote.

Local government is tiered from the county councils through smaller area district councils to parish councils. Inner London is comprised of borough councils. There are also metropolitan council areas in England.

Thus, if you live in a village in England there will be the local parish council and the district council and, perhaps a county council. Each one has certain roles to play. A council may have obligations set by statute and be empowered to act in certain ways. In other cases, a council has only the power to be consulted about matters; it can form opinions and submit observations.

Although a small parish council may not issue a leaflet describing its services, district, county, Inner London Borough and metropolitan councils will have brochures which at least set out their departments. To establish which department has responsibility for certain matters, it is often simply a matter of asking a few questions. A number of the files of local councils are open for public inspection and often photocopies can be purchased of relevant pages.

The officers of the council carry out the day-to-day work of the council and are answerable to the council, their employer.

Legal action can be taken against a council which has failed in its statutory obligations.

## Locks

You may want to change the external locks for security reasons. Do you need to add any locks, door or hinge security bolts, door chains, door viewers or intercoms?

Remember to lubricate the locks in your new home.

FURTHER INFORMATION: *See* **K**eys, **S**ecurity

## Lofts/attics

Most lofts are unfloored, so take great care when you are in the loft in case you step in the wrong place.

There ought to be a service gangway to the cisterns. Have good lighting: you may need a portable light.

The timbers used for roof construction have to be stress-graded and should carry stamp marks showing that they are. The timber used in lofts is generally knot- and split-free to ensure that the timber is of the specified strength.

The loft should be insulated throughout to the expected standard (now 150 mm of glass mineral wool) and may be quite cold in winter since the insulation prevents heat being lost into it through the ceiling.

You may wish to floor the loft. This has to be done carefully, particularly if there are loose electrical cables which go over joists. Be sure to identify and mark any coaxial cable joints in case the television aerial outlets need to be altered.

If there are any notches in timbers, these should be minor and should not go more than one quarter of the way through the beams. Do not notch timber without proper advice – you could drastically reduce the strength. Notching must always be done from the top, never the bottom.

The loft should be slightly ventilated with eaves and perhaps ridge vents. In very cold weather, opening the loft hatch to allow some heat to rise from the house should help prevent frost damage. Remember, even an insulated pipe can freeze.

CHECK THE FOLLOWING:

- Do the timbers appear sound and properly supported?
- Are the roof trusses tied to each other with cross battens and also to any gable walls?
- Is the underfelt in good condition?
- Is there any evidence of rain penetration or dampness?
- Check the brickwork or blockwork in the loft. Is it sound and tidily mortared?
- Are internal soil pipes secured and connected to any roof vents?
- Is there a television aerial inside the loft? Is it properly installed?
- Does the loft hatch close properly?
- Is the loft access located in a safe place? No truss should have been cut to accommodate the hatch opening unless the truss is strengthened.
- Is there a window in the loft? Is it secure and free from leaks? Does it open cleanly? Has it been painted?

# M

## Manholes

Are all the covers present, and does the installation seem correct? Usually the covers are for foul or storm water drains but in some cases the electricity, gas or telephone company may have its own chambers. Unless manhole covers are located where there is vehicular traffic, they are unlikely to be load-bearing.

FURTHER INFORMATION: *See* **Drainage**

## Maps

The developer may provide you with a street map, especially if the site is laid out with brand new roadways.

Various companies have databases which identify contaminated land and print outs have a map format. The National Radiological Protection Board is mapping the country to identify radioactive radon hotspots.

## Meters

Your new home should have an electricity meter (or possibly two, one for night-time); a water meter and possibly a gas meter and/or a liquid fuel meter.

You will need to have the keys for any meter cabinets.

If the housing for the meter breaks, contact the utility concerned.

Special keys are needed for the reinforced plastic housings used for outdoor gas and electricity meters. These should be supplied to you on entry. If not, you may be able to borrow one from a neighbour; the gas or electricity supply company should also be able to supply one as a spare part.

## Meter readings

When you move in, read all meters – water, electricity, gas

**Local street** maps and OS maps may take some years to be updated. So your new home might not be shown. However, the land and surroundings will be.

**Meter cabinets** may not be shown on the glossy sales literature which you receive giving an artist's impression of your house. They are easy to draw, yet often omitted because they are ugly. Ask where yours might be sited.

**Some landfill** sites have gas management systems installed when the tip is being created. Here, pipes are buried in the waste and are used to duct methane out for safe disposal, perhaps to a flame stack.

**Poor ventilation** can result in mould spores which can cause irritation to the lungs and can trigger asthma attacks in sensitised individuals.

**The local authority** planning department should know whether there are motorways, railways or even canals due to be built in your locality. This should be revealed in your pre-purchase enquiries. The situation can however change overnight if a new one is planned. All counties have a local development plan which shows areas which are zoned for various purposes. The plans will change as the government needs local authorities to find places for new homes.

and liquid fuel as appropriate.

Try to have the meter readings independently witnessed or preferably agreed in person, in writing (two copies, one each), by the developer's agent.

## Methane

Methane is the main constituent of North Sea gas. It is a colourless, odourless hydrocarbon gas which is often used for fuel. The odour of mains gas comes from thiophene, which is added so that the odour will be noticed in the event of a gas leak.

Methane is obviously highly inflammable. If you have a gas leak inside the house, your supply needs to be isolated immediately and the property ventilated. Extinguish all naked flames (lit matches, lit cigarettes, lit candles). Don't operate any switches – on or off.

Methane can cause potential problems in houses built on or near rubbish tips, ie landfill sites. Methane is generated as rubbish biodegrades. In some cases, this can result in a build-up of methane in basements or underfloor cavities. The problem is now taken very seriously.

Houses built on or near landfill sites are now constructed with this problem in mind. Additional underfloor ventilation is often required as a matter of planning consent or building regulation compliance. For example, a plastic flue pipe may be installed from the basement to the ridge of the house to help underfloor ventilation. These pipes sometimes have rotating cowls. Other methods of stopping methane entering a property include the placing of a gas barrier.

FURTHER INFORMATION: *See* **L**andfill

## Mice

*See* **I**nfestation p.93

## Mildew

Mildew develops in conditions of high humidity, typically in improperly ventilated showers and bathrooms. Unventilated wardrobes in cold bedrooms are also problem areas – clothes will become musty through time.

Shower rooms and bathrooms, with fans which operate for a set time after the light has been switched off, may not be sufficiently ventilated. Open shower doors to allow through air otherwise the cubicle will tend to be a damp area which will encourage mould growth.

If local patches of mould form on carpets or inside walls, signified usually by a gradual blackening, then suspect damp penetration. For example, a carpet beside a bath or shower which starts going black at the edge, suggests a leak which is keeping the carpet wet.

Proprietary mould killers are available but these are short-term palliatives and unsuitable for some surfaces.

FURTHER INFORMATION: *See* **V**entilation

## Mortgage

If you have a mortgage on your new home, the mortgage supplier will hold the deeds until the mortgage is paid off.

Mortgage surveys are mainly concerned with establishing that the property actually exists and that the value is sufficient so that in the event of you defaulting, the mortgage supplier will get its money back. The survey is somewhat cursory and is not normally a full structural survey.

Although your new home will probably have (limited) insurance against faults in construction, the lender will also insist on structural insurance, in case the building collapses or burns down.

FURTHER INFORMATION: *See* **I**nsurance

### Motorways

Motorways are the responsibility of the Department of Transport and the Welsh, Scottish or Northern Ireland offices as are major bypasses.

### Moving date

Have you arranged a moving-in date with all parties concerned?

If there are yellow lines outside your house and the removal van needs to be there for some time, ask the police well in advance for a certificate of exemption for the day.

Be sure you have the keys, and remember to read the electricity and other meters as soon as you move in.

# N

### Negotiating

Estate agents, sales people and after-sales service managers have probably been trained in negotiating methods. This may put you at a disadvantage. To learn how to negotiate, read some books on negotiating methods and sales techniques.

You may be surprised by some of the methods used to break down resistance! If you know about the methods, you can recognise when they are being used on you and take countermeasures.

One of the most common methods of closing a sale is for the sales person to fall silent and allow an uncomfortable silence to develop. By and large, people do not like silences and feel awkward. So, if you find this happening, just start mentally counting to sixty – this may turn the tables.

Before you negotiate, ask yourself what your second option is if the first fails. Have the second one up your sleeve and do not lose sight of it. It may be better to accept that only 80 per cent of what you want to be done will actually be done, rather than none at all.

When dealing with reported faults in your new home, it is important to report these clearly and in writing as warranty claims in accordance with the procedure. It is also important for you to be clear whether the after-sales service is agreeing to do the work. Beware of a mumbled reply and much fast scribbling which appears to be an agreement but is not.

FURTHER INFORMATION: *See* **A**fter-sales service, **E**state agents

### NHBC Building Control

The Building Act 1984 removed the monopoly of building control inspection

**In some cases** negotiating can become confrontational. This is not always helpful. If you do want to express exasperation, do so but don't let it get in the way of your objections. Sometimes it is better for both parties to cooperate to seek a mutually acceptable solution rather than battle.

**To avoid** head-on confrontations, use an independent referee or reference. For example, if the after-sales manager does not want to do a repair, you could point to the statutory requirements or a code of practice and say, "So and so has had the same repair done by you. Why are you not repairing my house?"

**An 'Approved Inspector'** can be an organisation or an individual.

**The technical manual** costs around £50 to buy, but NHBC publications will sell individual sections. Ask for a list of publications from the publications department. The guidelines are necessarily somewhat technical but some are reasonably understandable.

from local authorities, and allowed Approved Inspectors to operate.

NHBC Building Control Services Limited is a company devoted to building control inspection and is an Approved Inspector. Under the Approved Inspector scheme, the developer commissions and pays the approved building control inspector. The inspector should occasionally inspect the property as it is being built to ensure compliance with building regulations, and will then certify to the developer that it seems to comply. A copy of this certificate is provided to the homeowner.

Approved building control inspectors are regulated by Building Regulations in England and Wales. They advertise and compete for developers' inspection business with local authorities and one another.

Note that the certificate is no guarantee that everything in the construction within the scope of building regulations does absolutely comply. The inspector will only have visited the site occasionally. Read the declaration to see the exact wording.

The inspector can report faults to the site manager, but by the next visit, may rely on the signature of the site manager that the remedial work (perhaps since covered over) has been done. If a builder has difficulty in complying with a particular requirement using one form of construction, the inspector may suggest an alternative which does comply.

The inspector can, however, serve a statutory notice requiring the latest work to be removed so that the previous work can be inspected.

The NHBC Building Control Services Limited inspector may be the same person who inspects for NHBC construction fault insurance. So if there is a major fault, which breaches statutory building control requirements, then not only may the builder be actionable by you but the building control inspector may be actionable by the council as builder if the inspection has not been carried out with reasonable care. Unfortunately, you as owner will be the person to whom any enforcement notice will be issued.

The developer may also be in breach of the membership conditions of the building construction insurance scheme for failing to comply with NHBC Technical Standards. In some circumstances, the membership of the developer could therefore be challenged.

An approved building control inspector, who has not acted within the requirements laid down, could have that approval removed by the Department of the Environment.

## NHBC insurance

NHBC is a not-for-profit organisation, limited by guarantee, in England. It has been in existence for more than fifty years and claims to be the housebuilding consumer protection organisation. The Law Society, Royal Institute of Architects, Royal Institute of Chartered Surveyors, building societies, builder's associations and Consumer Association all have representatives on the Council. It is self-funding. NHBC claims to inspect each registered new house every three or four weeks but the inspections are said by NHBC not to be comprehensive. Purchasers who require a more comprehensive survey, must employ their own surveyor.

The same inspector or group of inspectors may also conduct a simultaneous inspection for building control purposes, if the builder has commissioned NHBC Building Control Services Limited (a subsidiary of NHBC) to undertake that inspection. The local authority building control department must receive notification forms from NHBC Building Control Services Limited, so you can check the point with the local authority.

NHBC insurance was created because of the need to curb the excesses of bad building practice. Its technical standards aim to raise the minimum standards which apply.

The insurance is a construction warranty scheme which covers most new homes (80–90%). An insurance inspector will check not just for building control compliance (but will have no authority to issue compliance notices); the inspector must also be satisfied that technical requirements (with which member developers must comply) have been obeyed. Only then will an insurance certificate for the property be issued.

NHBC then underwrites the cost of remedying of certain faults in construction, services and facilities as laid down by NHBC Technical Requirements and in accordance with the policy terms. It is not an unlimited warranty scheme and the small print should be read carefully.

Generally this is a Ten-Year scheme (though Twelve-Year Cover is now being offered). The first two years is the period when the developer should remedy the "teething troubles" at its own expense. You yourself have to notify the developer of faults within this time limit. Only if there is a dispute with the developer or if the developer has folded will NHBC be involved.

Depending on the relevant dates, you may find that you have one year's cover, not two. This could happen if the property was vacant for a year before being sold.

The remaining eight years are for major defects only, such as foundation problems. It is critical to this scheme that you report suspected faults within time. If you do not inspect your property or cannot be bothered to report a fault, bear in mind that serious faults may be found by a prospective purchaser's surveyor when you are trying to sell. The prospective purchaser may then walk away from the sale or try to negotiate the price downwards – the subsequent purchaser might not be able to claim for remedial work on obvious faults for which you should have made claim.

All registered members have to comply with the

**Many people** still think that it is the local authority which inspects for building control purpose. In fact the local authority's officers may not be used if the work is given by the builder to an 'Approved Inspector'.

**Under the NHBC** banner is: NHBC - the insurance company, NHBC Building Control Services Ltd, NHBC Services Ltd and PRC Homes Limited.

**Resistance** to the transmission of sound is covered by building regulations; and construction warranty insurers also have standards.

**Many airports** require noise abatement procedures to be employed by arriving and departing aircraft. These are designed to minimise noise pollution. A complaint to the duty officer at the airport can be made if there is excessive noise from a particular flight.

Membership Rules and these are available from NHBC.

NHBC produces a handbook for registered house builders. This sets out the technical requirements with which member developers must comply if they are not to be in breach of their membership undertakings. NHBC can invoke penalties for non-compliance, such as increasing the insurance premium for the builder, or throwing the builder out of the scheme. Several builders are struck off each year.

FURTHER INFORMATION: *See* **H**APM, **S**hield, **Z**urich Municipal

## Noise

Noise can be transmitted directly from a source, such as the sounds you hear standing beside water pipes or a noisy boiler.

It can also come though holes in walls – for example, if part of the mortar in a block wall is missing. It can also be transmitted along pipes, wood or plasterboard, so that noise emerges at a distance from the source.

Tracing transmitted noises may be difficult. Try placing the (blunt) blade of a large screwdriver against the suspect pipe and putting the handle against your earlobe. This will magnify the sound for you.

Plasterboard partition walls tend to act like drum skins and can easily transmit sound. It is common practice to fill the cavity with well-packed sound-deadening material, such as glass fibre; indeed technical standards apply. This method is used, for example, to reduce noise from lavatories in dwellings.

Copper pipes are efficient conductors of sound and noises can readily be transmitted to woodwork on which the pipes lie. Woodwork can be insulated by using rubber or similar anti-vibration supports for the pipes.

Noise can come from washing and dishwashing machines. Try supporting the machine feet on rubber mats rather than the bare wooden floor. A rubber car mat is cheap and could be cut to suit; use several layers of rubber. It is also important to make sure that the machine is not so close to fitted units or pipes that it vibrates against them. If a machine vibrates so heavily that it starts moving or thumping, it may be overloaded or faulty. Be aware that the movement will wear out the bearings too.

Noise from properties above or below can be reduced by adding further insulation. But this can be quite difficult to do once the building is occupied.

Noise will be greater in a room with smooth (perhaps tiled) surfaces, which echo. Deaden sounds by laying down carpets and hanging curtains. Sound waves emanating from one area can be reflected by a smooth surface. On motorway embankments, fences are sometimes tilted away from the road to bounce noise upwards.

Your local environmental services department may be able to offer advice about external noise pollution.
If you live near a motorway, the noise can be quite bad.

Double-glazing is a partial solution but not if you want to open your windows in the summertime. Noise-deflecting fences can also be erected. Trees and heavy foliage are beneficial, but can take years to grow; dense evergreens are preferable. Check the district authority planning file to establish whether the builder was supposed to erect fencing, trees or embankments.

If motorway noise is a problem, contact the local authority and government's transport department. Others in your neighbourhood may feel similarly; consider joining forces.Construction warranty providers and the BRE may have guidance notes for use during construction.

## Northern Ireland

Building and utility regulations are covered by local rules; NHBC has a Northern Ireland Technical Committee, so selected requirements apply. Legal actions are heard in Northern Ireland Courts.

For civil actions the county court or High Court of Justice is the likely venue; appeals are possible to the Northern Ireland Court of Appeal and thereafter the House of Lords. For indictable offences, the magistrates' courts are the first venue; the Crown Court, the Northern Ireland Court of Appeal and thereafter the House of Lords are then superior, in that order.

# O

## Overflows

Check all overflow pipes from cisterns (ie all lavatories and storage cisterns) for leaks and the general security of the fittings. Pour a jug of water through the pipes to make sure there are no blockages. Have someone outside to identify from which overflow pipe the spillage comes. Make a note of this; if there is a future spill you will immediately know which cistern is at fault.

Keep an eye on warning pipes in case they start to drip. The drips should fall away from the wall and not soak it.

## Overhanging branch

Are any branches of your trees overhanging a neighbour's property or the public highway? Are the branches causing a hazard to pedestrians or do they obscure road traffic signs? Are the branches obscuring a neighbour's view?

Are neighbouring branches overhanging your property? If so, you might be able to cut them back to the boundary line but to avoid disputes and upsets, talk to your neighbour first and try to agree what is to be done. It is important too that you know where your boundary lines are – you can only cut back to the boundary.

Check also for root damage, real or potential.

FURTHER INFORMATION: *See* **B**oundaries, **T**rees

# P

## Paintwork

Your home will have been painted by the developer and you should check the quality of the paintwork, both internally and externally. There may be

**Remember** that trees which are subject to a Tree Preservation Order cannot be lopped without the permission of the council – and then usually only by a registered arboriculturalist.

**It is worth** making sure that all toilet cisterns fill up correctly and do not overflow - sometimes cistern overflows have been blocked by rubbish.

**Be sure not** to build a path over a service hatch located on the ground. Hatches can be disguised with tubs placed above so long as there is access.

**Paths** can be laid in a variety of colours. Red slabs or bricks become redder when wet and can give an air of warmth to an otherwise bleak outlook in winter or wet weather. If you intend to add additional matching paths, ask the developer what paving material was used and where it can be obtained.

cracks or areas of bare wood or plaster.

Some of the paint colours you may like, others not. If you intend to keep the colours, ask the developer what shades have been used so that you know what to buy when you are ready to repaint. There are a number of coloured wood treatments available and it can be quite difficult to know which one has been used.

Knots on woodwork are usually filled and treated with knotting fluid to seal the resins into the wood. You may find brown knot stains showing through the paintwork as the years pass.

## Parish councils

Parish councils produce minutes of their meetings. These are usually displayed in public on a notice-board or are available for public inspection in the local public library or council offices.

You will find matters of local interest raised at the meeting. You can attend a meeting and raise matters yourself, even if you are not an elected member of the council. The press often attend council meetings. These councils sometimes have a role in new building developments and may be in contact with the builder.

## Parking

Provision for car parking will be covered in the planning application for your home. You can see details of the intended layout in the planning department's office.

Sometimes parking is provided in garages at some distance from the houses.

IF YOUR PROPERTY HAS A DRIVEWAY, CHECK:

- Is it level and solid?
- Does it drain properly or flood?
- What lighting provision is there and does it work?

Design practice nowadays is to integrate garages so that they are overlooked by at least some of the properties in a new development. This is intended to stop them being areas favoured by vandals and criminals. 'Secured by Design' is a major police initiative aimed at making developers think about the security implications of their designs.

FURTHER INFORMATION: *See* **D**riveways

## Paths

Paths and driveways may have been laid out by the developer in accordance with the plans approved by the council. Paving materials used include gravel, slabs and solid bricks.

- Are the paths level and do they drain properly in wet weather?
- Where are the surface water drains?

Paths need to have good foundations. These normally comprise compacted ground, perhaps with some compacted hardcore, on to which compacted coarse sand is laid. The coarse sand may be mixed with mortar and in some cases the underlay may be concrete. The slabs or bricks are then laid on top and vibrated to settle them in and make them even.

FURTHER INFORMATION: *See* **D**riveways

## Patio doors

The doors should run freely on their rails and be easy to lock. Is there a security lock and does it have a key supplied with it?

Is the glass scratched or scored? Is the sill watertight?

When it is frosty outside, is there undue condensation on any metalwork? Does the condensate trickle on to wood, plaster or even the carpet?

## Patios

It is important that a patio has a good base, otherwise the surface will distort.

Patios are usually impervious to water, so establish whether they drain properly when the rain is falling heavily. If there is flooding, contact the developer.

If the builder has laid the patio so that the damp-proof membrane course is only one brick height (75mm) above the patio, rather than the minimum two, then you may need to have the whole patio lowered. If a narrow trench is suggested, you need to be sure that the patio does not drain into it so that it becomes a moat around your foundations.

## Permitted developments

This phrase is used by local planning authorities for minor building developments (such as extensions to houses and greenhouses), which are small and behind the building line. Ask the planning department for details.

If you wish to have an extension and even if it is a permitted development, check the restrictive covenants on your property in case you have agreed not to erect an extension for a stated number of years.

There are also some building works which are declared to be exempt from building regulations. Ask the local authority building control department for information.

FURTHER INFORMATION: *See* **R**estrictive covenants

## Photographic records

If your new home has faults, you may wish to make a photographic record. If possible, place a card with both the date and a centimetre or metre scale clearly written to ensure they are visible in the picture. Photographs can provide valuable evidence; you never know when they might be needed.

## Piling

*See* **F**oundations p84

## Pipelines

The local authority should know where underground service pipes are and where their junctions to your property are.

## Pipes

Pipes are essential parts of the many supplies and services on which we rely. They can be large or small, and are variously used for channelling water, fuel, gas, effluent, flue gases and for ventilation. Pipes are also used to provide overflows or ducting through which cables and other pipes can pass.

They are laid throughout your property and are usually unseen. Because of their importance they should

**If the patio doors** are very large and all glass, you may wish to mark the glass with some tape or paper so that no one walks or runs into it.

**Sometimes planning** consent for developments on contaminated land may restrict the building of extensions for fear that contaminated soil is disturbed.

**Drainage** pipes of one sort or another often pass under a patio and their discovery can cause problems during the building of an extension.

**Ideally,** when the water (drinking and central heating) and gas services were being installed, the installer will have marked in pencil on the floorboards where underlying pipes are located. If you find unmarked pipes under the floorboards, mark the floor to show the route. If there are any concealed stopcocks, bleeding valves, switches, or junction boxes under the floor, then make a note in this manual and also mark the floor with a pencil or marker.

have been properly installed. Many regulations apply to these installations, so it is worth inspecting the pipes which you can see to make sure that the pipework does not appear to be damaged or unnaturally bent, and is properly secured.

Pipes which are sloping or horizontal should not be bowing unnaturally. If they are, a bracket may be missing or have broken. Codes of practice and manufacturer's instructions often indicate what the minimum supporting intervals for brackets should be. Check that the brackets are attached to the wall. If you see the rainwater pipe fall off a neighbouring property built by the same builder, check yours.

Remember, too, to take a common sense view of what you see. A soft plastic duct for electrical wires should clearly not be resting on a hot pipe.

Detecting unseen pipes can be difficult. If the pipe is metallic or if it carries live electrical cables, you can use a metal or voltage detector. These devices are available in hardware and DIY stores and give a beep when the detector is passed over a live wire or metal. They will also detect nails. But remember, the depth will vary according to the material used; some pipes will not easily be detected.

## Planning permission

The local authority has statutory powers to approve plans for new houses. The local authority should have some leaflets which describe the system in your area; individual council officials should also be helpful. Bear in mind that the local authority operates under certain rules and can only provide certain information, so don't expect it to provide any beyond that.

The local planning authority will have a file on your house. If you are in a group development, there may also be an estate file.

This file is on the public record and can be read by anyone. It includes not just the plans for your house, but also all official correspondence leading up to planning consent and the conditions attached to that planning consent. If objections were made, you will be able to see what these were and by whom they were made. This file may take some time to read and may reveal aspects of the history of your house or its plot of which you were previously unaware.

The local authority has to comply with the law and the file may be peppered with references to this or that Act of Parliament or local by-law. If there is a question in your mind about any of these items, you can trace back the cited document itself and read the relevant subsection.

The local planning authority will probably have a copy of the Acts and may be willing to let you see them. If not, you will need to note the name of the Act carefully and make enquiries at your local library or SO agent.

You will need to go to the Building Control Department to ask about building control for your house. The department may refuse to let you see the plans which they have approved for your house; if so, ask why.

You should at least be told whether the local authority carried out the statutory building control inspection or whether it was an Approved Inspector. Approved Inspectors have to tell the local authority's building control department if they are carrying out the inspection. If you find that there are defects in the building control inspection done by an Approved Inspector, then you may wish to express your concern to the local authority's building control department.

Planning consent is sought as a result of a planning application. Planning consent will take into account the Town and Country Planning Act; the local development plan; and whether the area is a conservation area, a park or site of special interest. It will also take into account any special amenities in the area, such as listed buildings, or trees protected by Tree Preservation Orders.

FURTHER INFORMATION: *See* **B**uilding control, **B**uilding regulations

## Plans

Various sets of plans for your site and the buildings will exist – plans lodged with the planning authority; plans with building control approval; and additional plans which are part of the developer's specification for your home and which go into greater detail about the fixtures and fittings. (Quite possibly you will never be allowed to see the latter, but they are what the site manager or Clerk of Works uses.)

In addition, organisations such as NHBC may have a system of giving Type Approval to new house designs. Once 'Type Approved', the developer can inform a local authority that it wishes to build house Types 1, 2, 3, 4 on a new development. The Type Approval standards comply with all relevant building legislation and requirements of statutory undertakings and the approving organisation's technical requirements. Building control vetting is reduced as the plans are for a standard production model.

Provided that the Type Approval has been given properly, you can expect that the precise plan was submitted to the local authority and to the building control inspector, and that what was actually built complies with those plans.

If you check; you may probably find that all is well but you may find that you are lifting a veil on what seem to be called 'trade variations'. In this case the house will vary from the precise plan. If you find this has happened, make a list of each point of difference and then determine whether any are important .

## Plot number

Until your house is built and has a street name and number, it will be known as 'Plot Number ...'. Indeed, the after-sales service may be completely thrown if you use your street name and number but not the Plot Number. So use both when dealing with the builder, developer and insurer,

**The plans** for your house will show the room sizes and ceiling heights.

**The local authority** can probably provide you with a copy of extracts from a planning file but these can be quite expensive and take some time. If you are inspecting a planning file, take along a notepad.

**Pop-up** waste fittings can jam or not lift if the rods at the back are not connected properly. The screw in the plug may also need to be adjusted. You can obtain replacements from plumbers' merchants but ask the developer for the make of sink and waste fitting - there are many varieties.

**If you are** in doubt about a plumber's credentials, you can always phone the Institute or other association of which the plumber is a member, and find out whether the plumber is registered. Beware that some associations are merely trade associations run for the benefit of members – they have insignificant disciplinary powers.

especially when the house is brand new.

FURTHER INFORMATION: *See* **B**uilding Regulations

## Plugs

- ELECTRICAL PLUGS: Check that the plug tops are secure; the cables are secure; the correct rating of fuse is in place. Check the state of the sockets, too. Does the plug overheat? Is the plug broken? Can it be inserted properly in the socket?

  You will need a coaxial plug for the TV aerial and a special plug for telephones. Do these plugs appear to be properly wired and unbroken?

- BLANKING-OFF PLUGS: these are found on radiators, tanks, cisterns and some plumbing fittings. Check whether they leak.

- SINK PLUGS: Check that they are all there; they are the right size and any chains are properly fixed. Do you have drainer plugs?

  If a plug jams in the sink, release it by using a rubber sink plunger. Put this over the plug, then lift; with luck the plug will free itself.

## Plumbers

Plumbers do not have to be registered to work on water and drainage services, although the Institute of Plumbing has a registration scheme. Plumbers who are registered with the Institute should comply with the high standards of registration (details of which can be advised by the Institute). If they do not and a complaint is made, they can be struck off the register.

The water by-laws must be obeyed, no matter who works on plumbing. A person who does not obey the law is liable to prosecution by the water authority.

If bad plumbing work has been done, consider commissioning a by-law compliance report from a registered plumber, or from the water and sewerage authority who can also take enforcement action. If a breach of the law is discovered, be aware that an enforcement order will be served against you as owner.

If you decide to ask the inspectorate of the construction warranty company to do an inspection, find out in advance whether the inspector has the relevant knowledge about water supply and sewerage regulations and whether the organisation charges for this. The warranty inspector should know what the organisation's technical standards are and be able to establish whether a given installation is right or wrong. The organisation should give guidance to the inspectors so that they are consistent.

If the developer proposes to send back the plumber who initially did the faulty work, you may wish to say that you expect the developer to provide you with a compliance certificate when the work is done – at the developer's expense.

## Pollution

Airborne pollutants can come from smoke stacks, traffic, industrial premises, cooked food outlets, faulty air conditioning systems, crop burning and garden bonfires.

In some cases, the local authority environmental services department may be able to help. For example, restaurants should have proper ventilation systems so that cooking smells can be expelled without adversely affecting nearby buildings. The planning consent file for the premises may reveal useful background information; you can then take a view as to whether the planning consents are being obeyed.

Pollutants can also be found in the soil (perhaps as a result of legal or illegal dumping), or in groundwater. Environmental services may be able to advise if there is a problem.

Rivers and streams can also suffer. The water or river authority should be able to answer any questions you have.

Noise pollution is increasingly the subject of legal restriction. You may find that the environmental services unit of the local authority has powers not only to issue enforcement notices but to confiscate equipment.

FURTHER INFORMATION: *See* **L**andfill, **N**oise, **S**mells

## Ponds

*See* **S**wimming pools and ponds p.148

## Postbox

An increasing number of properties are erecting private postboxes on their outer walls. This is especially the case if the property is security walled and gated so that postal deliveries cannot be made to the front door. Some post boxes are built into the walls and some are attached by heavy duty screws. These kinds of postboxes are available from architectural ironmongers.

## Post Office mail delivery

Have you redirected your mail?

To stop junk mail arriving, tell the Mailsort section of the Post Office. To find out exactly what personal data the Post Office stores about you, you can make a demand under The Data Protection Act.

## Potable water

Water in new homes should be flushed through the pipes to remove any debris which has entered during construction work. Thereafter, the mains water entering the property should be potable. If you have any questions about potability, you may wish to contact not only the developer but also the water supply company. If the mains pressure is too low or high this should be queried.

Every habitable property must have a supply of fresh drinking water. Usually, the supply comes into the property under the kitchen sink; the cold tap should deliver fresh water from the mains.

Depending on the layout, this may be the only tap in the property to provide water direct from the mains. The other cold water taps, cisterns and washing machine feeds probably come from the storage cistern.

How do you tell the difference? The water pressure may be different. Usually the pressure is higher

**Pollution** on land or in the air may cause the value of a property to drop.

**In apartment** blocks there may be banks of post boxes, one for each flat. Which one is for your apartment? Is your post box clearly numbered? Do you have a key and a spare? It is not very secure if your flats do not have personal post boxes and mail is just left on the hall table.

**Mains water** should not be fed into flexible hoses (for example, those for washing machines) unless regulations and the instructions state otherwise – the pressure is normally too high. If the hose bursts, there will be a serious flood.

**Buildings** of historic or architectural interest may be protected under the provisions of the Town and Country Planning Act. The Department for the Environment lists buildings which are important because of their intrinsic value to the country either due to their historic or architectural value.

**Your local library** may have a copy of a building price guide. If you are ever having work done, try estimating the cost of the job yourself, then ask for an estimate.

from the mains (unless you have a poor supply), and the water temperature may also be different.

The hot water system will usually be fed from the hot water storage tank, which in turn is filled from the cistern located in the loft (or at a higher level). Hot water for showers may be heated by a shower heater with its own power feed.

The pressure of the cold water and hot water feeds from the cistern will be almost equal so that the temperature in mixer taps does not fluctuate too much.

Provided that there is a cover for any cistern in the loft, there are unlikely to be any spiders or dead birds in the water. If the cistern is used constantly and the water is therefore not stale, it should be suitable for cleaning teeth. If in doubt, use the main supply.

### Preservation orders

Before moving in, you should be told if there are any preservation orders which apply to trees or anything else on your land. The local planning authority should provide details. Preservation Orders derive from the Town and Country Planning Act and the Town and Civic Amenities Act. If you receive a Tree Preservation Order, keep the papers because you must disclose the fact to a prospective purchaser whenever you decide to sell. Protected trees on a building site should be protected by a fence. If whole trees are removed by a builder for relocation, the whole root ball must be taken out intact.

FURTHER INFORMATION: *See* **T**rees

### Preservative treatments

Timber is vulnerable to insects and rot. Certain timbers may therefore have been treated; by law. The woods used for roof tiling, fences or exterior battens are always treated, structural timbers in the roof and floor only sometimes.

### Pricing

There are a number of detailed guidebooks used by the building and other trades for estimating prices of work. These are also used by quantity surveyors when they price the cost of building a property.

The cost of building (or rebuilding for insurance purposes) can be surprisingly low relative to the price being asked. The difference represents the builder's profit, in part, but bear in mind that the value of the land is another factor. It is helpful to establish the prices for similar properties in an area; and also instructive to discover what the builder is charging for the same house in another part of the country.

Pricing is not an exact science because the unexpected can occur.

FURTHER INFORMATION: **E**stimates and quotations

### Professional advice

Sometimes it is necessary to seek professional advice. Obtaining this advice always means paying a professional fee – which can be expensive.

The best professional advisers are registered with a professional society or institute. The membership regulations are mandatory and a breach can result in the adviser being struck off the register or otherwise disciplined. The professional body is independent and should have teeth.

Other 'professional' advisers may not have any qualifications. Letters after a name may have been obtained more or less as a matter of paying a joining fee.

Professional advisers will usually have professional indemnity insurance against any claim. Limited insurance is a limited safeguard for the insured; it is between the insurance company and a professional adviser to work out what cover the adviser has. The adviser can also be sued for something not covered by insurance.

Legal costs often swallow up more than the amount awarded – or, at least, reduce it. Unexpectedly high fees are the cause of many complaints. So, before you choose an adviser, ask for a brochure and fee sheet; consult several advisers and choose the most suitable. Describe what service you want, then ask how much it will cost, how long it will take, and who will do the work. Costs are difficult to predict, but try at least to get a general estimate.

The adviser may wish to charge by the hour. So consider setting a financial limit in writing for a sum not to be exceeded without prior consent by you. You may also wish to state in writing that this ceiling figure is inclusive of expenses and VAT (which otherwise could be surprising extras).

The adviser will, of course, expect you to be able to pay and to settle your bills promptly. Discuss any problems with your adviser face to face; in many cases there may be a genuine misunderstanding which can be amicably sorted out. (Remember, you may be wrong.)

If you really have grounds for complaint, be sure that you have the facts to make a good case.

### Public records

A lot of information can be obtained from public records, including local authority files; membership registers of professional and trade bodies; and registrations made under the Data Protection Act.

# R

### Radiators

Central heating radiators are usually water-filled. As hot water is pumped around the system, the radiators should become hot. A temperature of up to 43°C is considered to be reasonably safe should a young child or elderly person overbalance and be trapped against the radiator; terrible burns can result from a scalding hot radiator.

If you have a water-filled central heating system, it is important that the radiators are balanced throughout the property. This means altering the flow-regulating valve on each radiator (at the opposite end to the on-off valve) so that the right volume of hot water is pumped through the system. This will give an even heat balance throughout the house.

The valves in the lounge and living quarters are

**Central heating** is usually comfortable but can make the atmosphere dry. You can buy a humidity meter from an ironmonger or a garden centre if you want to measure the relative humidity.

**In water-carrying** radiators, air or, if there is corrosion, hydrogen gas can accumulate at the top.

**Having** the boiler temperature too high will cause additional scaling problems in hard water areas. Excessively hot water will also mean that your house creaks and groans as pipes expand and cool – which might interrupt a good night's sleep.

**The National** Radiological Protection Board is mapping this country to establish radioactive radon levels.

**A body** of evidence has been gathered, mainly since the early 1990s, to link the inhalation of radioactive radon with deaths from lung cancer.

**The British** Geological Survey has also produced a map of areas affected by radon and a technical report. The Building Research Establishment has issued a guidance note on protective measures for new dwellings. The Radon Council (established in 1991) is composed of professionally interested organisations, and issues a Code of Practice. It also produces a list of contractors who specialise in such work.

usually set wider to allow more water flow to provide higher temperature in those rooms than in the bedrooms. There are optimum temperatures recommended for each kind of room.

It is important that when the wall thermostat is set, the house attains an even temperature throughout. The thermostat should never be above a heater. It must be in an even average temperature location. Some houses have a number of thermostats and each zone has to be balanced as well as the individual radiators within each zone.

If a room is colder than it should be and the radiator is full of tepid water, then open the flow valve to allow more hot water to circulate and warm up the room. Always make a note of the initial setting and count the number of turns which your adjustment to the valve involves. Then, if you do encounter a problem, you can always reset the valve.

Cold radiators may be caused by a blockage; alternatively they may be air-filled and require to be bled; the radiator's own thermostat may not be working or be incorrectly set; or a valve may not have opened. If the radiators always feel cold there may be a thermostat on the boiler which has been set too low. If you are turning up the temperature on the boiler, do it gradually. It is not a good idea to turn it up to maximum. That is likely to send extremely hot water into the system, and toddlers and the elderly risk being burned if they fall against the radiators.

If the house is still too cold, then apart from having the system checked you might also wish to establish whether the boiler fitted has the correct thermal output rating. A small boiler is not going to heat a mansion. The building control plans should indicate the intended boiler size. It is also possible for a specialist to calculate what the boiler size should be for a particular house.

The same general principles apply to underfloor heating systems which use hot air.

At the top of the radiator at both ends are blanking-off fittings, one of which will have an air bleeding valve. This requires a special key. A radiator which needs to be bled is cold at the top but warm at the bottom. You can measure where the water level is by feeling where the temperature changes suddenly.

## Radon

Radon is usually present in the atmosphere in such a small quantity that it can be ignored. It cannot be seen or smelt.

Radon is a chemical element which is formed in rocks such as granite which naturally contain uranium in very small levels. The radon forms as a result of natural radioactive decay and the radon isotope which is formed is also radioactive. As radon is a gas it outgasses from the granite. The level of radioactivity is normally very low and for practical purposes can be ignored.

The problem for some house owners occurs because

radioactive radon may accumulate in the underfloor void. It escapes from fissures in the underlying rock which supports the house. Part of the reason for the problem is that houses are much better insulated than they used to be, so air is trapped in the houses for longer.

The National Radiological Protection Board is an independent statutory body set up by the Radiological Protection Act of 1970. It is currently mapping the country to establish where high levels of radioactivity from radon are encountered. There are affected areas throughout the UK, including parts of Anglesey, Cornwall, Denbighshire, Devon, Dorset, Flintshire, Lincolnshire, Northamptonshire, North Somerset, Oxfordshire, Pembrokeshire, Powys and Shropshire.

Clearly, the permeability of the ground to radon gas is an important factor. The indoor levels also tend to fluctuate during the day and depend, for example, on the degree of ventilation in the property; the levels tend to be higher at night.

In the most affected areas, houses are now built with barriers across the area covered by the building to stop radon passing into basement areas. In those areas, and in lesser affected areas, a sump and extract pipe from ventilated floor void areas are used. Once the radon escapes to the atmosphere it dissipates and is of no concern.

FURTHER INFORMATION: *See* **F**oundations

### Rainwater

Rainwater should drain freely from roofs and not penetrate into the property. Check the gutters and rainwater pipes. During heavy rain, check to see if the gutters cope. Any overspill which sometimes happens in torrential downpours should be near the outlet (unless, of course, water is deliberately cascading down a roof from an higher outlet).

Rainwater should not flood against the foundations of your home.

### Rats

*See* **I**nfestation p.93

### Record keeping

Your new home may be your most valuable asset. It is important to keep records, especially if there are any faults, so that you and the developer know what the faults are, when they were first identified, and what action has been taken to remedy them.

It can be helpful to take a photograph which includes a card with the date and a dimensional scale. These also provide a record of what has happened if ever you need to make a complaint.

FURTHER INFORMATION: *See* **P**hotographic records

### Refrigerators

The noise from fridge and freezer compressors can be obtrusive at night. To reduce noise, stand the fridge on rubber feet and make sure that the fridge does not lean against timber or plasterboard. Alternatively, any plasterboard wall may be packed with mineral wool to provide sound deadening.

**If using a professional** adviser consider asking for itemised monthly billing if a long job is involved. This will keep the adviser constantly aware of costs and will also allow you to query any figure close to the time it was incurred rather than a year later.

**Make sure that** you have the instructions and warranties for refridgerators and freezers. Do you have a service contract? Do you need insur-ance cover for the contents in the event of a power failure?

**When moving** home, put a label on the top side of each box or container so that you know the contents and destination room.

**It is always** a busy time when moving in to a new home, so why not designate one room as your haven where you can escape to relax for a short time?

**If you have** removed a faulty part and replaced it with another while under warranty, keep the old part and the receipt for the developer when you make a claim. But before you make the repair, read the warranty terms, because your repair could invalidate the warranty.

## Removal firms

Removal firms will provide you with tri-wall boxes and containers. Remember that if you keep any, you will have to pay for them; indeed, you may have to pay return transport.

When you are filling boxes always make them flat topped, otherwise they will not stack properly.

Although the cardboard is quite strong, it will quickly collapse under excessive weight or if wet. Books are very heavy so use smaller boxes. Fill each box evenly and flatly, then seal it. The next box of books will then be supported by the books underneath rather than relying on the box walls which are there only to hold the books together as a group.

## Repairs

It is, of course, important that repairs are made properly. Check that a faulty condition is not repeated on repair. Sometimes repairs are done which still fail to correct the underlying cause.

Try to agree in writing a specific date and time when repairs will be made. Don't let the developer drift with vague promises.

Sometimes you or someone else may have to carry out a temporary repair pending proper repair.

It is probably acceptable to make an urgent repair without breaking the terms of any warranty though the repair must be of the correct standard. If you have a bill, send this to the developer with your claim for recompense.

## Representations

Before you buy a property, you will no doubt ask many questions of the salesperson. Many of your questions will be important and the answers you receive will affect your decision.

If you rely on important information provided by the vendor when you buy and it turns out that the information is wrong, you can take legal action against the vendor for misrepresentation. If the vendor goes out of business in the interim you cannot take direct action.

Many people (including the salesperson or estate agent) will be involved in providing you with information on the vendor's behalf. Commonly, the purchase contract will then include a clause which wipes out all representations made to you unless they are written into the contract.

So, if there is something important that has been said to you, it is in your interest to have this recorded in writing and for this to be written into your purchase contract. The vendor's solicitor will probably want to avoid this as the solicitor may not know what the salespeople or estate agents or glossy brochures have stated. Glossy brochures usually carry small print to the effect that they are not legally significant as a representation or part of the contract. In other words, the glossy brochure could be misleading.

During your initial enquiries, ask whether the salesperson is aware of anything adverse such as contaminated land, structural defects, or motorways or airport expansions. The answers you receive are important. If nothing else, your time will be wasted if you find a critical answer is not in fact true.

Answers which are put in writing can be taken to be representations – unless words in the letter disclaim that any representations are being made.

Try also try to ask questions of those who are local and who perhaps have already moved onto the new development. This should give you some less biased opinions, as well as giving you a chance to meet your new neighbours.

### Responsibilities

Many people have been involved with the construction of your new home. For each fault it is important that you identify who (if anyone) is liable in civil law to you. This may be different from the person who created the fault or the supplier who provided any faulty goods. For example, if the plastering work is poor, it is probably the vendor of the property (backed up by any warranty scheme) who is liable to you for correcting the faulty work.

The vendor's liability is unlikely to be unlimited. It may be limited by time as a result of your purchase agreement, or there may be time limits imposed by law which mean that you cannot take legal action against the other party. These legal time limits are often measured in years rather than weeks.

Remember, too, that there may be a chain of responsibilities and liabilities which passes through a number of parties, only one of whom is directly contracted to you. Suppose the developer engaged a construction company to build the property, and the construction company contracted the plastering work to a plastering company, which in turn employed the plasterer who did the work. It is nonetheless the vendor who is responsible to you.

When you discover a fault, it is important you deal with the person liable to you rather than with companies or individuals who may have had a part to play in the creation of the fault but have no direct responsibility to you.

### Restrictive Covenants

When you buy a property, you will find that you have to agree to a number of things – perhaps not to keep a caravan in the driveway or to build an extension.

These are called "restrictive covenants" in England and Wales, and "real burdens and conditions" in Scotland. They can result from conditions applied by the planning authority when controlled consent to build was given or from conditions which the present or a previous owner of the land has applied. Restrictive covenants tend to be revealed to you only at the very last minute, once you have psychologically committed yourself to buy and are going over the details with your solicitor.

You may find yourself having to agree to them, but if you do not like any, try to

**Ask as many** questions as possible so that anything negative is smoked out quickly. If you get evasive answers, you can ask for a prompt written reply.

**As often happens** in the building trades, companies come and companies go. So, it is quite possible that, say, a plastering company which did work in your home could have gone into liquidation, or the construction company, or the developer. This is why construction warranty schemes are important; even though the warranty terms are limited, you should be covered for some things.

**Consider writing** to the seller or seller's agents, setting out what you have been told about restrictive covenants by the salesperson and saying that your further interest in the property is on the basis that what you have been told and have summarised in the letter is accurate.

**Some landowners** are happy to allow people to cross their land but do not wish to have a public right of way established. The landowner can therefore erect a sign to say that it is not a right of way; and close the path for one day every year (perhaps on 2 January), keeping a note of this along with the name of an independent person who could testify to this in the event of a legal challenge. Take legal advice to ensure whatever action you take is sufficient and legal.

reject them - some restrictive covenants may be such that you could not possibly agree.

Indeed, had you known, you would have walked away at the first instance. If you have invested considerable time and effort in trying to buy the house, it is not always so easy to walk away and start again.

One of the first questions which you could ask is "What are the restrictive covenants which apply to this property which you hope to sell to me?"

If the salesperson still does not act on your request, complain to a senior person in the organisation. Customer complaints rarely help salespeople's standing in their own organisation.

If the salesperson tells you verbally what the restrictive covenants are, then ask for an immediate letter confirming what you have been told. The salesperson may be misinformed or be making it up.

Once you know what the restrictive covenants are, you can decide whether to proceed and whether to make a different offer for the property.

You may find that the land on which the property was built was contaminated and that one of the restrictive covenants is that you are asked to agree never to build an extension or swimming pool. This may not matter to you. But how would you feel about discovering that there is a right of way through the property?

## Rights of way

Rights of way are paths along which the public may pass without obstruction. These should be shown in council and Ordnance Survey maps. If necessary, you can study old maps to find rights of way.

If the public use a path across land as a short cut and this is unchallenged for many years, a right of way can become established by virtue of the landowner's inaction. This can then be confirmed by a court.

If those on a right of way stray on to adjoining private land, then they may be guilty of trespass. Consider erecting a sign which says that your land is private while also clearly marking out the right of way. It is important that the boundary of the right-of-way path be clearly defined and the way be safe.

It is an offence to block a right of way. Local conservation groups often make a point of marching along rights of way at intervals and recording this so that the landowner cannot say that the right of way has fallen into disuse.

FURTHER INFORMATION: *See* **E**asements

## Rising damp

It is very important to make sure that your property cannot suffer from rising damp. Other than being structurally sound, the other essential requirement for a building is that it be watertight. Building regulations require measures to prevent rising damp. Such measures are usually unseen in new houses but are something which the building inspector should be checking thoroughly.

For the normal property which has brick foundation

courses and a brick or block wall on top, the damp-proof course must be at least 150 mm above the immediately surrounding ground level. It can come as a shock to find a new house certified for building control and construction insurance purposes where the clearance is only half that.

Yet less clearance than this or, worse, ground which is in contact with the wall above the damp-proof membrane, will cause dampness in the wall. This, among other effects, may cause the inner skin to become wet or to be so cold that condensation forms with the result that mildew starts to grow.

Check where your home's ground level is and look for traces of the damp-proof membrane. It is probably black in colour and running horizontally at least 150 mm above the ground or patio level.

If you cannot see it immediately, check the walls all around your property and have a look at neighbouring properties to see if you can spot their damp proof courses. If you still cannot find it, stand back and try to establish whether the mortar course which holds the DPC has been mortared over. The mortar will be slightly different in colour below the course than above. If necessary, scrape the mortar at the damp-proof course level to see if you find the black layer or dig some soil away from the wall to see if it is just under the present ground level.

The mortar course might have been deliberately concealed if the level is less than 150 mm and therefore does not comply.

If, in spite of all your efforts, you still cannot find the level, ask the developer. You should be able to see something. So don't be put off by waffle suggesting the brick quality is marvellous and a DPC is not needed.

If seriously in doubt, ask the building control officer responsible for certifying your property or an inspector from a construction insurance company.

In cases where the level is hidden by a few spadefuls of soil lying against the outer wall, this is a simple matter to remedy. But be sure that any small trench beside the wall does not act as a moat for rainwater.

You may find that all of your lawns, paths and patios have been laid out at the wrong level. If so, they all have to be lowered. The developer may be unwilling to do this. So contact your insurer.

Some damp protection can be provided by using low porosity bricks called 'engineering bricks' as a barrier to rising damp. Engineering bricks are quite often use to cap walls.

## Roads

For public roads, the local highway department is responsible for their upkeep and any street lighting, traffic signs, salting and drain cleaning.

Trunk roads are the responsibility of The Department of Transport, Welsh Office, Scottish Office or Northern Irish Office or Highways Agency.

**To check** horizontal and vertical alignment, use a builder's level and a plumb line.If you want to check levels which are far apart, stretch out a garden hose filled with water but keep the openings pointing upwards. Fill with water from a jug. When both ends are just spilling over, they are level.

**Note** that pieces of damp-proof membrane may be placed above an airbrick. Airbricks are sometimes much higher than the damp-proof course, so double check. And if your house is on a slope, the damp-proof course level will be stepped.

**Any utility** which digs up an adopted road or pavement must reinstate it to the previous condition once work is done. During work the excavation must be safely fenced off from the public.

**Try to check** inside the loft space for any water penetration. If water is coming in, it may run down timbers causing dampness at some distance from the source.

**Roof sagging** can be caused by bad design (the supporting timbers are too weak), overloading (tiles or slates are too heavy); or insect attack; or illegally cut rafters or joists. Any sagging needs to be investigated immediately in case the roof collapses.

**Planting trees in** the highway margin can result in damage to the underground service pipes as the roots grow and even to the destruction of the road. People who plant trees in the margin without consent can thus expect some heavy bills in future years.

However, in new housing estates and even some older ones, roadways have been created which have not been adopted over by the council, usually because they have not yet been built to the technical standards required. The council will take over maintenance only after adopting a road. The developer may privately own the road until such time as the council agrees to accept ownership.

In new housing developments the roads may be reasonably well made up but suffer some damage from site traffic. Once construction is complete, the developer will normally arrange for the top surface to be laid and the roadway and highway margin to comply with the council's standards.

This may take some time. During this period access to your home is over private land owned by the developer. When you buy your home, your contract should have a clause allowing you to pass over the land for access purposes. If you have bought without that agreement, the developer could refuse to let you pass over the land (which becomes a "ransom strip") – see p.44.

Unadopted roads may have multiple ownership, with each house owning half of the roadway in front of it and each owner agreeing to allow access to others. Such roads are often signed "Private" and can be in poor condition. The owners are jointly responsible for the cost of maintenance and could be held negligent if the road deteriorated to such an extent that damage was caused to an individual or vehicle.

Adopted roads are bordered by highway margins. These are verges or pavements and usually clearly defined. If you are in an open-plan estate and have lawns running to the kerb, it is possible that the margin around the kerb will be the highway margin and this (which may be a metre wide) should be marked with a boundary block.

The highway authority will inspect the roadway and margin at intervals; and will spot if anyone is trying to take the margin into private ownership, perhaps by planting trees, shrubs or rocks. An accident caused by these illegal plantings will render the person liable for prosecution. Similarly, any tampering with the lids of telephone inspection chambers in the highway margin could result in prosecution.

A complaint to the council can be made if someone is attempting to take public land into private ownership.

FURTHER INFORMATION: *See* Temporary roads

## Roofs

The roof in your home is very important as it keeps the weather out! It is very heavy and is held in place by stress-graded timber, which is typically covered by roofing felt, battens and tiles.

None of the roof timbers should be seriously split or bulging.

Check also the ridges and valleys and overhangs to make sure they are in good condition.

The ridge tiles form the apex and there can be chimney, attic window and ventilation pipe exits. Are the roof vents and joints with chimneys or roof windows intact?

From the outside check that all the roof tiles or slates are in place and evenly set. None should be out of line, missing, broken, flaking or badly stained. If you find that there is a rattle from the roof during windy weather, a tile may be loose and need to be fixed securely. Clay and cement roof tiles will usually have the maker's name and the type embossed in an under-surface. Ask the builder for the make and type, in case you ever need any for an extension.

Look at the guttering to make sure it is properly fixed. When there is a downpour, do the gutters collect the rain properly?

If there is flashing present, does it seem in good condition? Sometimes rainwater can run behind flashing causing a wall to become wet. It is often difficult to trace the source.

There will be a number of cross-battens in the loft. They may be in awkward positions and should not be cut. Similarly, unless you have the proper advice, do not be tempted to cut any roof timbers – for example, to provide better headroom in the loft space. This is because the roof timbers are carefully designed to carry loads. Given that the developer has probably used the minimum size, you do not have a huge safety margin if timbers are cut.

Flat roofs can give leakage problems if the covers are not properly in place. This can be insidious and the fault may manifest itself a distance away from the hole – for example, by causing a damp patch on a ceiling.

It is important that flat roofs drain properly. There should be no lakes after rainfall, although there may be some minor puddles. Check the outlet; any debris around it will obviously slow down drainage. The outlet pipe should be protected with a cage to stop leaves entering the pipe and blocking it.

### Rot

Dry and wet rot are the main enemies. All building materials slowly decay, however, dry and wet rot are less likely to occur in a newly built house.

Despite its name, the dry rot fungus thrives by damp and humid conditions. It slowly makes its way through the core of timber and can grow through porous brickwork to reach more timber.

Proprietary treatments may hold back a minor attack but the only permanent solution is to cut away affected timber and replace it with treated timber. The brickwork and any adjacent woodwork must also be treated

Wet rot occurs in untreated timber which is continuously exposed to water – rain perhaps. Eventually the timber crumbles and has to be replaced. Many timbers in houses are treated nowadays, especially the battens used to hold roof or cladding tiles.

**Walking** on the roof may cause the cover's surface to crack. Some flat roof covers are not strong enough to support people and crawling boards have to be used.

**Any timbers** which sit on damp brick piers should be isolated by means of a damp-proof membrane. Otherwise the timber will become damp and rot.

**If you have** moved old wooden furniture into your new home, check it for woodworm.

**If you sign** a satisfaction form, keep a duplicate copy of the form. The agent may say that a copy will be sent to you, but it will be up to you to ensure that you obtain a copy of this satisfaction form.

**If you do wish** to note some faults on the satisfaction form, you could do so. It is important to state that the property is unexamined if that is the case.

Remember also to check that the paintwork is good and that any mastic or other seals on door and window frames do keep any water out.

It is important that roof timbers are not soaked with leaking water. Timbers nowadays are much thinner than they used to be; roof truss members are sometimes formed from two pieces of timber butt joined by side plates.

Hardwoods are more resistant to attack than softwoods such as pine but are vulnerable to woodworm and death-watch beetle. The insects burrow inside, leaving the tell-tale signs of small, usually circular, holes and (in some bad cases) fine sawdust.

When you inspect the loft, have a look at the timbers for insect damage. There are propriety insecticides available but you should consider having timbers treated. Remember to ask the developer if the timbers have been pre-treated – there is no point in paying twice.

### Run-off

The surrounding land should be able to handle the run-off of rain water so that it does not accumulate against the property in puddles. Unless a suitable drain has been supplied, paths should drain away from the walls rather than towards the walls. The local planning authority files should give you some details of the surrounding land and the drainage provisions.

If run-off is a problem, then more land drains may be the solution. Any soakaway provided must not be closer to the building than specified by regulations.

If you ever intend to hold back the land by building a small garden wall (no more than a metre high), be sure to provide adequate drainage, otherwise water may accumulate behind the wall and its weight cause the wall to give way. As a rough rule, the garden wall's thickness should be at least one third of the wall's height.

Large retaining walls are subject to building regulation approval and, in some circumstances, planning permission. If your property has a retaining wall with the public highway, it is important to know who is responsible for the upkeep.

## S

### SAP energy rating

*See* **E**nergy rating p.77

### Satisfaction form

Developers or their agents may ask you to sign a satisfaction form when you are given the keys. Broadly, the form asks you to confirm that you are satisfied with the house and gives you the opportunity of noting any faults.

Discuss with your solicitor what you should do if presented with one of these forms. Your solicitor may advise you not to sign, or to enter the word 'Unexamined'.

Remember, you may lose part of your warranty cover if you say that the property is in good condition but the next day find all sorts of faults. The developer might be able to claim that these faults occurred after you signed the form and may try to avoid some responsibility.

## Scale

Scale from hard water is a problem in many areas. Hard water contains calcium and magnesium salts; when the water is heated to above 68 degrees celsius the soluble salt is chemically altered and forms an insoluble white salt – scale. Some water purifiers can remove soluble calcium salts.

In hard water areas, water readily scums with soap; kettles need to be descaled; and central heating boilers may sing and clog.

In a new boiler, set the boiler thermostat to a lower setting to minimise scale formation in the heating chamber.

Hot water central heating systems are closed systems which recirculate water, requiring only a top-up from the storage cistern as the water evaporates. Scale can block and corrode pipes. Proprietary descalers are available for central heating systems and also proprietary preservative solutions which can prevent scale and internal corrosion as well as sealing minor leaks.

## Scheduled Monuments

Strict laws apply to alteration, repair and conversion. Contact English Heritage, for further infomation.

## Scotland

The legal system in Scotland differs from the rest of the UK: some Acts of Parliament apply only to Scotland; some apply to the whole of the UK. Scottish courts will, however, interpret relevant legislation in accordance with Scottish legal practice.

Note that Scotland has a different set of Building Regulations from those in England, Wales and Northern Ireland. Scottish companies are registered at the company registry in Edinburgh; although registered details can be obtained from any Companies House registry in the UK.

## Screws

Although largely unseen and ignored by many people, screws will have been used in the construction of your new home. A missing screw can mean a problem.

Check if any screws are missing – eg. from hinges. Check if any screws are the wrong type – eg. roundhead instead of countersunk – or are badly rusting. Check also the safety of screws on door handles and plates, carpet grippers and elsewhere in case they are protruding or have jagged edges.

To save time, screws are sometimes hammered into place, largely destroying the heads, and then given two final turns for security. Many screws are now put in place using power drills. Check that the crossheads are intact, that the screws are square to the work and driven in fully.

## Sea level

An OS map will indicate the approximate elevation of your property above sea level.

## Sealants and mastics

Many sealants are used to seal window and door frames, to stop rainwater penetration. The seal between panes in double glazing units should be hermetic. If there is any condensation between the

**Soft scale** mixed with detergent and fluff may accumulate in both the flexible and fixed waste pipes used by your clothes washing machine. Check the U-bends and upright collection pipes every few years to save a flood.

**Building Regulations** for Scotland differ from those in the rest of the UK. NHBC has a technical subcommittee for Scotland.

**There are** adjusting screws on the hinges of assembled furniture such as bedroom and kitchen units. These can be altered if a door is not closing properly, but take care in case the door falls off the hinge.

**Keep an eye** open for unexpected dampness in the first few weeks, for example in cupboards under kitchen worktops or around the shower.

**There is often** a panel at the side of the bath and a panel under the shower tray which can be removed. This provides access to the waste fittings and also allows you to see whether there is any dampness problem.

**For security,** low-energy lamps provide good illumination at night for a low running cost. Exterior and interior lights can be programmed to come on at night if you have a timeswitch. Some timers operate lamps at random intervals.

panes, there is a problem. It is important to check that the seals are intact.

Other sealants such as silicone sealants are used to seal the edges of baths and showers, kitchen work tops and vanity basin surrounds. Where there is likely to be a significant amount of water, it is important to ensure that the seals are good and that no water can bypass the seal. Even small gaps in the sealant used in showers can result in damp penetration. It is worth taking time to inspect the seals in showers closely.

Do also check that there is a waterproof seal around any taps or mixer units provided in the shower. Also check the seals where the shower head itself is held up by a holder drilled into the wall. Seals in showers may seem to be fine but water can leak through pinholes, eventually causing the tiles to buckle and the plasterboard to become mouldy and crumble.

Worktops are made of compressed fibre. Unless sealed, the edge will soak up water, expand and possibly crack the melamine cover. Keep an eye open for any sudden slight bulges around the sink or basin. If this happens, a scrupulous drying regime is needed because continuous wetting will mean that the work surface will shatter.

Kept dry, the damage may be reversed over a week or two, and only new sealing material will then be needed.

Seals on gutters, rainwater pipes, waste disposal fittings on sinks, wash-basins, baths, bidets and lavatories should also be checked for drips.

FURTHER INFORMATION: *See* **D**amp

## Security

Architects of new estates are increasingly having to design layouts with security in mind. This means, for example, providing good illumination and no blind spots. The criteria are based for example on a British Standard, the Police Architectural Liaison Manual and NHBC guidance on security (see NHBC technical manuals). Also commended is the 'Secured By Design' initiative run by police forces.

Survey your new home from the security aspect. What is the weakest aspect? Where is it most vulnerable? Consider extra door furniture, perhaps a door chain, a door viewer and even an alarm button which you can press.

Consider having security lighting installed – floodlights which are triggered by PIR (passive infra-red) movement detectors. These have daylight sensitivity adjustments, and sometimes heat adjustments too. It is a good idea to have such lighting for the doorway – perhaps a PIR lamp which operates only when some-one passes.

The angle at which the detector is pointing is important. The sensitivity is highest for movement across the detector rather than in a line towards it. Security lights can provide a valuable deterrent, but be careful to position the PIR detector so that it cannot be reached and covered.

Also available are electrically operated curtain systems which open and close curtains automatically.

Outside your house, are there any valuables in the

garden or garden shed? Are ladders and tools securely stowed? How secure is the perimeter fence and gate?

Does the garden layout need to be changed to remove any hiding places?

To deter intruders, plant shrubbery which is thorny and dense to act as a barrier. Ask at your local garden centre. Be careful, though, not to plant such shrubbery too close to the wall of a house; this may provide a hiding place.

If you wish to plant a tree, choose one which has a narrow trunk even when mature and which has no low foliage – or cut it away.

FURTHER INFORMATION: *See* **T**heft, **T**rees

### Self build

Many people build their own houses either by buying in plans or having an architect propose drawings. The homeowner then acts as the site developer.

NHBC and Zurich Municipal offer self build guarantees.

### Septic tank

These usually have capacities of 600 to 800 gallons. Does the tank have a cover? Check the overall installation for workmanship and damage. Are there any keys? Do you have any instructions?

Who will empty it? Do you have a contract? If not, ask your neighbours or refer to the local trade directory.

### Service Contracts

New homes are generally supplied with a considerable amount of electrical and gas equipment. Most of these items should have instruction sheets supplied by the manufacturer; in addition, there may be guarantees. Ideally, developers should give new house owners complete sets of instructions and guarantees. Faulty goods should be rejected immediately.

Manufacturers of washing machines and similar "white" goods like to persuade purchasers to take out service contracts for between one and five years. This provides a healthy profit for them, even if the spin put on it is that the guarantees "help you".

If you add up the annual or the five-year costs for the washing machine, fridge, freezer, dishwasher, microwave, cooker, filter hood, and whatever else you have, a tidy sum of money is probably involved. Is it worth it?

If a multiple-year, after-sales insurance policy is pushed by the vendor's sales department - with money required up front, of course - you can ask the salesperson how reliable the item is, and if it really needs such expenditure. Beware, too, of deadlines set by the insurers - "You must insure now or it will be too late." This is a crude sales method.

The quality standards used for many 'white' goods are relatively high; if something is going to go wrong, it will probably do so within the first year. So run the machine in by using it thoroughly in the first year, so any faults will then be repaired under guarantee.

The first year's cover is probably the best value and may even be included in the standard purchase price.

If the company will not

**Take care** what you sign. Take time to read the small print in case it has clauses which work against you.

**If you are** ever told by a service engineer that you need a new washing machine, ask for an explanation in clear english, about what has gone wrong in your old one. If the reply is too technical, ask again and again until you get an answer which you understand. Then find out the cost of replacing and installing that part (VAT included). Many perfectly serviceable and expensive electrical items are thrown away because of the failure of minor parts, such as fuses or switches. Remember, service engineers may be on commission, so it is in their interest to tell you an appliance needs to be replaced.

**It is difficult** for anyone to be completely sure what lies underneath a plot of land, but the building control officer should be satisfied that the site is likely to be stable.

**Groups of houses** may share a common, privately owned sewer system which connects to a public sewer some distance away. Responsibility for maintenance of the private sewer should be described in your deeds. Repairs to private sewers are often expensive.

insure the item after a set number of years, this probably indicates that your appliance has that length of working lifetime. Manufacturers tend to know their own models' service histories. Obviously however, the lifetime will depend on how heavily it has been used (or misused) and on the reliability of the machine parts. Appliance manufacturers publish the average lifetime of their machines, so look at the trade press.

If you ever have a problem with spare parts, try a trade directory. Many stockists have mail-order services too.

## Settlement

Some settlement is likely to occur after the property is built unless it is on rock foundations. This may lead to some very minor cracking. Refer to the Building Research Establishment's scale, used by NHBC, to rate the seriousness of any cracks which you see. Minor cracks may also be caused by natural shrinkage of materials – for example, kiln-dried wood may dry out further. These cracks are usually inconsequential and can be filled with a proprietary filler when decorating.

Subsidence of the land supporting the foundations is, however, much more serious. When foundations are designed, great care should have been taken to establish the underlying geology.

If the house is built on solid rock, the foundations are unlikely to move. But many houses are built on other types of soil – sandy, clay, chalk, and so on. Some natural forms of land are unsuitable unless special precautions are taken; this applies to shale and marshland. The land may not be natural but rather have been formed by the builder, such as a soil cap placed over a landfill site. There may also be underground springs, old wells or abandoned workings. Also of importance is whether the plot is at the top, middle or bottom of a ridge or slope.

## Sewerage

Sewers are provided in the public highways. Approved residential developments are connected to them if their installations comply technically with the mandatory regulations. Foul waste disposal is covered partly by building regulations and partly under the water supply by-laws.

Sewers must be constructed in accordance with Building Regulations and in accordance with water regulations. Domestic sewerage pipes are usually tested for leakage before being covered over. Rainwater is not always ducted into sewers, but may be directed to a river or soakaway.

A new home should not have any leaking or upwelling foul waste chambers. Nor should there be any backflow problems with the lavatories. If a sewer is blocked, pressure of waste from houses up the sewer line can lead to unfortunate events in houses lower down. This can present a health risk and prompt action is required.

The local council has a map showing where sewers are.

## Shared walls

Responsibility for shared garden or perimeter walls should be identified in the deeds of the property and also in Land Registry files.

In flats, common walls may be jointly owned, with the boundary between the properties being the midline of the wall (unless otherwise agreed in the the deeds). Refer to the Party Walls Act.

## Shelves

If you are installing shelves, remember that the shelves may be required to take a considerable weight. Books are particularly heavy.

Heavy-duty, adjustable shelf systems are available in many furniture and DIY stores. It is crucial that the fastenings to walls are strong, and are appropriate to the kind of wall.

Dry-lined and partition walls can present a particular problem. In dry-lined walls, plasterboard sheets are attached to the underlying blockwork by plaster blobs. Plasterboard on its own is too weak to support even a medium shelf, and has a nasty habit of failing suddenly. So take care to fasten the shelf so that the fastenings go through the plasterboard into the blobs and then into the blocks – there should be no air spaces which the fastening is bridging.

To find where the plaster blobs are, knock the wall with your finger and listen to the sound. As you knock in lines across the wall the sound will change according to the position of the fixing blobs. Using this simple but effective method, you can map the wall by sound and work out where to put the fastenings.

For partition walls, knock across the wall and from top to bottom and you will find the location of the wooden studs. Screw the shelf supports into the studs.

## SHIELD

This is a structured defects insurance scheme for housing associations. It is a partnership between Schal Property Services, Sorema (UK) Ltd and Burlee Ford Insurance Brokers Limited.

## Showers

Is the water pressure at the shower head adequate? Does the mixer operate properly. What happens to the mixed water temperature when other taps are run? Does the temperature suddenly change?

If the flow from shower head jets is uneven, this may be due to scale. Shower heads can usually be dismantled for cleaning. Be sure not to lose any rubber washer. Before you take the shower head off, cover the waste outlet, in case you drop a screw or washer down the plughole. Remember, too, that descalers are acidic and hazardous unless used properly. Read the instructions.

✸Check the wall panels and tiles for security and water tightness. Are all silicone or other seals intact and working? Is the door securely fixed? (take care in case it falls off when you are checking.) When showering is there any evidence of water leaking? Is there any evidence of floorboard wetting or

**Is the ventilation** in the room adequate to disperse water vapour after the shower has been used? Even if there is a properly working fan it needs to have air coming into the room and a good outlet vent (which you will need to clean occasionally).Ventilati on systems are designed to give a certain number of changes of the air in the room per hour.

**When fixing shelves,** in all cases, take care in case there are pipes or wires. Use a metal or voltage detector to scan the walls. They are comparatively cheap relative to the danger and damage which will occur if you drill in the wrong place.

**Some companies** offer a database service which can tell you some of the history of your site, especially if there have been industrial works or landfill nearby. Remember, though, that information coming out of these databases is only as good as that entered.

**Excavation** on the site might also reveal the existence of archaeological ruins or historic artefacts, even treasure trove! If anything of this nature is found, the local council must be informed and the local council's archaeologist may be involved.

**Site preparation** is governed by the Building Regulations. So is moisture exclusion.

carpet dampening? Is there any evidence of water damage to any ceiling beneath the shower?

- If you have shower curtains, are they properly installed? Are there any cuts or tears?
- Are they sufficiently long to be tucked inside the bath or shower tray without danger?
- Does the track seem securely fixed or is it drooping?

Is the shower tray stable and unmarked? Does it drain cleanly? Is it really well sealed against the tiles? If not, water may leak down behind and soak the plasterboard. The tiles will then loosen. There will also be a musty smell. This problem might take a few years to manifest itself.

Are the plumbing fittings tightly mounted? Do check that any mixer tap which comes out of the tiled wall is well sealed with silicone to stop water getting in behind the tap.

If there is an electric heater, does it work? Have you read the instructions and warning leaflet? Do you have the warranty card? Is it sealed against water penetration?

## Signposts

Signposts external to your property are usually the responsibility of the local authority or Department of Transport. Check whether any foliage from your plot obscures any traffic or other signs. If it does you may be held liable.

The erection of Neighbourhood Watch signs on lamp-posts may require planning consent.

There may be ground signposts which denote the limit of the highway boundary. Fire hydrant signs attached to any boundary walls must not be removed or obscured. Contact the local fire authority if there is a problem.

## Site

The site on which your new home is built will have an history. The planning authority has past details of your plot, as may the Land Registry.

Some details can also be obtained from local maps including OS maps. Try the local library first.

The site may be close to other work planned by the local council; you can ask to see the development plan for the area. The council's environmental services department will be able to advise on site pollution, whether suspected or real.

Sites may or may not be suitable for building. Even though planning consent will be needed for legal development, the fact that planning consent has been given does not mean that it is practically feasible to build on the land. Site investigations may be needed to establish what the soil is like. This can involve digging trial pits and drilling boreholes.

It is required under building regulations that a site be properly prepared before building.

FURTHER INFORMATION: *See* **B**oundaries, **B**uilding Regulations, **P**lans

## Smells

Offensive smells can obviously come from a variety of sources. Identify whether the odour comes from outside or inside your house, on or off your plot of land.

Inside the property, bad odours can come from drainage systems. Check that U-bends have water in them; without a water seal, harmful vapours will enter your home.

Odour can also come from stale overflow pipes on sinks, wash-hand basins and baths. Simply clean with a disinfecting solution.

Mould smells emanate from permanently wetted wood, wetted plasterboard, or wetted carpet. The shower cubicle is a common source of leaks.

Kitchens, bath and shower rooms where lots of hot water vapour is produced and which are poorly ventilated, also give rise to problems of mould growth. Disinfecting solutions can give temporary alleviation of the problem but in the long term, the underlying cause must be remedied.

Electric waste disposal units used for macerating waste vegetable peelings and so on, tend to accumulate deposits in the inner chamber and need to be cleaned regularly. An electric waste disposal unit is potentially dangerous so follow the manufacturer's instructions. Before starting any cleaning make trebly sure that there is no possibility of the power to the unit coming on when you are cleaning it.

Many waste units have a rubber ring below the plug. Does yours have a ring and plug? If the ring is not present, water will cascade out when the unit is operated. These rubber rings can become unhygienic and need to be washed at intervals. Never put any corrosive chemicals down the waste disposal unit unless following the manufacturer's instructions, as the spindle will probably corrode and jam.

Dry rot is also malodorous. This tends to accumulate in unseen humid places such as underneath floorboards. This spreads slowly but should not be present in a new house. Ask the developers whether the timbers have been treated with preservative.

If the problem is traffic fumes, you could think about buying an air cleaning appliance.

Cooking odours can sometimes be mitigated by using the cooker hood.

FURTHER INFORMATION: *See* **A**ir quality

## Smoke alarms

Smoke alarms save lives. Often in fires, it is the smoke which kills and an alarm will give anyone in the building early warning of a potential fire risk.

Houses do not normally have fire alarm systems although larger buildings where there are flats will have them. If there is a system installed, find out where the nearest alarm points are and also who is responsible for checking that it works. Ask if there are supposed to be fire extinguishers present by law. Even if there is a fire alarm system, you should install some smoke alarms of your own. These are quite cheap and widely available in

**Look at old maps** of the area and ask local people who may have some useful information about the history of your site. The Mines Inspectorate, which is part of the Health and Safety Executive, may also be able to provide some information. Mining companies should also have details, even if the files have been inherited from another company.

**Even** if you decide not to use an electric waste unit, you should still clean it occasionally to mould growth and to keep the spindle from seizing.

**If the odour** comes from outside your plot, the local council environmental services department might be able to help.

hardware stores. Always buy long-life batteries and remember to change them as necessary. When you move into your new home, check that any smoke alarm already installed has a fresh battery, that you have the instructions and that the alarm actually works.

Sometimes smoke alarms are positioned wrongly, perhaps too close to a toaster, and trigger unnecessarily. The solution is to move the smoke alarm to a better place.

If you hear occasional short beeps in your home and cannot quite trace the source, it may be that your smoke alarm is telling you that the battery needs to be replaced.

If you have gas appliances, consider buying a carbon monoxide monitor or alarm.

FURTHER INFORMATION: *See* **C**arbon monoxide

### Soakaways

Soakaways are pits dug in gardens, filled with rubble and covered over with a good depth of soil.

Drain pipes are laid to allow rain to drain into the soakaway. The rainwater can then be drained away locally without having to go into the foul waste disposal system. Foul waste must never be ducted to a soakaway. Soakaways are often employed for garden shed and greenhouse rainwater drainage.

They should never be close to the foundations, and should be at least 3 metres away at their nearest point.

When a soakaway is constructed, it is important that water entering the soakaway should be able to drain away. This means that the soakaway should be cut into a readily drainable, permeable layer. If the soil is clay, there may be sublayers of sand to soak up the rainwater.

It is important that the water table of the land is sufficiently low to allow the water to drain away. If the water table is high and close to the topsoil, the soakway may fill with water and not do the job intended. It may be possible to pump the water to another location for discharge.

Soakaways may also attract the roots of trees and shrubs which seek water and this can gradually clog the soakaway as years pass.

**In heavy clay** areas, it may be necessary to drill a borehole. This can be lined with a perforated plastic pipe and water drained into this. Again, the surrounding water table must be sufficiently low.

### Soil

The nature of the soil on which your property sits is very important. The building control officer should have taken pains to ensure that the foundations for your house match the soil type. The building control officer should know what foundations have been used. The plans submitted to the local authority should also indicate these too, unless they were amended by building control. The developer should also be able to tell you as should the insurer.

Some soils need to be stabilised sufficiently before building. This can involve drainage, impacting, vibrating and grouting work.

Construction warranty insurers may have technical guidance notes on methods which have been used. You can also find details in books written on building construction and site preparation.

**For more details** upon the connections between the foundations and soil types, look at textbooks on building construction and insurer's technical guidance notes.

The soil around your house may have been brought to the site by lorry and then smoothed out by earthmoving equipment. You may find that there are rubble drains under the surface, as well as builder's rubbish. Depending on what is there, the soil may be poor or reasonable in quality.

Soil test kits are available from garden centres.

You may have to add humus and in some cases you may even wish to buy in topsoil for the garden and lawn.

FURTHER INFORMATION: *See* **T**opsoil

## Soil heave

Soil heaves when physical forces cause it to move upwards and sideways.

Wet soil will heave when there is a heavy frost. This is the reason why many flower tubs crack during frosty weather.

House foundations are designed to be of sufficient depth that soil heave from frost is unlikely to cause a movement problem. A garden path laid with poor foundations (perhaps directly onto compacted soil) may heave as the surrounding and underlying soil heaves with frost.

A further form of soil heave occurs in areas of shrinkable soil, such as clay soil. During a drought the clay shrinks and cracks and this can cause the foundations to crack, which in turn may cause a fracture in the superstructure of the building. When the rains return, the clay expands again and exerts strong forces which may mean that the new crack is diminished in width.

## Soil pipes

Check for leaks, odours and building in arrangements. Also check waste pipes.

## Solar heating

Solar heating systems have developed considerably during the last twenty years.

Many houses now have solar panels which capture solar radiation. The infra-red, heat radiation of the sun may be captured to heat water. Or light energy may be used to generate low voltage electricity, which is then used to charge batteries.

Does the system appear to be unbroken and properly installed? Do you have the instructions for the system and any guarantees?

FURTHER INFORMATION: *See* **E**nergy conservation

## Solicitors

Solicitors who practice in England and Wales, or Scotland or Northern Ireland are registered with the appropriate Law Society, which also has a disciplinary system. There is also a Legal Ombudsman.

If you are considering appointing a solicitor, it can be helpful to have a recommendation from a friend or acquaintance. It is important to control the costs of the work done by your solicitor. When you want to employ a solicitor ask how much the case will cost you (get an estimate), how long it will take and what the worst scenario outcome for you could be. A solicitor may not

**In some areas** where the homes are built on land which is later suspected of being contaminated, the local authority may require the land to be covered over in such a way that the soil is not accessible (perhaps by paving the land).

**Before you lay** gardens or lay paths, install what drains you need as it is always more difficult to do that once a garden is established.

**What means** are there for disposing of ashes (which may be hot)? Hot ashes will melt plastic bags and wheelie bins, and are liable to set fire to any combustible waste. If in doubt, place the ashes in a galvanised bucket and take this outside to cool down.

**In the unfortunate** event that you are having a court battle with the developer, the building's specification may be a useful reference document. You may be able to access it by means of the legal concept of 'discovery'.

be too forthcoming about prices or volunteer information but will expect you to raise the subject. If there is a prospect of litigation, ask about your liabilities if you withdrew at various stages. For example, could you be landed with the other party's bills?

Even if you think that your case is cast iron and the other side will end up paying, remember that it is you who instructs the solicitor and you who are liable for the bill in the first place. So what will happen if you win your case but the company you have sued, goes into liquidation? Will you have the money or will you have to sell your home?

If your solicitor wants to charge by the hour, find out what the rate is and whether there will be any 'uplift' ie charges of up to 50% more for out-of-hours work, etc. Remember that over and above the fees, charges will also be made for expenses, travel, researchers and VAT.

Why not ask for monthly billing? Consider, too, setting a cash limit of an all-inclusive sum, which is not to be exceeded without your prior written approval.

In the event of a dispute, legal charges can be referred to the local taxing master (often a judge), who will vet the bill to see if it seems reasonable in the circumstances.

FURTHER INFORMATION: *See* Legal information

## Solid fuel

Information about solid fuels can be obtained from the Solid Fuel Advisory Service. Smokeless fuels must be used to comply with the Clean Air Act.

The installation of heat appliances which burn solid fuel and, indeed, other fuel is governed by Building Regulations and also by NHBC Technical Standards. Check the installation: is it properly installed; have fire bricks been used? Does the flue draw smoke or blow it back? Does the fuel burn cleanly in the grate without flames licking areas clearly not intended to be in contact with the flames?

Are the fireguards adequate and secure? Do you have a spark guard for use with log fires?

Is there an instruction leaflet – for example, for a solid fuel cooker?

Is the storage place for fuel dry and properly built?

## Specification

The developer of the property will have a very detailed specification for your house. This specification will consist of the plans and a list of materials, constructional details, fittings and fixtures. It will have been used for placing any contracts with contractors; for planning and building regulation compliance applications; and for the preparation of the sales details. In essence this is the technical definition of your house but it is something which you are unlikely to see unless you have commissioned an architect who has to clear the specification with you before contracts are placed.

Once specifications and plans have been set, so-called 'trade variations' are allowed.

This means that there may be departures from the initial specification. Although minor alterations are of no consequence, significant changes can be introduced which may also be disguised as 'trade variations'. However, it lies with the person responsible for the variation to show that the variation is truly a trade variation and does not involve any unauthorised departure from planning or building control consent.

Count the number of trade variations from what was approved and gauge their individual and cumulative significance.

### Stair carpets

Check that the carpets are properly secured to the runners and that there are no bulges or loose ends which are likely to cause someone to sustain an injury. Are there any joins and do they hold together without presenting a trip hazard? Are there any tacks, staples or nails protruding?

Newly laid carpets will relax and stretch so you may have to have the carpet relaid in due course.

### Stair lifts

Does the installation seem properly attached to the walls and can someone get on and off the lift safely? Do you have instructions and guarantees?

### Stairways

Stair construction is subject to building regulation control. There are limits set for the steepness, curvature, tread width and height. To prevent tripping, it is important that the top stair is flat with reference to the surrounding flooring.

Check the security of treads and risers, the banisters and posts. Do the stairs squeak? Check the security and smoothness of the handrails. People grip handrails quite securely and also slide their hands along the rails. So inspect for raised slivers of wood and metal.

FURTHER INFORMATION: *See* **B**annisters

### Steps

The height of steps – whether in stairways or leading into the house from the garden – is subject to regulatory limits. Check the steps for stability.

### Stonework

Stonework can give a natural appearance to a building. Stone from quarries – whether slate, limestone, marble or granite – varies enormously in its nature and composition. Some variability is to be expected, which is part of the appeal. Walls are often clad with polished stone panels which hide the common bricks behind. Polished marble is generally too expensive for all but commercial premises. It comes in a variety of shades and markings, and no two pieces are identical. It is highly water-resistant but will deteriorate if rain is acidic. Polished granite is also popular in commercial premises and is much more resistant to acid erosion.

Reconstituted stones are also available. These are synthetic products: crushed stone is combined with cement and set in moulds under pressure. The

**For safety reasons** always ensure that the stairwell is satisfactorily lit.

**Stairways** and ramps are governed by building regulations. The stairs can be private or common.

**Stonework** has a natural attraction. The stonework used in buildings is often characteristic of the locality. Queries are listed in trade directories.

**Stone quarries** are members of a trade association, which produces a directory of members. If your property has natural stonework finishings, ask the builder for the name of the quarry, in case you ever want to buy some more.

**Ask the developer** for the name of the cupboard manufacturer in case you wish to buy some extra units in the coming years. Sometimes the cupboards come from obscure trade sources. Do the cupboards have shelves and shelf support plugs?

reconstituted stones are generally of a uniform size and laid in courses. They are usually less porous than fired bricks and can be artificially coloured with cement colourants.

Stonework is often used as flooring. The stones are laid, perhaps in a pattern, which is then abraded with a polisher until the surface is smooth and flat.

Slate is a laminar material which is widely used for roofing and cladding. Nowadays it is cut into regularly shaped portions by special stone saws.

Random ashlar walls are walls built of natural stones which are rectangularly shaped but of different sizes. The different sizes are mainly the result of the sizes available from the quarry. Coursed ashlar is more costly. Here the stones are of uniform size and laid like bricks.

In some properties, flintstones are set into a wall with mortar in order to give an historic character to the property. The structure must, however, comply with building regulations and adequate thermal insulation must be provided, perhaps by an inner skin of aerated blocks.

In the garden, gravel stones can be used for paths. These create a crunching noise when walked upon and this can have a security value.

Brick pavoir blocks are increasingly being used for driveways and paths. They are made from a blend of crushed stone, sand and cement, and they are heavy and strong owing to the compression of the materials.

Some stones are porous and need to have good capping. Dampness is usually indicated by the presence of moss. Salts which occur naturally in some porous stones, and salts which pass into the wall from the soil or result from acid rain, can cause porous stonework to deteriorate.

## Stopcocks and stop valves

Your home will have a number of stopcocks and valves which are used in the water and gas supplies. Make a note of where they all are and what they do. The water supply to the dwelling is usually delivered by an underground pipe, probably made of plastic. It will usually enter the kitchen under the sink, and there must be a stopcock. Can you find it? Can you turn the handle easily?

If not you will be unable to turn off the water supply quickly in the event of a leak. Does the gland drip?

There is probably also a turnkey stopcock in the street or in your driveway. This is likely to turn off water to the whole property. In an apartment block, all flats may be affected.

Clearly isolating valves should appear to be in good condition, operate and not leak.

A number of stopcocks will be found beside the hot water tank. Some may be in the loft space or under the floor. Radiators have individual isolating valves; some may be thermostatically controlled.

Water-fed appliances, such as washing machines or

dishwashers, should be fed by flexible hoses which must be of the approved grade. These are connected to outlets which should have isolating valves.

Isolating valves should also be provided beside all cisterns so that the cisterns can be isolated for servicing.

Do you have a key for isolating the main gas supply at the meter? Each gas appliance should have an isolating valve which is accessible.

## Storage

Minimum storage requirements are established by the Technical Standards of NHBC and perhaps also by technical standards issued by other construction warranty insurers.

Check whether the cupboard and wardrobe doors are correctly fitted and that there are no chips or damage to the outer surfaces. Are the cupboards stable and is any cornicing and coving firmly placed?

Is there a broom cupboard? What provision is there for an ironing board and for keeping cleaning materials?

Do drawers run smoothly on their runners and are all handles properly attached?

## Storage heaters

Electric storage heaters are heated with cheap night-time electricity. The accumulated heat is then released at a controlled rate during the day.

Each storage heater should have its own isolating switch. It may also have one or two thermostats.

Do you have the instruction leaflet and guarantee?

## Storage tanks

Storage tanks or cisterns are usually provided to store water. These can be in the loft to provide cold (non-mains) water, which also feeds the hot water system. There may be a central heating water tank as well. Each lavatory has its own individual cistern.

Every tank or cistern should automatically fill up to the level marked on the side by the operation of a float-operated valve. The filling rate should neither be too fast nor too slow. The float should not bounce, nor should it be too noisy.

Each tank must have a warning pipe to allow extra water to flow away safely should the float valve fail to shut off the supply. Tanks should have local isolating valves to allow the tank to be serviced.

Fuel oil storage tanks must also to be checked for stability and for leaks. The tank should have a vent pipe which prevents rain entering and a lockable filler port. It should also have an isolating valve which can be operated if there is leak further down the line.

## Streams

Find out from your local OS map where the stream comes from and where it goes. Ask locals if it is known to flood.

Your property deeds will tell you if you have any rights or obligations in relation to the stream. The Land Registry, local council or river authority records should

**Storage cisterns** are heavy when full of water. They need to be supported properly, usually with their weight spread over a number of joists by means of load-spreading beams.

**In the attic**, the tanks must have a lid and be insulated. Pipes in the attic must also be fully insulated.

**Underground** streams may be present in your area. The local building inspector may be able to provide information.

**While** the subcontractor may be recalled to make repairs, it is likely to be the developer who is liable to you as owner – unless warranty terms, or other terms to which you have agreed, state otherwise.

**The majority** of subsidence claims are attributed to trees and shrubs which are too close to the property.

reveal who the owner is and who, for example, has control of fishing rights.

### Street lighting

This is the responsibility of either the local council or sometimes the highway authority. Street lighting in private roads is a matter for the owners. Your property deeds will tell you whether you have any obligations in this respect.

### Stress-grading

Timber used for structural purposes, such as in roof trusses, has to pass strength tests. Timber which has passed the test has to be stamped to that effect; and the grade may also be indicated.

Using timber which is not stress-graded could result in a collapse of the property.

### Strip foundations

*See* **Foundations** p84

### Structural walls

Some walls in a property are load-bearing. Other walls may be acting as buttresses to stop the walls bulging.

Load-bearing walls must be structurally sound and should not be cut or removed without proper advice.

FURTHER INFORMATION: *See* **Lintels**, **Load-bearing capacity**

### Subcontractors

It is common practice in the building industry for subcontractors to be brought in to do specific tasks, such as painting or installation of plumbing work.

With respect to the workmanship, the subcontractor is legally bound to the company placing the work order. It must also do work which complies with the law. (For example, the Building Regulations for England and Wales have an Approved Document relating to workmanship and materials.) Construction insurers also insist on certain standards.

Some subcontractors may not be qualified, and their work may have to be inspected before being passed for regulatory compliance. Other subcontractors set standards of excellence in their work.

A home owner's problem with subcontractors often stems from incompetent site management. The site manager has to authorise payment to the subcontractor but should do this only if the work has been correctly done in accordance with the written specification in the site manager's hands.

### Subsidence

Subsidence can have a devastating effect on a house's structure and value. The land may have to be stabilised and action taken to safeguard or repair the foundations.

Underpinning of the foundations is a common but very expensive solution. Remember, though, that any significant remedial work will require building control approval.

The foundations in your house should be specified in the local authority plans and building control plans. A proper site survey should have been undertaken before building control approval was given. Any unapproved design or material variation is a potentially serious matter, as is poor workmanship.

Areas where there have been mining are also at risk from subsidence. Although local authorities take account of this before granting planning and building control permission, the information which the local authority has about the location of shafts and workings may not be accurate.

FURTHER INFORMATION: *See* **F**oundations, **L**and, **T**rees

### Substructure

This is the part of the building you cannot see. The building plans will show the planned substructure. Hopefully, the plans match the reality.

### Sulphate

Natural sulphate from the soil can attack and deteriorate brickwork and concrete. Special measures are taken in areas where there are high sulphate contents in the soil to reduce this.

FURTHER INFORMATION: *See* **S**oil

### Surveyors

Surveyors can variously survey land, buildings or quantities of materials for use in constructions. Clearly if you employ a surveyor, the surveyor needs to be competent relative to what you want surveyed. So choose one with the correct professional skills.

For example, a building surveyor will be able to provide a general view on the structural stability of a building but may not be competent to comment on the subject of soil contamination, or to say whether particular features do or do not comply with building regulations, water regulations, gas regulations, and so on.

A surveyor will always be commissioned at your expense by the lender before a mortgage is given. The mortgagor is primarily concerned that the building actually exists and is of suitable quality, and also that any money loaned can be recovered in the event that you default on payments. In other words, the survey is primarily a valuation survey and is usually relatively superficial.

You are unlikely to see this survey, and even if a fault is reported, you may not be told. As the surveyor's client is the lender, the surveyor cannot advise you of the content of the report without the client's approval.

A so-called "full" structural survey will never be truly full as many parts of the building will be hidden under floorboards and will, for all practical intents and purposes, be inaccessible. The report may also be accompanied by various disclaimers. Always read the small print and disclaimers carefully.

Be aware that a building surveyor may very well say nothing about the land on which the building sits, even if the surveyor knows that there is a potential problem with underground streams, landslip or contamination. This may be because the subject is outside the scope of the surveyor's indemnity insurance.

Professionally qualified surveyors should be covered with professional indemnity

**Chartered Surveyors** have been asked by local authorities to provide valuations of properties for council tax banding purposes.

**Insurance claims** for subsidence run to many hundreds of millions of pounds per year. Underpinning costs about £400 to £500 per square metre of the house and must comply with building regulations. Insurance companies do not pay out for preventative maintenance. You need to wait for the problem to be happening before you make a claim.

**Check ponds** and swimming pools for safety especially if you have young children or pets.

**In some regions**, an aerial on the set or one in the loft will give adequate reception. In areas of weak signals, a booster may be required.

**If the road** is not adopted by the council, there may be charges which you have to pay to bring it up to the council's standard before it can be adopted.

insurance in the event that the surveyor has made an error or omission or has been negligent.

Survey fees should be discussed in advance.

### Swimming pools and ponds

Check the safety of pools and ponds, especially if there are children and pets around. Do you need a fence or pool cover? If the area is fenced off, do you have a lock on the gate or door?

Keep an eye on the water level in the pool in case there is a leak. The water supply company will probably have installed a meter. Alternatively, you may have to pay a supplement on your water rate.

Has the swimming pool been properly constructed with no obvious faults? What construction guarantees do you have? Do the pumps and lights work? Do you have the operating instructions?

Where are the filters located? Are the chemicals needed to treat the water stored safely?

Are the filters free from rubbish?

Is the pool free from rubbish and broken glass?

Have you marked the depths so that diving is safe? Are the surrounding walkways safe, especially for people in bare feet?

# T

### Taps

Taps should be properly marked to show hot and cold. The handles, body and spout should be undamaged. The tap body should not move. The flow from the spout should be an even stream. If irregular, there may be swarf behind the diffuser; this can usually be easily unscrewed and cleaned. Mixer taps need to mix properly.

Dripping can be caused by a faulty washer, seal, an uneven metal bed or something trapped under the washer. In hard water areas, scale may build up on the bed which may have to be reamed if the constant passage of dripping water through a small channel causes a larger channel to be formed.

FURTHER INFORMATION: *See* **B**aths

### Telephone poles

If you have any of these on your property, you may be entitled to a small annual fee. Refer to the property deeds, which should reveal an agreement with the telephone company.

The same applies to a cellular radio network tower.

### Telephone service

Have you arranged a new account with a service provider?

Establish what facilities you need– for example, extension phones.

Just because the house has new telephone connection points, do not assume that the wires are actually connected to the sockets. Even if you ask the telephone company to connect your house, the telephone engineer will probably only connect your main socket to the service wires. Extension sockets may be left unconnected without your knowledge, particularly if you are supplying your own telephones.

### Television

Remember to change the address on your television licence or to buy a licence. If you are moving into a new area, the television channels may have to be retuned to local stations.

● Check that you do have a television (and, if necessary, a satellite) aerial. Check, too, that the television aerial sockets are actually connected to the coaxial cable run into the socket. This cable must be connected to the aerial or there will be no picture or sound.

Television stations broadcast on a number of predetermined broadcast channels. (This broadcast channel number is different from the channel number used on the TV set for each station.) Contact the Engineering Services department of the broadcasting company to find out the channel number for your area. Modern TV sets will scan for the channel themselves, in which case there is no need to know the channel number.

### Temporary roads

In a brand new development, the roads may be temporary and not properly topped with asphalt. A temporary road may be owned by the developer until it is of a technical standard acceptable to the local council, which then agrees formally to adopt it and take over responsibility for its upkeep.

When you enquire about a new property, find out about the roads and whether the council has agreed in principle to adopt them. The precise details should be provided to you before any contract is signed – but, as this is often late in the day, find out soon. Ask the salesperson when you make your initial enquiries. The local planning authority should let you see the wording of the planning consent given for the development, and the plans will show what the road layout should be.

Temporary road surfaces may have protruding manhole covers and high kerbs, so take care.

FURTHER INFORMATION: *See* **R**oads

### Thatch

If your new home has a thatch roof, this will have to comply with building and planning regulations. Wheat straw thatch usually lasts for about 12 years and reeds for 30. The roof ridge should be checked every 12 years unless there is an obvious problem earlier.

Your building and house contents insurers should be advised that the house has a thatched roof.

### Thermal insulation

There are minimum standards for thermal insulation. In accordance with building regulations, these apply to the external walls, ceiling and windows.

The size of windows is partly governed by thermal considerations. SAP energy ratings (see page 77) are now calculated for each new home prior to actual construction.

Construction warranty insurers may require

**If your home** has a thatched roof then fire is a worry, so in addition to normal precautions, why not install extra smoke alarms and fire extinguishers?

**Roof tiles** gradually gain a patina of moss and lichen. A new tile will weather in over time. Sometimes the spreading of water which has been used to wash adjacent old tiles onto the new tiles can help to spread moss and lichen and thus age the new tiles faster than normal.

**Floor** and carpet tiles need to be properly laid. It is very important that edges do not protrude and form a trip hazard.

**Bear in mind** that the instant you become owner of the property, you are responsible for its security. This has implications if you do not intend to move in immediately.

**Timber-framed** buildings have an attraction for developers as several months can be cut off the construction time. In the early 1980s over 20 percent of new houses had this form of construction but strict quality control on site was not maintained. These abuses were exposed in the mid-1980s and this nearly destroyed the market.

additional measures to be taken.

Pipes, cisterns and tanks which carry water, need to be thermally lagged.

FURTHER INFORMATION: *See* **E**nergy ratings, **I**nsulation

## Tiles

Roof and wall tiles are used to keep out the rain and snow. Check that they are whole and properly fixed. (For tiles which are located up high, you may find binoculars helpful.)

Collectively, the tiles on a house are likely to be very heavy. The supporting roof trusses will have been carefully calculated to support the weight. Tiles are usually held in place by timber which has been treated to withstand rot. In roofs which are not too steep, every alternate or every third course is nailed. This means that with gentle levering of the adjacent tiles you can sometimes just lift out a tile, if you need to replace it.

In steep roofs every tile is nailed; typically aluminium nails are used since they do not easily corrode.

Tiles which are used to clad walls are supported by treated timber battens. Usually every tile is nailed. Specially shaped corner and ridge tiles are used, and some tiles may have been cut to fit into corners.

The product name of clay and cement tiles is usually pressed into the back of the tiles, perhaps as a code. This should help to identify the brand if you need replacements.

Tiles in showers and around wet surfaces in kitchens and bathrooms should have been properly grouted and the edges sealed to stop water penetration. Any cut-outs in the tiling for switches or taps should also be sealed properly.

Are any tiles broken or chipped? Are there any bulges? Shine a torch beam along the surface – any shadows will represent bulges.

## Timber-Framed Buildings

The timber-frame sections can be fabricated off-site, like roof trusses, then assembled onto the foundations. The timber forms the inner skin; the outer skin is typically brick- or blockwork.

The timber-frame is protected from the outer wall by an impermeable membrane. Glass fibre may be used to insulate the frame.

Timber-framed buildings are used by some local authorities for public housing. Just under half of those are built in Scotland. Their use is, however, still limited because the practical risks seem to outweigh the advantages.

Strict site control is essential during construction. It is very important that timber used for external walls should be kept dry before erection, and that precautions are taken to stop rising damp and rain penetration. One critical element is the plastic sheeting which backs the whole frame. Poor site control means that the plastic may very well be badly torn and not properly repaired. The design of the building must also take account of the need to control the spread of fire and limit noise transmission. Timber dwelling houses need to comply with building regulations just as brick-built houses do.

If you have a house of this kind, the local authority plans will indicate the general structure; the building control plans will go into greater detail. Refer to the NHBC technical guidance notes on external timber-framed buildings for more technical background.

When inspecting the house check that the timbers are good and not significantly split. Are there any obvious defects or damp patches?

## Topsoil

Topsoil is soil which is suitable for cultivation as it is rich with nutrients. Subsoil is not suitable for cultivation and should not be dumped by any builder over topsoil. Developers clear away topsoil from sites before they start work and then replace it afterwards – in theory.

Even so, the soil which has been replaced may be far from suitable for cultivation. It may have its fair share of building debris: planks of wood, broken bricks, bits of tiles, strapping and sheets of polythene. As much of it will be under the ground level you are likely only to find it when you garden. When planting, dig deeper than you need to in case you are planting your new plants on top of broken bricks, bonfire debris... Sometimes a brown or badly growing patch on a lawn can indicate debris underneath.

NHBC has laid down basic requirements for garden areas for properties which it insures.

FURTHER INFORMATION: *See* **S**oil

## Towel rail

Is the towel rail securely mounted and unscratched?

If electrically operated, is the isolating switch in a safe position?

If filled with hot water, do the valves work? Is it hot at the top? If it is cold at the top but hot at the bottom, the radiator probably needs to be bled. Check that there is an air bleeding vent. You might be able to loosen this with a screwdriver rather than a special key. Never withdraw the bleeding screw completely; do not be impatient if the air comes out slowly. When bleeding out trapped air from the rail, have an old towel handy to collect any spray which emerges once the air is fully evacuated.

## Trade variations

It is normal in the building trades for there to be some variation from what was planned – for example, there may be a variation in the colour of a paint. Recognised substitutes must be used.

If you have questioned something and the developer just says, "It is a standard trade variation", that may be the case. However, it is a vague term and can be bent to have a wider meaning by the less scrupulous. The onus of proof lies with the person using the term so do not let anyone bluff by using the term.

A view can be taken of the number and nature of variations. Refer to approved plans, regulations and codes of practice, which can all provide firm points of reference.

FURTHER INFORMATION: *See* **S**pecifications.

**Remember,** fire is a greater risk in timber houses, so insurance will probably cost more. Check all fire precautions, such as smoke alarms and their batteries. You may wish to add additional smoke alarms and even fire extinguishers.

**Trees** with thick trunks and dense foliage can provide hiding places for intruders; for security reasons, trees with thin trunks and no significant lower foliage are preferable.

**Trees in clay** soil near a building can set alarm bells ringing for foundation stability. Usually, the Building Control Officer will insist on piled or raft foundations.

**Trees which** make high water demands include elm, oak, poplar, and willow (which is notorious for damaging both foundations and drains). Moderate demands are made by leyland cypress, apple, cherry, plum, pear, horse chestnut, plane, sycamore, ash and maple. Holly, beech and birch make low demands.

### Trading standards

If a developer or builder is trading in an improper manner, a complaint can be made to the Trading Standards Office of the local council.

Trading Standards departments may also become involved when estate agents and insurance companies have acted improperly.

### Treasure trove

If you come across treasure trove in your new plot, take the trove to the police and report it. To keep it is illegal. Once the official wheels have turned, you might have it legally returned to you.

Make a note of the exact spot in which you found it. This might be useful for the county archaeologist.

### Trees

Trees generally are pleasant features in an area but, on the negative side, they can cause foundation problems or disputes with neighbours if branches are overhanging their land or blocking their views. Their roots can also penetrate drains and block them.

If your plot is already established with trees, it is to be hoped that the builder has not damaged the roots during excavations for foundations and drainage. This may cause the tree to become unstable over time. A variation of the ground level around the tree and the compaction pressure from contractors' vehicles can also affect tree growth.

Conservation Area Orders or Tree Preservation Orders mean that some trees must be preserved by law. The trees in such orders may be individually identified on site plans accompanying the order, so it will be known if one has been damaged or cut down without prior approval. The trees themselves will not normally be marked. Check with the local planning authority before felling any tree which is becoming dangerous or which you do not wish to retain. If a protected tree on your land falls down during bad weather, advise the local council so that the tree can be inspected.

Before buying a house, check whether there are any trees or hedges subject to such orders and see if they are actually there! If the developer has cut them down, the developer rather than you should bear the responsibility.

Different species of trees exert very different water demands on the ground. A mature deciduous tree will draw about 50,000 litres (just over 10,000 gallons of water from the soil) every year. The effect is most severe on shrinkable soils like clays. Once a tree is uprooted (or cut down), the soil will gradually expand and may heave as it becomes wet again.

Different species of trees grow to different heights (many have a mature height of more than 20 metres) and the roots spread to different depths and widths. No tree should be planted closer than 5 metres to a house, whether yours or a neighbour's. Note that a willow tree should not be planted within 40 metres, a poplar within 35 metres or an oak within 30 metres.

Most tree roots are within the top metre of soil.

If neighbouring houses are affected by your negligence in planting a tree you can be sued.

If there is already a tree close by when your house is built, steps should probably be taken to keep the tree about the same size rather than let it grow unrestricted. Bear in mind that the foundations of your house will have to be laid after appropriate calculations taking into account the type of tree, the shrinkability of the soil and the climate in that part of the UK. Of course if a tree is planted unplanned after the house is built, the foundations cannot be changed and the tree could become an agent for foundation damage.

Over the last few decades, there have been considerable improvements in foundation design. It is to be hoped that these will be sufficient. For further details, the Building Research Establishment has a Guidance Note about this.

FURTHER INFORMATION: *See* **F**oundations, **O**verhanging branches, **P**reservation orders

## Trespass

It is important to know where public highways and private land boundaries lie so that it is clear whether a particular piece of land is publicly or privately owned.

The owner of private land has the right to control who comes onto the land. In England an action for trespass can be taken if an act of trespass has occurred. If trespassing is a potential problem, the landowner can erect a sign which declares the land to be private. This may act as a deterrent to trespassers.

## Turf

Building and foundation work causes great disruption to surrounding land. A simple landscaping solution is to smooth the land and lay turf.

The underlying ground ought to be properly prepared before turf is laid. However, developers, who are keen to provide a new instant lawn, may just smooth out the existing soil and lay turf on top.

The soil attached to grass roots in the turf is not very thick and the roots can readily dry out, especially at the edges. It is important to water new turf to keep it damp but do not deluge the new turf – this just washes nutrients away and can flood the soil. Good underground drainage is also important.

If a brown patch appears in an area of new turf, this may be because the underlying soil is not holding water or is poisoned. The builders may have buried debris there.

When you order turf, specify what kind you require as different kinds have different durabilities.

## Type Approval

*See*: **P**lans p.119

# U

## Underground springs

The local building control inspector will know whether underground springs are a problem in your area.

**Turf tends** to crumble, so commercial suppliers often use a fine nylon net to hold the sward together. Be careful - exposed portions of nylon can catch and cut children's fingers or pets' paws.

**Trees subject to** a protection order must be kept intact and should be undamaged by building operations. You should also probably assume that all trees on your plot are subject to a preservation order unless the council tells you otherwise.

**Building services** include: electricity, water, sewerage, gas and telephone services.

**Insurers** may specify minimum levels of services to be provided in new houses which they insure. Refer to their Technical Standards.

Typically springs come up through channels in chalk or clay and the upwelling water is usually impossible to stop by plugging. The best approach is to divert or duct away water, perhaps using a rubble-filled drain if it is a minor problem.

The worst situation is to create a dam, even unintentionally, as that may lower the load-bearing capacity of the soil. The soil might then move under the weight of the building, laterally.

FURTHER INFORMATION: *See* Foundations

## Underground workings

Ask the local council if you think that there may be underground workings (such as mines) in the vicinity of your house. However, not all mineshafts are mapped and the maps are sometimes inaccurate.

## Upper floors

Upper floors in buildings are suspended and made either of timber or pre-cast concrete. Timber floors are generally made from joists that are either clad with tongued and grooved floorboards or decked with chipboard.

Between different dwellings (such as in a block of flats), it is important that the separating floors are both thermally and acoustically insulating. There are guidelines specifying the level of sound which can be transmitted from one dwelling to another. The construction insurer may have mandatory standards.

The way buildings are constructed affects the transmission of sound. For example, joists at party walls are usually hung from metal joist hangers built into the wall. The joists do not pass from one dwelling into another; each floor is thus to an extent separated acoustically from a neighbouring one.

Gaps between neighbouring flats should also be sealed – for example, where pipes pass through walls.

## Utilities

The installation of services within a building is a separate act from the building of the construction and requires tradespeople with different skills. Services must be installed in accordance with the minimum requirements of law.

Some installers may be good, others bad. If you have encountered a few problems in your home with a particular service – say, the plumbing – then it is worth inspecting all the plumbing work closely in case there are other problems lurking. You might also wish to talk to neighbours to see if their new homes have had similar or even other problems.

The installation of each of the main services – electricity, gas, water and telephone – is covered by separate Acts of Parliament. There are corresponding sets of regulations in force, and usually Codes of Practice too. If something deviates from a Code of Practice this should be for a sound reason and not due to negligence.

If you want to find more about services, buy or borrow

a current trade textbook which gives an interpretation of the relevant Act.

A developer may engage subcontractors to install services and the subcontractor, if short-staffed may further contract out some of the work.

If there is a problem, you as the house owner, may claim for remedy from the vending developer, not the subcontractors. In bad cases the developer could even sue the contractor, and the contractor the subcontractor.

You, as the home owner, will however be served with any statutory enforcement notices as the property is ultimately your responsibility.

Sometimes problems can arise at the interface of trades, even if each service appears to be correct in its own way. For example, it is obvious that you could be electrocuted if you were able to touch an electric light fitment while in the bath. However, the electrician may have installed a pendant light in the bathroom before the plumber installs the bath underneath. On a development, all bathrooms may have been fitted out that way.

It is really the job of the site manager to spot these problems but there is no excuse for tradespeople not reporting a potential problem to the site manager.

In addition to the minimum statutory requirements, you may be provided with additional facilities which are not matters of statutory regulation. In this case, the limited technical standards of the construction insurance company may apply for a time. These standards might cover the minimum number of sockets in a room, the provision of minimum cupboard accommodation, and so on.

The utility companies bring the services to your property along the public highway and provide a connection point. As a rule, service pipes or cables on your side of the connection point are your responsibility.

Many services are now brought into properties underground and there are minimum depths at which these are buried. If the ground has been later scraped away, the minimum level may not be attained and that could be hazardous.

If you have a meter box, you should have been provided with an access key. You might need the key in an emergency if you have to isolate the gas supply – so keep it handy.

# V

## Valves

Your new home will have water-flow control valves in the cold water, hot water, and hot water central heating systems. There are also likely to be liquid fuel and mains gas valves.

Valves are used either to alter flow rates or to stop the flow completely.

Check all valves. Remember to set them back to the position in which you found them. When checking a gas valve, ensure that you are not turning off apparatus further down the supply line

**It is important** to remember that legislation, regulations and standards are always changing. Those which apply to your house are those in existence when your house is being constructed, not later. It may be difficult to obtain a copy of 'old' standards if they have been replaced by a new edition. Copies might, however, have been supplied to The British Library.

**Avoid** planting trees over service access lines. The roots might eventually cause the supply to fail and you may be landed with a large bill plus much inconvenience.

**Valves** in new systems may jam open because of a small piece of swarf which has been swept into the valve mouth.

**A room feels** less fresh if it is badly ventilated and the relative humidity is above 70%.

**By placing your** head against a wall and looking down its length, you can see whether its planarity is good or perhaps if there is a bulge.

(such as a cooker ring).

If you are opening a multiple-turn water valve, it is generally preferable to back the valve off slightly from the fully open position. Valves may jam when turned hard against the stop.

In the central heating system, some valves diverting hot air or hot water are electrically operated. Clearly, if the electricity fails the valve will not operate. Some of these have manual overrides.

Central heating systems often have thermostatic valves on radiators. Do you have the instructions?

If a gas valve leaks, turn off the gas and call the emergency service. Don't use anything electrical and extinguish any flames and cigarettes whihc could cause an explosion or fire. Open the windows to ventilate the room.

If a water valve leaks around its spindle, tighten the nut a little with a spanner. Overtightening will, however, jam the spindle. If it continues to leak, try taping a band of folded kitchen towel around the pipe, pending repair. If you wish to check whether a water leak is still occurring, dry the site with a paper towel and then wrap a dry paper towel band around the pipe. Check to see whether it becomes wet.

FURTHER INFORMATION: *See* **B**all valves

## Ventilation

Good ventilation is important in the early days of your new home, to dry out the dampness which has inevitably arisen from building work (plastering, for example).

What is best is natural ventilation provided throughout the day by open windows (subject, of course, to security). The water in the plasterwork will evaporate into the air and this damp air will then be carried outside and replaced with drier air (which can absorb more water). It is a slow process and, clearly, it requires constant ventilation.

Some fans have to be switched on and off manually, some have time switches. Others come on once the main light in the room is switched on and may remain on for some time thereafter. Check that the fan works and that you have the warranty card.

It is important for the underfloor void in a suspended floor to be properly ventilated to prevent dampness. Air bricks (see p. 46) usually allow sufficient ventilation, provided there is the correct number in accordance with the plans.

Lofts also need to be ventilated; there are likely to be eaves or soffit vents (with fly screens) and roof ridge vents.

If methane or radon levels are likely to be a problem, planning consent may be conditional on the installation of a ventilation system. Usually this means running a wide plastic drain pipe from the void to the roof ridge. At the top, the pipe has a cap designed to cause air to be sucked up from the void. This passive system of ventilation does not use electrical energy to assist the ventilation process.

FURTHER INFORMATION: *See* **A**ir bricks, **M**ethane, **R**adon

### Vibration

Traffic vibration can be a problem for those living near roads. Usually the vibration is a result of the movement of air but it may also be caused by ground vibration.

Airborne sound can sometimes be reduced by having dense hedges or trees, but care should be taken that these do not damage the foundations. It is difficult to reduce ground-transmitted sound.

### Voltage

The UK voltage is about 230 volts. Appliances which only operate on 110 volts must not be used. Some appliances have switches to alter the voltage.

# W

### Wales

The legal system in Wales is common with that in England but different from that in Northern Ireland and Scotland.

The Welsh Office, based in Cardiff, has ministerial responsibilities for a number of matters, including local government, housing, water, sewerage and town and country planning. Companies House has a main office in Cardiff.

### Wallpaper

It is generally inadvisable to paper walls of a new house for a year or two until the walls have had a chance tó dry out and settle down. If you wish to decorate the walls in the interims try some stencils.

### Walls

A key requirement for an external wall is that it be structurally sound and water-tight. Internal walls also need to be structurally sound. Check the walls of your new home carefully in terms of materials used and workmanship.

External cavity walls are tied together at specified intervals with wall ties to stop the two skins bulging. Wall ties should be concealed in the structure and not be protruding. If they are, the bricks may have to be cut out and the wall ties replaced. If this happens, check that the replacement bricks match those removed. (Wall ties are difficult to detect but can be located by a metal detector). Any significant bulge in a wall or unintentional leaning requires immediate action.

Check the quality of the bricks and mortar. It goes without saying that the bricks should be good and not cracked and that the mortar be properly mixed and pointed. Ask the developer for the name of the manufacturer of the external bricks and find out what type they are in case you wish to build a matching extension or garden walls in future years.

Mortar is always mixed on site as needed, and is typically a mixture of sand and cement. Lime may also be added, as may colorants, setting controllers and materials to prevent frost damage.

The less cement used, the weaker is the mortar and the more like sand it is. The cement to sand ratio should be about 1:4 parts by weight.

**If you wish to** read about bonding and the kinds of bricks and blocks available, refer to a DIY book or, better, a textbook used for training tradespeople.

**Building walls** are usually vertical and should be relatively even. Use a plumb bob if you wish to check the verticality. Shining a torch beam along the surface of a wall when it is dark can also reveal bulges.

**Dampness** in walls may sometimes be indicated by the growth of green moss along the mortar. This takes time to develop but can suggest a problem, especially if localised.

**The terms** "warranty" and "guarantee" are used almost inter-changeably in the industry and this practice has been continued in this book. To be more accurate, the builder gives a 'warranty' to the house purchaser that the builderwill rectify faults at least when the property is young. For a further period and if the builder should fail during the period, the insurer, in its capacity as a third party, gives a limited "guarantee" to the house purchaser that it will step in under certain conditions to effect repairs.

You can roughly test the strength of mortar by trying to drive a screwdriver into it. If the mortar crumbles easily, there may be a problem.

It is also possible to have mortar analysed for cement content; the dust from a drilled hole is collected and analysed in a laboratory.

A number of batches of mortar are used in any building. Not all (or even any) may be faulty. Tinting colours can also vary if badly mixed.

Brick and block walls which are built in cold weather should have been covered with canvas or sacking to prevent frost damage. A wall that is carelessly bumped before it sets will show a mortar crack line.

The design of wall structures of your home should be in the planning authority and building control files. Bricks and blocks are laid in such a way as to provide structural strength. Different types of bonding may be used.

Interior partition walls can be made from brick; block, (which may be plastered,) plasterboard; or wood composition board. The density of a wall can be determined by tapping it and gauging the extent of sound transmission through the wall.

Some walls are load-bearing; others are not designed to be load-bearing and will collapse if required to bear a substantial load. Upper floors are supported by structural piers or beams which themselves must be properly supported. It is quite common for brick and block walls to be used internally downstairs. These load-bearing walls support walls which are immediately continuous in the upper floor. Similarly, ceilings are supported by walls and structural piers.

External brick or block walls should be watertight. On a flat-topped garden wall or parapet, the topping should be made from brick or other material that is impervious to rain. Engineering bricks (which are not porous) are often used for cappings, these being placed edge on, across the wall. Alternatively, concrete copings are sometimes used; these must be properly bedded in mortar.

The capping should extend over the wall and have a groove that allows water to fall to the ground rather than wet the wall. It is important that the mortar sealing the capping is intact, otherwise water will penetrate and cause local damage over the years. Sometimes the capping is mounted on a damp-proof membrane. Lead or other flashing may also be used to cap walls.

At ground level it is important that walls do not become damp from water in the soil. This is why the damp-proof layer should be at least two brick courses above ground level. If there is green moss growing on the bricks and mortar above the damp-proof membrane, check this carefully in case there is a damp penetration problem.

Walls which are north-facing will be more prone to moss growth than south-facing walls. Shaded walls will be more prone too. Take these factors into account and try to distinguish a general patina which will occur gradually in properly built houses from moss growth that is caused by perpetual dampness.

Garden or retaining walls which are over a metre high may be subject to building regulations and require construction design approval before erection.

## Warranties

A building warranty is a limited promise made by a party as a result of a direct or indirect payment made to it, to repair or rectify a fault. A warranty is always time limited and may also include a number of exclusions.

The organisation giving the warranty does so only because it believes the financial risk of offering such a warranty or guarantee is acceptable. If it did not conclude that, no warranty would be offered.

A warranty provides a limited assurance that a fault will be rectified but only under certain circumstances. (It does, of course, rely on the party giving the warranty still being in business when the claim is made!)

The party giving the warranty also has to agree that the claim is valid and this means there is a potential for dispute.

The NHBC supplies one of the best known limited warranty/guarantee systems for new houses. This was introduced because of the appalling workmanship which ordinary people were discovering in new homes. Zurich Municipal also has an underwriting scheme. This is in competition with the NHBC scheme. The Zurich initiative comes from a profit-making insurance company. The NHBC is an organisation which makes no profit.

HAPM and Shield have also entered the market, both for private and social housing. The market is clearly being shaken up, a fact that will keep the insurers on their toes as reputations will be at stake.

Try to understand the limited warranty arrangements for your new home. If the builder is a one-person firm, try to obtain warranty assurances, as well as some form of additional guarantee cover should the builder cease trading altogether.

Despite all of the legislation and regulation of house building, the NHBC receives thousands of warranty claims annually. Bear in mind that these claims are likely to be in the two- to ten-year period covered by the warranty since the NHBC does not normally become involved in the claims made against developers within the first two years.

In the case of fitted electrical appliance warranties, you may find that hard-selling tactics are used to persuade you to take out breakdown service contracts, perhaps lasting three or five years. It is doubtful that these are really good value unless the appliance requires the attention of service engineers at three-monthly intervals over five years.

If you are thinking of entering such a scheme, add up the total expenditure for each appliance. This represents what you will definitely spend for

**If you suspect** dampness in any wall, tap it with a light hammer – a dry brick will ring but a damp brick will give a dull thud.

**The purchaser** of the warranty has a duty to report the fault in the correct manner if repair is sought, and to make the property available for repair at such a time as specified by the person providing the warranty.

**Quite often** appliance service schemes are pushed to potential customers in a way that an immediate decision is required. Take care not to be bounced into something you might regret.

**Some waste** disposal units will overheat if overloaded with vegetable waste. You will hear that the motor is not running freely at high speed.

**If the waste disposal unit hums** when switched on, it is jammed. Switch it off immediately, otherwise you may burn out the motor. If the unit does not operate when the power is on, there may be a resetting switch on the motor housing. Switch off the power while you look for it. When you find it, press the button and switch the unit on again.Read the instructions first.

insurance, although everything may work perfectly for the five years. Only you can decide whether the suggested expenditure is acceptable or whether you would rather keep the money and carry the risk yourself.

Usually these domestic electrical appliances have a one-year partial warranty which is free of charge. This is the period when a breakdown is most likely as the apparatus has not been used until then.

Accidental damage, misuse (which includes not following the instructions), and unauthorised repair are common exclusions to limited warranty terms.

## Washing machines

Are they plumbed in properly? Where are the isolating switches and appliance isolating valves for cold and hot water? Are the drain tubes connected and do these have U-bends? If the washing machine is fitted inside kitchen units, do the doors close?

Do the appliances work properly? Do you have the instructions and any warranty cards?

In hard water areas, slushy scale (ie scale with detergent and fibres) may accumulate in the drain pipes. It is worth cleaning the vertical pipe and its U-bend every few years. Also clean the flexible tube from the appliance.

## Wasps

*See* **I**nfestation p.93

## Waste disposal

Your local authority's environmental services department will tell you on which days solid rubbish is collected and if there are any recycling schemes in operation.

## Waste disposal units

Electric waste disposal units are useful devices for macerating soft vegetable and similar waste which is then flushed away to the sewerage system via the sink drain.

Do you have the instructions? Where are the operating and isolating switches? Does the unit operate? Take care when switching it on for the first time in case it is faulty or jammed; stand back in case there is something solid near the rotor arm.

The unit should have a rubber ring with flaps. This ring acts as a flexible barrier allowing peelings to be passed through but preventing splashes coming into the sink. Check, too, that there is a plug.

Underneath the sink, check for leaks in case the unit's flange is not properly mounted and sealed on the sink body. Also check that the motor unit is not loose on its supporting flange. The drain pipes and their connections should not be leaking.

Check the electrical wiring. This should be in good condition with no cuts and the outer cable sheathing should be tightly held in the cable clamp. Coloured insulated wires should not be showing. The connecting wires should be slack, not strained. All of the electrical parts should be completely dry.

Many waste units now have thermal overload cut-outs which switch off power to the motor if the temperature in the casing becomes too high. These thermostatic switches may be inside the casing and not visible unless the unit is dismantled. Some have reset buttons on the casing.

So if the waste disposal unit suddenly stops working, a thermal cut-out or overload switch may be operating. It may automatically reset when the unit has cooled down and the waste unit will start again. Modern units have a manually resettable switch to prevent the motor suddenly restarting.

Does the unit come with a guarantee?

### Water hammer

Water hammer is a loud banging sound which occurs when air is trapped in water-carrying pipes. Water hammer exerts considerable pressure on pipework and should be attended to promptly. There ought to be a bleed valve somewhere.

A vibration in a tap may mean that the wrong kind of washer has been used or that the water pressure is too high for the fitting.

### Water meter

Many properties now have water meters. Does your property have one? If so, where is it?

What is the reading when you move in? Try to have the reading witnessed in case of a dispute with the vendor.

If you wish to have a water meter, contact the supplying company but be mindful of your construction warranty terms.

### Water penetration

One of the fundamental requirements is that a habitable building should be watertight against rain and rising damp.

Check that mastic seals around doors and windows are good, that rainwater does not enter, and that timber which is not supposed to be wet is kept dry. Also, check the loft after heavy rain, in case there is a problem.

If there is a running or dripping water penetration problem, the place where the water accumulates and shows may be some distance away from the actual leak. Some detective work will then be required to trace the source.

### Water tank

This is likely to be in the loft. Its weight should be evenly supported, spread over several roof trusses by spreader beams. The tank should also be at a height to allow sufficient pressure for taps and a shower head, unless a pump is used.

There should be a warning pipe for ducting spilling water. Check the float operation and that the level of water in the tank is correct when filled (according to marks on the tank). Read the manufacturer's instructions which should be on a label attached to the tank.

The tank should have a loose lid and be thermally insulated. All pipes should be insulated too. There should also be isolating valves.

There may be a secondary, smaller tank in the loft for the central heating system. This should also be checked.

For more details, refer to the water supply by-laws and

**If too much** noise is transmitted, try mounting the appliance on a rubber support. Cut up a rubber car mat if necessary. If the appliance is very close to a hard surface, it might vibrate when used and knock against the surface.

**In cold weather** it may be desirable to open the loft hatch to let in heat because the heavy insulation necessary now on ceilings for energy conservation means that freezing is more likely. It is therefore all the more important that pipes are insulated.

**Contact** the local council planning department if you are not clear about ownership. There may be fishing rights, mooring rights, navigation rights and water extraction rights which apply. The river or navigation authority should also have information.

**If you cannot** reach a window to clean it, you might be able to use a pole to which a cloth has been attached.

any insurer's technical standards. The tank supports must comply with Building Regulations.

Check that the tank is clean – uncontaminated by rubbish, dead birds, etc.

### Waterways

If your property adjoins a river, stream or canal, there is likely to be a person or organisation which owns the river or stream. Their rights may apply to part of the embankment too. It is also possible that you own part. Whatever the case, it is important that you know where the boundary is and also, if there are walls, who is responsible for their upkeep. The Land Registry should have details of the boundary.

Take care not to pollute a river or stream. Analytical methods are nowadays very sensitive and legislation is tight.

Try to find out what happens in heavy rain. Is there a flood plain and is your house in the middle of it? What has been the highest local flood level? Is there a local flood warning system; if so, try to obtain details. The water table around your house is likely to be similar to the river level.

Are there any materials which you need or precautions which you can take now to prevent damage in event of a flood? Consider having bags to fill with sand and some sand, waders, portable gas lamps, and so on.

Some houses are built on land which has underground springs. This water should not be drunk: it is probably not pure. The existence of the springs may make it necessary on clay soil to put in a piled foundation. On chalky soil, the springs may have run for centuries and have cut channels into the chalk or limestone.

A problem which can occur with these springs is that excavation work may block the spring. In this case, water can gradually build up and the pressure may soften land eventually causing a landslip.

### Wet rot

*See* **R**ot, p.131

### Windows

Are they properly installed? Is the glass scored or cracked? Are the window units sealed to prevent rain penetration? Is there any sign of water between the panes of the double glazing? Do the windows rattle in the wind?

Do bathroom and lavatory windows have frosted glass? This may be a planning consent requirement.

Can the window be opened freely. Is there a window lock? Is there a security lock? Does it have a key? Does any safety catch work?

From the security aspect, which is the most vulnerable window? Does the security need to be improved? If there are alarm switches on each window, do they work?

FURTHER INFORMATION: *See* **G**lass

### Wiring

No bare electrical wires should be visible in a new house, except perhaps for some electrical earth strapping in cupboards.

The developer may have left insulated mains wires jutting out from an outside wall so that you can connect an outside lamp. These wires might be live if the switch is on. There is, therefore, a risk of electrocution if the wires are touched. Be especially sure that children and pets cannot get to them.

If the conductor wires become wet through rain, the lighting circuit protectors may trip.

If you wish to screen off an area with barbed wire, check the legal position first, in case someone is hurt and sues you.

### Wiring regulations

The Institute for Electrical Engineers produces the IEE Wiring Regulations, which is now in its 16th edition.

The regulations cover fundamental requirements of safety; earthing methods; protection (from damage, undervoltage or overcurrent); circuit isolation and switching control; circuit design; testing; and inspection.

The construction warranty provider should have technical standards which specify minimum numbers of sockets, and so on, in each room. If you have an NHBC registered property, the NHBC Technical Manual in force at that time will let you know what the requirements are.

Electrical installation inspection work can be carried out by registered members of the National Inspecting Council for Electrical Installation Contracting (NICEIC).

### Woodwork

Is the woodwork in good order, free from splits, gashes and scores? Has the interior woodwork been properly sanded?

Is there any sign of dampness?

Wooden floors may be made from tongued and grooved planks or from a decking medium such as chipboard.

### Woodworm

*See* **Infestation** p. 93

### Workmanship

It is a requirement of Building Regulations that there be proper workmanship employed (for matters within the scope of the Regulations). At present this seems to be interpreted by the authorities as relating to health and safety matters rather than 'quality'.

# Z

### Zurich Municipal

The Zurich building guarantee scheme was launched in 1993, partly to compete with NHBC and HAPM. Its surveyors carry out site inspections and policies cover newly built homes (for private sale, self-build, or rent) and conversions for sale or rent. Builders and developers are required to register and in doing so comply with the membership requirements. Zurich Municipal also publishes its own Technical Standards for construction. Zurich Municipal's insurance cover has limitations and policy holders should be clear in their mind what they are. Zurich Municipal is an approved assessor for the National Home Energy Rating system and can provide SAP ratings for new dwellings.

**The Wiring** Regulations tend to be incomprehensible to the average person. It may be more useful to seek out a written guide to the Regulations.

**Zurich Municipal** is a trading name of Zurich Insurance Company of Switzerland.

# Further Research and Reading

You may wish to obtain more information about certain subjects. This list (which is not comprehensive) is divided into subject headings to make your task easier. In this list the years of publication are not given because new editions of many books are published at intervals.

The list also tells you where you can obtain useful catalogues of relevant books: catalogues are ideal for quickly finding the latest books and wider ranges of books on specialist subjects.

It is suggested that you telephone any organisation mentioned, just in case it, or its address, has changed.

Comprehensive directories of all books which are in print are available in major public libraries. Most bookshops have on-line or microfiche access to the current listings. Those which serve universities or colleges offering specialist courses usually stock a good range of technical and legal books.

Comprehensive specialist catalogues are published by organisations such as The Building Centre, The Stationery Office Ltd, The Building Research Establishment Ltd, The Institution of Electrical Engineers, RIBA, RICS,and WRc. Professional and trade organisations sometimes also have lists of publications relevant to their membership.

Government departments and local authorities publish information on various subjects.

Manufacturers of products used in new buildings produce installation and/or user literature, and sometimes product catalogues. Product catalogues can be found in wholesalers and retailers or obtained directly. Sometimes manufacturers have to supply health and safety data sheets with the products.

The Science Reference and Information Service section of the British Library has a very wide collection of technical reference books and periodicals relating to the construction industry. The British Library Document Supply Centre in Boston Spa can provide books on loan and photocopies of articles.

## Appliances

– Refer to the manufacturer's product literature, and the installation and user guides. Codes of practice, standards and mandatory requirements for installation sometimes also apply.

## Arbitration

– RICS Books catalogue. RICS Books, Surveyor Court, Westwood Way, Coventry CV4 8JE.

## Architecture

– RIBA publications list. RIBA Publications, Finsbury Mission, Morland Street, London EC1V 8BB.
– RICS Books catalogue.
– The Building Bookshop catalogue. The Building Centre, 26 Store Street, London WC1E 7BT.
– The Stationery Office Ltd (formerly HMSO), Sales Department, PO Box 276, London SW8 5DT, or its agents in main cities.

## Brickwork

– *Brickwork*, 2 vols, G Lynch (Donhead Publishing). Very readable.
– *The Maintenance of Brick and Stone Masonry Structures*, ed. A M Sowden (E & F N Spon).
– The Building Bookshop catalogue.
– See also STONEWORK.

## Building Contracts

– RICS Books catalogue. Standard contracts are widely used in the industry. Usually building contracts include a clause to allow a three- to six-month period for snagging, even if there is no warranty or guarantee scheme.

## Building Control

– *Journal of Building Control* (Institute of Building Control). Periodical. Back copies for public reference only are held by the Science Reference and Information Service of The British Library, London.

## Building Regulations

– Building Act 1984. This generated the Building Regulations and from these come Approved Documents and Mandatory Rules of Escape: there are also British Standards and Codes of Practice. Other Regulations may come into force and be updated. The Act also generated Building (Approved Inspectors) Regulations; Building (Disabled People) Regulations; Building (Inner London) Regulations and Building (Prescribed Fees) Regulations. Other Regulations may come into force and be updated. It applies to England and Wales only.
– *The Building Regulations: Explained and Illustrated* (latest edition), V Powell-Smith and M.J Billington (BSP

Professional Books). This is a very good, if naturally somewhat technical, work, said to be the leading title in the field. It applies only to England and Wales. The first part of the book concerns legal and administrative matters and gives an overview of building control, building regulations for England and Wales, plus sections on local authority control, private certification and liabilities. The second part relates to technical aspects in some detail. Do be sure to use the volume which corresponds to the regulations applying when your home was built, as the regulations are constantly being updated.
– For other relevant Building Acts and Regulations, contact The Stationery Office Ltd, The Building Bookshop, RICS Books or a public library. Scottish Building Regulations and those for Northern Ireland are available from the Stationery Office agents.
– *The Scottish Building Regulations Hamilton,* et al, (Blackwell Scientific Publications).

## Building Technology

– *Building Construction Handbook,* R Chudley (Newnes). A very good book.
– *Building Technology* (latest edition), Ivor Seeley (Macmillan Press Ltd). Very readable. Refers to British Standards and BRE Digests. Comprehensive guide .
– *Construction of Buildings, 5* vols (latest editions) Barry (Blackwell Science). Very wide ranging and clear.
– *Mitchell's Structure and Fabric,* J S Foster (Longman Scientific and Technical).
– The Building Bookshop catalogue.
– See also other headings.

## Building Services

– *Illustrated Encyclopaedia of Building Services,* D Kent (E & F N Spon).
– The Building Bookshop catalogue.
– See also ELECTRICAL INSTALATIONS, GAS SERVICES, PLUMBING TECHNOLOGY AND WATER AND SEWERAGE.

## Carpentry and Joinery

– *Carpentry and Joinery,* G Mitchell (Cassell).

## Company Reports

– Building companies that are listed on the Stock Exchange produce annual reports and accounts which they will send on request.
– Companies registered in England and Wales, Scotland and Northern Ireland have to register and submit annual reports to the appropriate Registrar. Much of the basic information is in database form and any Companies House can supply initial details, at about £5 per company record.
– *Key British Enterprises* (Dun and Bradstreet Ltd).
This lists thousands of British companies, giving basic data. Try your main public library. Updated annually.
– *Kompass Trade Directory,* UK (Reed Information Services Ltd).
This annual provides basic information about many UK trading companies and the products which they produce. Main public libraries probably have a copy in the reference section. It is also useful for tracing parent and subsidiary companies. It will provide you with an address and telephone number; the names of executive directors; current financial performance. The information in the entries is supplied by the companies, who also pay for their entries in the directory each year.
For more up-to-date information on company reports, ownership and directors contact Companies House.

## Conservation and Heritage

– See useful review in *Whitaker's Almanack.*
– Building Bookshop catalogue

## Consumer Issues

– Association of New Home Owners Ltd., 22 Abbey Road, Steyning, West Sussex BN44 3SQ. Send an SAE with any enquiry.
– The Consumer Councils: various publications.
– Consumers' Association: *Which* issues reports on many varied subjects of relevance to new house buyers. Your local library may have back numbers.

## Contaminated Land

– Local authority reports and files.
– Database searches: available from some specialist companies and Environment Agency. Check trade directories.
– RICS Books catalogue.

## Conversions

– *Converting Old Buildings,* Alan Johnson, (David and Charles).
A very useful book about converting old buildings such as barns, churches, warehouses, stations, mills, schools. Sections cover permissions and building procedures, the construction-

al characteristics of period buildings and a number of building defects and their treatment. It has lots of examples.
– *Investigating Old Buildings,* L Smith (B T Batsford Ltd).
– *Cleaning Historic Buildings,* N Ashurst (Donhead Publishing).
RICS Books catalogue.
– See also BUILDING AND STONEWORK.

## Data Protection Act

The UK Registrar in Wilmslow, Cheshire can provide you with information about your rights as a data subject. There are also a number of guide books available.

## Defects

– *Defects in Buildings,* (Property Services Agency).
– *Dampness in Buildings,* A Oliver, (BSP Professional Books).
– *Remedial Treatment of Buildings,* B A Richardson (Butterworth-Heinemann).
– RICS Books catalogue and Building Bookshop catalogue.
– Construction warranty provider's technical guidance notes.

## Dilapidations

– RICS Books catalogue.
– The Building Bookshop catalogue.

## Disabled

- Building Regulations
- Insurer's Technical Standards
- Construction Publications catalogue (CRC Ltd)
- Special interest groups

## Electrical Installations

– *Wiring Regulations.* The Institution of Electrical Engineers (IEE) issues these at intervals. The latest is the 16th Edition. The IEE's Wiring Regulations are virtually incomprehensible to the layperson. There are however lots of trade guidance notes and books available which are marginally better.
– National Inspecting Council for Electrical Installation Contractors (NICEIC): sets inspection standards and performs inspections.
– The Building Bookshop or IEE Books catalogues.
- A Handbook on the 16th edition of the IEE Regulations for Electrical Installations (Blackwell Scientific Publications). Quite technical.

## Environment

– Stationery Office catalogue, RICS catalogue, The Building Bookshop catalogue and WRc catalogue.
– Environment Agency or Scottish Environmental Protection Agency for leaflets.
– Local council's local environment report.

## Flats

– *Building Acts and Regulations Applied to Flats,* C M H Barritt (Longman Scientific and Technical).
– RICS Books catalogue.
– The Building Bookshop catalogue.

## Foundations

– The Building Bookshop catalogue.

## Gas Services

– *Domestic Gas Appliances* (Construction Industry Training Board).
– *Gas Service Technology, 3* vols (Benn Technical Books).
– The Building Bookshop Catalogue.

## Health and Safety Publications

– Health and Safety Executive Information Centre, Sheffield S3 7HQ, or Stationery Office.
– RICS Books catalogue.
– The Building Bookshop catalogue.

## Heating

– *Stoves, Hearths and Chimneys,* Keith Williams (David and Charles). A useful guide to solid, liquid and gas fuel heating systems.

## Information Sources

– *Directory of Information Sources in the UK,* (Association for Library Management, ASLIB).
– *Britain* [year], An Official Handbook (Central Office of Information).
- *Whitaker's Almanack.*

## Landscape

– RICS or The Building Bookshop catalogue.

## Leadwork

– *The Lead Sheet Manual* (Lead Development Association and Lead Sheet Association). Flashings and flat roofs.

## Legislation

– Acts of Parliament, Statutory Instruments, Regulations, Approved Documents are available from The Stationery Office Ltd.
– Guidebooks: see, for example, the RICS catalogue which covers building law, property and land law, landlord and tenant law, liability and negligence. It includes a section on Scottish law. See also the Building Bookshop catalogue and the

WRc (water) catalogue. Try the legal section of local bookshops for more general guides to the law.
– *The New Penguin Guide to the Law* (Penguin Books) gives a very good guide to the law in England and Wales. It covers many aspects relating to housing including conveyancing. It also covers consumer rights, how courts work and even DIY litigation.
– *Whitaker's Almanack* (J Whitaker and Sons Ltd), The Stationery Office Ltd. Published annually, gives a useful overview of recent legislation and the names of courts.
– *Chambers and Partners Directory of the Legal Profession* (Chambers and Partners Publishing Ltd). See latest edition. Covers all of UK and gives summary of fee rates.

## Maintenance

– Your local public library or bookseller should have a range of books about maintenance tasks. Construction warranty schemes will obviously not pay for repairs needed due to lack of maintenance.

## Noise

*Noise Control in Buildings*, C M Harris (Mc Graw Hill Inc.). US practice but informative.
- Insurer's technical standards.

## Organisations

– Directory of British Associations, (CBD Research Ltd).
– *Centres and Bureaux* (CBD Research Ltd).
– *Councils, Committees and Boards* (CBD Research Ltd).
– *Whitaker's Almanack* lists national and local government statutory bodies, professional societies and institutes, regulators and ombudsmen.

## Party Walls and Rights of Light

– RICS Books catalogue.
– The Building Bookshop catalogue.

## Planning

– Local authority's planning consent files and area development plans are open to public inspection.
– Books: local public library, RICS Books or The Building Bookshop catalogues.
– Local authority development plans.
– Government development plans (Environment Agency, Welsh, Northern Irish or Scottish Office publications.
- Royal Town Planning Institution booklist).

## Plans

– Various plans may be kept by different people – architect, developer, clerk of works, builders, service fitters, subcontractors, local authority building control and the local authority planning department. Any construction warranty provider should have a set of plans, perhaps a Type Approved set of plans for your property if not unique.

## Plasterwork

– *Plastering, A Craftsman's Encyclopaedia,* W D Stagg and B F Pegg (BSP Professional Books).

## Plumbing Technology

– *WRc* Books catalogue.
– *Water Bye-Laws* (WRc plc). A very clear guide.
– *Hot and Cold Water Supply, An Illustrated Guide,* British Standards Institution (BSP Professional Books). A very clear guide.
– Trade guides and manufacturer's instructions.

## Quantity Surveying and Pricing

– Various publications are available which estimators use to price work. See, for example, RICS catalogue and the following:
– *Griffiths Building Price Book* (Barton Publishers).
There is a companion volume for landscapes and gardens.
– *PSA Schedule of Rates for Building Works* Property Services Agency (HMSO and TBV Surveying).
– Spons Building Price Guides (E & F N Spon). Various titles.

## Roofs

– *Roof Construction and Loft Conversion,* C Mindham (Blackwell Scientific Publishers).
– See also BUILDING TECHNOLOGY (CARPENTRY AND JOINERY AND LEADWORK).

## Self-building

– There are a number of books and periodicals which are very informative for newly built, newly renovated or newly converted properties, as they cover the whole process and are usually very readable. Specialist periodicals have lots of interesting advertisements.
– *Practical Housebuilding,* Robert Matthews (Blackberry Books).
– *The 96/97 Housebuilder's Bible,* M Brinkley.
– *Built It* magazine (Build It Publications Ltd).
– *Individual Homes* magazine (Ascent Publications Ltd).
- *Building Homes* (The Builder's Group): Periodical

- *Journal of Building Control* (Institution of Building Control): Periodical.

### Stationery Office Ltd,(The)

[previously HMSO] Norwich NR3 1PD and PO Box 276, London SW8 5DT.

– The best source of all Government publications. Acts of Parliament, Statutory Instruments, Building Regulations, Health and Safety. Sales agent for publications by National Radiological Protection Board and European Union. Catalogues are available on various subjects such as building, housing and planning. Most cities have agents.

### Stonework

– *Stone Cleaning*, R Webster (Donhead Publishing).
– *Practical Stone Masonry,* P R Hill and J C E David (Donhead Publishing).
– *Masonry Walls*, K Thomas (Butterworth-Heinemann).
– See also BRICKWORK.

### Subsidence and Underpinning

– RICS Books and The Building Bookshop catalogues.

### Surveying and Valuation

– RICS Books catalogue.

### Technical Manuals

(construction warranty)
– The NHBC and Zurich Municipal produce their own Technical Manuals in which they set construction standards above the legal minimum, to which builders on their respective registers are supposed to comply. The standards apply to the technical attributes of the land, the construction of the building, the services and, to a lesser degree, fitments (such as numbers of sockets and cupboard space).
The manuals are looseleaf and cost about £40–£50 but you might be able to buy one section if only one is of interest.
Note that only those standards which are in force when your house was built will apply. Years later, it can be a problem determining exactly what the standards were at the time.
These guides are necessarily somewhat technical but if you have a construction warranty provided by a construction fault insurer, this is the warranty inspector's reference document, even if sometimes the wording might be woolly.
New entrants into the construction warranty business will probably also publish technical standards.

### Trade Directories

*Talking Pages.* This is a telephone version of *Yellow Pages.* Freephone 0800 600 900.
– *Kompass Directory of UK Companies and Products.* (Reed).
– *Kelly's Directory.*

### Trade Journals

Trade and professional organisations often produce regular journals such as *Building Control* (Institution of Building Control). The British Library has huge holdings of these. Some may be held in the Science Reference Library, Holborn, London but the collection is due to move to St Pancras.

### Underpinning

– *Underpinning and Retention* eds. Thorburn and Littlejohn (Blackie Academic and Professional).
– *Underpinning, A Practical Guide*, R Bullivant and H W Bradbury (Blackwell Science).

### Water and sewerage

– WRc plc (formerly the Water Research Council) produces a comprehensive catalogue of publications. It is the UK national centre for environmental toxicology, and is a research, technology and consultancy company. It has a very extensive list of books, reports and manuals relating to the water industry.
WRc also distributes all of the Water Industry Specifications and Information & Guidance Notes for the water industry.
– *Water Supplies Byelaws Guide*, WRc plc (latest edition) (Ellis Horwood Publishers, Chichester).
This is recommended as your first reference to water supply bye-laws in the UK. Although dealing with technical matters, they have been explained in a very clear way which should be understandable by laypeople.

### Whitaker's Almanack

– Produced annually (J Whitaker and Sons Ltd & The Stationery Office Ltd).
A reference copy may be in your local public library. It is full of useful and reasonably current information about the organisation of national and local government, law courts and conservation bodies, and gives the names of many organisations. It also indicates what Act of Parliament covers which regulatory body. A very useful source of information.

# Useful Organisations

Before writing to any organisation mentioned below, do check the latest telephone directories in your local public library to confirm that the names and addresses are still current.

ADVERTISING STANDARDS AUTHORITY
2 Torrington Place
London WC1E 7HW

ARCHITECTS AND SURVEYORS INSTITUTE
15 St Mary Street
Chippenham
Wiltshire SN15 3WD

ARCHITECTS REGISTRATION BOARD
73 Hallam Street
London W1N 6EE

ASSOCIATION OF BUILDING ENGINEERS
Jubilee House
Billing Brook Road
Weston Favell
Northampton NN3 8NW

ASSOCIATION OF NEW HOME OWNERS LIMITED
22 Abbey Road
Steyning
West Sussex BN44 3SQ
A small organisation set up by Christopher Lorentzen in 1993 to help home owners because of problems with newly built homes, despite the long existence of other well-known consumer associations. Send a large SAE for details.

BRITISH BOARD OF AGRÉMENT (BBA)
PO Box 195
Bucknalls Lane
Garston
Watford WD7 7NG

BRITISH COUNCIL OF ORGANISATIONS OF DISABLED PEOPLE, THE
Litchurch Plaza
Litchurch Lane
Derby DE4 8AA
Details of organisations for those who need help with building facilities.

BRITISH LIBRARY, THE
96 Euston Road
London NW1 2DB
Map collection and historical publications.

- Document supply service,
Boston Spa
Wetherby,
North Yorkshire
LS23 7BQ

- Newspaper Library
Colindale Avenue
London NW9 5HE

- Science Reference and Information Service
25 Southampton Buildings
London WC2A 1AW
Holds many trade journals for the building industry.

BRITISH STANDARDS INSTITUTION
389 Chiswick High Road
London W4 4AL

BRITISH WATERWAYS
Willow Grange
Church Road
Watford
Hertfordshire WD1 3QA
Navigation authority for canals and rivers.

BROADS AUTHORITY, THE
Thomas Harvey House
18 Colegate
Norwich NR3 1BQ
Norfolk and Suffolk Broads.

BUILDING CENTRE, THE
26 Store Street
London WC1E 7BT
Has a good bookshop and catalogue.

BUILDING REGULATIONS ADVISORY COMMITTEES:
England and Wales – Department of Environment (qv)
Northern Ireland – Cawood House, Arthur Street, Belfast BT1 4GF
Scotland – Scottish Office Environment Department Building Control Division
New St Andrews House
Edinburgh EH1 3TG

BUILDING RESEARCH ESTABLISHMENT LTD
Garston
Watford WD2 7JR
Technical guidance for the building industry. Bookshop also has publications from National Radiological Protection Board and Department of Environment guides. Privatised.

CHARTERED INSTITUTE OF BUILDING
Englemere
Kings Ride
Ascot
Berkshire SL5 7TB

CHARTERED INSTITUTE OF HOUSING
Octavia House
Westwood Business Park
Westwood Way
Coventry CV4 8JP

CHARTERED INSTITUTION OF BUILDING SERVICES ENGINEERS
222 Balham High Road
London SW12 9BS

CITIZENS' ADVICE BUREAUX – See local telephone directory.

COAL AUTHORITY, THE
200 Lichfield Avenue
Mansfield
Notts NG18 ARG
Has responsibilities for mining subsidence and abandoned coal mine shafts.

COMPANIES HOUSE
37 Castle Street, Edinburgh
EH1 2EB;
Crown Way, Cardiff
CF4 3UZ;
55-71 City Road, London
EC1Y 1BB

CONFEDERATION FOR THE REGISTRATION OF GAS INSTALLERS (CORGI)
140 Tottenham Court Road
London W1P 9LN
Gas installers must be registered with CORGI or an equivalent.

CONSTRUCTION INDUSTRY TRAINING BOARD
Bircham Newton
Nr King's Lynn
Norfolk PE31 6RH

CONSTRUCTION INDUSTRY TRAINING BOARD FOR NORTHERN IRELAND
17 Dundrod Road
Nutts Corner
Crumlin BT29 4SR

CONSTRUCTION RESEARCH COMMUNICATIONS LTD
151 Rosebery Avenue
London EC1R 4QX
Construction publications catalogue.

CONSUMERS' ASSOCIATION
2 Marylebone Road
London NW1 4DF
Back numbers of Which? may be available in your local public library.
(Which? Ltd, PO Box 44,
Hertford SG14 1SH)

COUNCIL FOR LICENSED CONVEYANCERS
16 Glebe Road
Chelmsford
Essex CM1 1QG.

COUNTRYSIDE COMMISSION
John Dewer House
Crescent Place
Cheltenham GL50 3RA

COUNTRYSIDE COUNCIL FOR WALES
Plas Penrhos
Fford Penrhos
Bangor
Gwynedd LL57 2LQ

CROFTERS COMMISSION
4–6 Castle Wynd
Inverness IV2 3EQ

CROWN ESTATE
16 Carlton House Terrace
London SW1Y 5AH

DEPARTMENT OF THE ENVIRONMENT AND TRANSPORT
2 Marsham Street
London SW1P 3EB
– Building regulation
– Environment Agency
– Directorate of Air Climate and Toxic Substances
– Energy Efficiency Unit
– Highways Agency
– Ordnance Survey
– Planning Inspectorate (with Welsh Office)
- National Groundwater and Contaminated Land Centre
See also Scottish Environmental Protection Agency.

DEPARTMENT OF THE ENVIRONMENT FOR NORTHERN IRELAND
Clarence Court
10–18 Adelaide Street
Belfast B2 8GB
Ordnance survey of Northern Ireland: Historic Buildings Council for Northern Ireland, Council for Nature Conservation and The Countryside: Planning Service.

DEPARTMENT FOR CULTURE, MEDIA AND SPORT
2-4 Cockspur Street
London SW1Y 5DH
Historic buildings.

DEVELOPMENT CORPORATIONS
– refer to *Whitaker's Almanack*

DOMESTIC HEATING COUNCIL
34 Palace Court
London W2 4JG

ELECTRICAL CONTRACTORS ASSOCIATION
34 Palace Court Road
London W2 4HY

ELECTRICAL CONTRACTORS ASSOCIATION FOR SCOTLAND
23 Heriot Row
Edinburgh EH3 6EW

ENGLISH HERITAGE
(Historic Buildings and Monuments Commission)
25 Savile Row
London W1X 1AB

ENGLISH NATURE
(Nature Conservancy Council, England)
Northminster House
Peterborough PE1 1UA

ENGLISH PARTNERSHIPS
(Urban Regeneration Agency)
16–18 Old Queen Street
London SW1H 9HP

ENVIRONMENT AGENCY
Hampton House
20 Albert Embankment
London SE1 7TJ
National Rivers Authority, Pollution Inspectorate, waste regulation: England and Wales. Environment Act 1995.

EUROPEAN COMMISSION
Offices in Belfast, Cardiff, Edinburgh and London. Publications available through The Stationery Office.

FACULTY OF ADVOCATES
Advocates Library
Parliament House
Edinburgh EH1 1RF

FEDERATION OF MASTER BUILDERS
14 Great St James Street
London WC1N 3DP

FORESTRY COMMISSION, THE
231 Corstorphine Road
Edinburgh EH12 7AT

GAS CONSUMERS' COUNCIL
15 Wilton Row
London SW1V 1LT

GENERAL COUNCIL OF THE BAR
(England and Wales)
3 Bedford Row
London WC1R 4DB

GEORGIAN GROUP, THE
6 Fitzroy Square
London W1P 6DX

HAPM (Housing Association Property Mutual Ltd)
International House
26 Creechurch Lane
London EC3A 5BA

HEALTH AND SAFETY EXECUTIVE
Rose Court
2 Southwark Bridge
London SE1 9HS

HISTORIC BUILDINGS COUNCIL FOR SCOTLAND
Longmore House
Salisbury Place
Edinburgh EH9 1SH

HISTORIC BUILDINGS COUNCIL FOR WALES
Brunel House
2 Fitzalan Road
Cardiff CF2 1UY

HOME OFFICE, THE
50 Queen Anne's Gate
London SW1H 9AT

HON. SOCIETY OF THE INN OF COURT OF NORTHERN IRELAND, THE
Royal Courts of Justice
Belfast BT1 3JF

HOUSING CORPORATION
149 Tottenham Court Road
London W1
Registers housing associations.

INCORPORATED SOCIETY OF VALUERS AND AUCTIONEERS
3 Cadogan Gate
London SW1X 0AS

INSTITUTE OF BUILDING CONTROL
92-104 High Street
East Street
Epsom
Surrey KT17 1EB

INSTITUTE OF CHARTERED FORESTERS
7A St Colme Street
Edinburgh EH3 6AA
Tree surveys, land use and conservation advice.

INSTITUTE OF CLERK OF WORKS OF GB
41 The Mall
London W5 3TJ

INSTITUTION OF GAS ENGINEERS
2 Portland Place
London W1N 3AF

INSTITUTE OF MINING ENGINEERS
Danum House
6A South Parade
Doncaster DN1 2DY

INSTITUTE OF PLUMBING
64 Station Lane
Hornchurch
Essex RM12 6NB

INSTITUTE OF REVENUES RATING AND VALUATION
41 Doughty Street
London WC1N 2LF

INSTITUTION OF CIVIL ENGINEERS
Great George Street
London SW1P 3AA

INSTITUTION OF ELECTRICAL ENGINEERS
Savoy Place
London WC2R 0BL
Issues the Wiring Regulations.

INSTITUTION OF STRUCTURAL ENGINEERS
11 Upper Belgrave Street
London SW1X 8BH

INSURANCE OMBUDSMAN BUREAU
City Gate One
135 Park Street
London SE1 9EA
Building insurance complaints.

JOINT NATURE CONSERVATION COMMITTEE
Monkstone House
City Road
Peterborough PE1 1JY
Links the national conservancy councils. English Nature, Countryside Commission for Wales, Department of Environment for Northern Ireland and Scottish Natural Heritage.

LAND REGISTRY HM (England and Wales)
Lincoln's Inn Fields
London WC2A 3PH
Branches: Birkenhead, Coventry, Croydon, Durham, Gloucester, Harrow, Kingston-upon-Hull, Leicester, Lytham, Nottingham, Peterborough, Plymouth, Portsmouth, Stevenage, Swansea, Telford, Tunbridge Wells, Weymouth and York.

LAND REGISTRY (OF NORTHERN IRELAND)
27 - 45 Great Victoria St
Belfast BT2 7SL

LAND REGISTRY (SCOTLAND)
Registers of Scotland
Meadowbank House
153 London Road
Edinburgh EH8 7AU
Executive Agency of Scottish Office.

LANDS TRIBUNAL FOR SCOTLAND
1 Grosvenor Crescent
Edinburgh EH12 5ER
Disputes about the valuation of land, restrictive covenants, rating levies and tennants rights.

LANDS TRIBUNAL OF ENGLAND AND WALES
48–49 Chancery Lane
London WC2A 1JR
Disputes about the valuation of land, restrictive covenants and rating levies.

LAW SOCIETY FOR ENGLAND AND WALES
113 Chancery Lane
London WC2A 1PL

LAW SOCIETY OF NORTHERN IRELAND
98 Victoria Street
Belfast BT1 3JZ

LAW SOCIETY OF SCOTLAND
26 Drumsheugh Gardens
Edinburgh EH3 7VR

NATIONAL ASSOCIATION OF ESTATE AGENTS
Arbon House
21 Jury Street
Warwick CV34 4EH

NATIONAL CONSUMER COUNCIL
20 Grosvenor Gardens
London SW1H 0DH
Publications include *Controlling the Cowboys.*

NHBC (NATIONAL HOUSE-BUILDING COUNCIL)
(Insurance)
Buildmark House
Chiltern Avenue
Amersham
Buckinghamshire HP6 5AP
This is the registered office. There are regional offices in Belfast, Bury St Edmunds, Clevedon, Clifton, Edinburgh, Milton Keynes, Sevenoaks. Also covers Isle of Man.

NHBC BUILDING CONTROL SERVICES LTD
Buildmark House
Chiltern Avenue
Amersham
Buckinghamshire HP6 5AP
Approved Inspector for Building Regulations in England and Wales. Competes for inspection work with local authority building control departments.

NATIONAL HOUSING AND TOWN PLANNING COUNCIL
14 Old Street
London EC1V 9AB

NATIONAL INSPECTION COUNCIL FOR ELECTRICAL INSTALLATION CONTRACTING (NICEIC)
Vintage House
36–37 Albert Embankment
London SE1 7UJ

NATIONAL LIBRARY FOR SCOTLAND, THE
George IV Bridge
Edinburgh EH1 1EW

NATIONAL LIBRARY OF WALES, THE
Aberystwyth
Dyfed
SY23 3BU

NATIONAL RADIOLOGICAL PROTECTION BOARD
Chilton
Didcot
Oxon OX11 0RQ

OFFICE OF FAIR TRADING
Field House
Bream's Buildings
London EC4 1PR

OFFICE OF THE DATA PROTECTION REGISTRAR
Wycliffe House
Water Lane
Wilmslow
Cheshire SK9 5AF

OMBUDSMAN, OFFICE OF BANKING
70 Gray's Inn Road
London WC1X 8NB

OMBUDSMAN, BUILDING SOCIETIES
Millbank Tower
Millbank
London SW1P 4X5

OMBUDSMAN FOR CORPORATE ESTATE AGENTS
4 Bridge Street
Salisbury
Wiltshire SP1 2LX

OMBUDSMAN, LOCAL GOVERNMENT
Commission for Local Administration in England
21 Queen Anne's Gate
London
SW1H 9BU

OMBUDSMAN, LOCAL GOVERNMENT
Commission for Local Administration in Scotland
23 Walker Street
Edinburgh EH3 7HX

OMBUDSMAN, LOCAL GOVERNMENT
Commission for Local Administration in Wales
Derwen House
Court Road
Bridgend CF31 1BN

OMBUDSMAN, OFFICE OF THE LEGAL SERVICES
Oxford Street
Manchester M2 3WQ
Oversees complaints against solicitors, barristers and licensed conveyancers.

OMBUDSMAN, OFFICE OF THE SCOTTISH LEGAL SERVICES
2 Greenside Lane
Edinburgh EH1 3AH

ORDNANCE SURVEY
Romsey Road
Maybush
Southampton
SO16 4GU

PLANNING INSPECTORATE EXECUTIVE AGENCY
Tollgate House
Houlton Street
Bristol BS2 9DJ
Appeals on local authority planning application decisions in England and Wales.

PRC HOMES LTD
Buildmark House
Chiltern Avenue
Amersham
Buckinghamshire HP6 5AP
An NHBC-associated company which specialises in pre-cast concrete structures.

ROYAL INCORPORATION OF ARCHITECTS IN SCOTLAND
15 Rutland Square
Edinburgh EH1 2BE

ROYAL INSTITUTE OF BRITISH ARCHITECTS (RIBA)
66 Portland Place
London W1N 4AD
Book catalogue

ROYAL INSTITUTE OF CHARTERED SURVEYORS (RICS)
12 Great George Street
London SW1P 3AD
Good books catalogue.

ROYAL TOWN PLANNING INSTITUTE
26 Portland Place
London W1N 4BE
Planning and environmental books catalogue.

SCOTTISH CONSUMER COUNCIL
Royal Exchange House
100 Queen Street
Glasgow G1 3DN

SCOTTISH ENVIRONMENT PROTECTION AGENCY
Erskine Court
The Castle Business Park
Stirling FK9 4TR

SCOTTISH HOMES
Thistle House
91 Haymarket Terrace
Edinburgh EH12 5HE
Scottish national housing agency.

SCOTTISH NATURAL HERITAGE
12 Hope Terrace
Edinburgh EH9 2AS
From merger of Countryside Commission for Scotland and Nature Conservancy Council for Scotland.

SCOTTISH OFFICE
Dover House
Whitehall
London SW1A 2AU
and
St Andrews House
Edinburgh EH1 3DG

SHIELD DEFECTS INSURANCE
Partnership between Sorema UK Ltd, Schal International Management Ltd and Burlee Ford Insurance Brokers Limited (17 Stanley Street, Liverpool L1 6AA).

TRADING STANDARDS
See your local authority directory of services or your local telephone directory.

VICTORIAN SOCIETY, THE
1 Priory Gardens
London W4 1TT

WELSH CONSUMER COUNCIL
Castle Buildings
Womanby Street
Cardiff CF1 2BN

WELSH OFFICE
Gwydr House
Whitehall
London SW1A 2ER
and
Cathays Park
Cardiff CF1 3NQ

WRc PLC
Henley Road
Medmenham
Marlow
Bucks SL7 2HD
Produces a good catalogue of publications on all technical aspects of water.

ZURICH MUNICIPAL
6 Southwood Crescent
Farnborough
Hampshire GU14 0NJ
Building guarantee insurer and approved building control inspector: in competition with NHBC, since 1993.

# Index

Items which are emboldened appear as separate entries in the A-Z section (pages 43-163).